Single Mother

Single Mother

The Emergence of the Domestic Intellectual

Jane Juffer

NEW YORK UNIVERSITY PRESS
New York and London

NEW YORK UNIVERSITY PRESS
New York and London
www.nyupress.org

Library of Congress Cataloging-in-Publication Data
Juffer, Jane
Single mother : the emergence of the domestic intellectual /
Jane Juffer.
p. cm.
Includes bibliographical references and index.
ISBN–13: 978–0–8147–4279–2 (cloth : alk. paper)
ISBN–10: 0–8147–4279–3 (cloth : alk. paper)
ISBN–13: 978–0–8147–4280–8 (pbk. : alk. paper)
ISBN–10: 0–8147–4280–7 (pbk. : alk. paper)
1. Single mothers—United States.
2. Single mothers—United States—Public opinion.
3. Single mothers—Government policy—United States. I. Title.
HQ759.915J84   2005
306.874'320973—dc22   2005029006

New York University Press books are printed on acid-free paper,
and their binding materials are chosen for strength and durability.

Manufactured in the United States of America

c 10 9 8 7 6 5 4 3 2 1
p 10 9 8 7 6 5 4 3 2 1

To Alex, with all my love

Contents

Acknowledgments

I can't remember when I decided to write this book. The plan must have emerged, gradually, over the last decade or so, in between or during trips to the park, the emergency room, the children's library, the soccer field, and the take-out restaurants. Ideas interspersed in the loads of laundry, the packing of lunches, the Lego projects. Notes jotted down here and there, on bits of paper and napkins, thoughts about single mothers on television and in film. Conversations with other mothers, single and married, interwoven with academic discussions of care of the self and domesticity. In the spring of 2002, I realized that I had inadvertently started writing this book. And I have my son Alex to thank for leading me through the craziness of everyday life.

I owe so much to all of the single mothers I talked with along the way: women at the Rebecca Project in Washington, D.C., along the U.S.-Mexican border in Texas, and at the Puerto Rican Cultural Center's Family Learning Center in Chicago. There were also mothers at home, in State College, Pennsylvania, who inspired and sustained me. Among them, I am most indebted to Julia Kasdorf, a paradigmatic domestic intellectual. For her tireless commitment to reciprocity and community, to an ethics of caring and curiosity, I am forever grateful (not to mention all the home-made meals, gifts picked up at thrift stores, and just-in-time e-mails and phone calls). She also read and scribbled comments and questions on almost every page of the manuscript, even when caught up in her own busy life of mothering and writing.

My parents, Ron and Peg Juffer, have supported Alex and me, making the long trip from Iowa to Pennsylvania without complaint and adding much love to our household. My mother transformed many a dull day into a fun time with her wit and laughter and skill at games, and my father did the same with his unfailing left-handed hook shot and belief in the Cubs.

For research assistance, I am indebted to Jennifer Hergenreder, who not only found dozens of useful legal articles but also read them carefully and asked exactly the right questions (often answering them at the same time). Vilma Shu also displayed considerable initiative and creativity in her research. On the road, I was assisted in my interviewing by Jonathan Jones, a committed activist and organic intellectual at Proyecto Libertad, and by his colleagues Nathan Selzer and Nilda Prado. In Chicago, my friends of almost fifteen years, Margaret and Melinda Power, provided moral, political, and intellectual support as well as a place to stay. Thanks also to the Puerto Rican Cultural Center folks, especially José Lopez and Marísol Morales, for their time and patience. And to my other Chicago ally, Esteban Cruz, thanks for the endless energy and good humor.

At Penn State, my colleague Ralph Rodriguez sustained me throughout the march to tenure, illustrating that smart people can also be committed organizers, activists, and friends. Vincent Lankewish has made me laugh at even the most dire of moments. Thanks to Jeff Nealon for his acerbic wit and clear analysis into all sorts of issues. Evan Watkins gave me trenchant feedback on a variety of writing projects. Susan Squier has been a valuable friend and mentor. I also have benefited from conversations about what cultural studies is (still an open question) with Megan Brown, Amy Mendenhall, and other graduate students in my seminars over the past five years.

My editor, Eric Zinner, believed in this project from the start. Thanks also at NYU to Emily Park and to freelance copyeditor Alice Calaprice as well as to the anonymous readers for their suggestions. An early version of my argument was published in *Cultural Studies* 17(2): 2003.

Finally, to Grant, *amor de mi vida,* thank you for coming into our lives, for your passion, and for helping me see where to go next.

Introduction
Domestic Intellectuals: Freedom and the Single Mom

The year is 1992. On the campaign trail, Vice President Dan Quayle blames single mothers for the dissolution of family values. He derides Candace Bergen's character Murphy Brown, a successful television anchorwoman, for flaunting fatherhood and making the decision to become a single mother "just another lifestyle choice." Quayle's denunciation is echoed in policy-making circles by conservative guru Charles Murray and others, who characterize single mothers as lazy, promiscuous, and nearly unredeemable.

A decade later. The Family Friendly Programming Forum, a consortium of advertisers that funnels seed money to promising shows, subsidizes for the fourth straight season WB's *The Gilmore Girls,* which features a never-married mother and her teenage daughter who are integral members of a tight-knit community. Jennifer Aniston's girl-next-door character on *Friends,* Rachel, gets pregnant and decides to keep the baby but not marry Ross, the father. *Sex and the City*'s Miranda also decides to become a single mom. The winner of the 2004 American Idol contest is Fantasia Barrino, a nineteen-year-old single mom from High Point, North Carolina, who one night brings her one-year-old daughter Zion up on stage and urges all single moms to believe that they can do whatever they want. The runner-up is sixteen-year-old Diana DeGarma, daughter of a single mom from Snellville, Georgia. Wal-Mart, site of family values, runs a commercial showing a woman trailed by her children, saying: "I'm a single mom, and I depend on Wal-Mart to get by."

Wal-Mart also appears as a champion of single mothers in the film *Where the Heart Is,* in which Natalie Portman plays a penniless pregnant teenager named Novalee Nation. Abandoned by her boyfriend in Sequoia, Oklahoma, Novalee chooses the local Wal-Mart as her temporary home, sneaking into the store to sleep at night. She gives birth amid the racks of clothing and promptly becomes a national media celebrity, mother of the "Wal-Mart baby." The president of Wal-Mart sends her $500 and promises a job at any store in the country. Paying homage to the nation that embraces rather than judges her, Novalee names the baby "Americus" and proves that she can indeed embody the entrepreneurial spirit of her daughter's birthplace, becoming a prize-winning photographer and building her own home. Americus is no bastard child. She redefines the nation that Wal-Mart once stood for—the nation of nuclear families buying American. Now, any family that can "buy American" merits respect.

Dan Quayle seemed especially irked that Candace Bergen's character was treating mothering as a "lifestyle choice." Now, the very notion of single mothering as a lifestyle choice has been used to validate the practice, to lift it out of the realm of dependency and shame into the realm of freedom and full citizenship.

Such is the claim made by Single Mothers by Choice (SMC), the nation's largest support network for single mothers. They define a "single mother by choice" as "a woman who decides to have or adopt a child, knowing she will be her child's sole parent, at least at the outset. Typically, we are career women in our thirties and forties. The ticking of our biological clocks has made us face the fact that we could no longer wait for marriage before starting our families." The group was started in 1981 by Jane Mattes, a "single mother by choice," and now claims several thousand single women around the world as its members. They share resources and information through the Internet and local chapters, advising women about assisted reproductive technologies, sperm donors, adoption, and how to raise a child without a father. The group distances itself from any form of dependency. Says Mattes, we are "single women who chose to become mothers, single mothers who are mature and responsible and who feel empowered rather than victimized," "we are at least as able, if not more able, to support a child and ourselves as is the average man," "without recourse to public funds" (10).

Low-income single mothers as activists demonstrate a more ambivalent relationship to the discourse of self-reliance. At the Rebecca Project in Washington, D.C., a group of mainly single mothers goes through addiction treatment programs and then, upon recovery, may become grassroots organizers on Capitol Hill and elsewhere, lobbying for more just welfare policies that include monies and time for addiction treatment. In 2003, they succeeded in persuading senators to propose welfare legislation that allows six months of treatment time to be considered as work under the welfare-to-work requirements, a small but significant victory. Rosetta Kelly, an addict for thirty-seven years and single mother of three, describes how her life changed through the intersection of personal responsibility and public policy:

> When I was using, I never had food in the house or clean clothes for the kids. Now, putting policy into my life, I'm more responsible. The cabinets, refrigerator, the freezer are full of food. . . . To go to the staffers and tell them my story and for them to see it really wasn't what they thought it was and to hear someone tell their stories who's actually lived it—that is fulfilling to me. Now I have a belief system—I get on the pulpit and I preach—those are the things I do now. My life is full. I have a son now who turned anger towards me into love, and I've learned how to love him. Those are the things I do now. I'm just trying to be a responsible member of society.

For Kelly, demonstrating that she is a responsible mother and citizen is not antithetical to a project of community building that locates each individual within a support network.

There is no typical single mom. Yet at the same time, single mothers in the United States at the turn of the century all live with the imperative to demonstrate self-sufficiency. With that demonstration comes an erasure of the stigma that has historically marked single mothers in this country and even the recognition that single mothers don't always have to be self-sacrificing in order to qualify as good mothers. Borrowing a term from the Italian antifascist activist and theorist Antonio Gramsci, I argue that single mothers are the new "organic intellectuals." As he postulated, "Every social group, coming into existence on the original terrain of an essential function in the world of economic production, creates together with itself, organically, one or more strata of intellectuals which give it homogeneity and an awareness of its own function not only in the economic but also in the social and political fields" (301). I am also redefining the term to encompass the work of mothering, as Gramsci didn't attend to the domestic sphere. Single mothers are "domestic intellectuals," operating within the usually denigrated realms of child care and housework to rearticulate these realms as ones of political, economic, and social possibility. Fantasia Barrino, the women of the Rebecca project, and the members of Single Mothers by Choice are all domestic intellectuals; they have emerged at a particular point in history, at specific locations, and have begun to articulate a sometimes homogeneous but often contradictory identity category. Single mothers are the exemplars of the shifting American family, showing that women can raise children in nonpatriarchal households. They are also the representatives of the neoliberal dream of self-sufficiency, identified by President George Bush as no longer outsiders to the nation: "I believe Americans in need are not problems; they are our neighbors. They're not strangers; they are citizens of our country," he said, while campaigning for welfare reform in 2002 (Meckler A1). Single mothers "do heroic work" in raising their children alone, Bush added, even as he proposed still stricter welfare-to-work requirements than were passed in the 1996 Personal Responsibility Act.

Single moms put together everyday life at a complex conjuncture of social, economic, political, and cultural forces. And there are more of us every day. The 2000 U.S. Census and other demographic studies show a remarkable growth in single-parent families due to both divorce and new births; by some estimates, one-third of all babies are now born to single moms, and less than 25 percent of all families conform to the nuclear configuration. New possibilities for mothering without men are due to the feminist and gay movement's challenge to patriarchal notions of family, the liberalization of divorce laws, an increase in numbers of financially independent women, and developments in new reproductive technologies. Single mothers emerge as a respected identity group in the context of the neoliberal production of the self-regulating citizen-consumer-subject. This conjuncture of forces can be seen in the remarkable explosion of positive media representations of single moms over the last decade; from *Austin Powers* to *The Cat in the Hat*, single mothers are the new darlings of popular culture.

At the same time, the project of neoliberalism and its insistence on cutting social programs and expanding private enterprise has been making life increasingly difficult for many single mothers. Governmental support for low-income mothers has been steadily declining for years, signified most dramatically in the 1996 Personal Responsibility Act (PRA) that turned welfare administration over to the states in the form of Temporary Assistance to Needy Families, which limits aid to five years and institutes strict work requirements during that time. The poverty rate in women-headed households is higher than it is for any other demographic group.

The Bush administration proposes marriage as a solution; the PRA included numerous provisions to "promote marriage, reduce out-of-wedlock births, and 'encourage the formation and maintenance of two-parent families'" (Mink 73). Access to child care for all single mothers is woefully inadequate. There continues to be discrimination against mothers, especially lesbians, in custody cases, where they are held to higher standards of "good parenting" than men. In many locations, single women are not treated as equals to married women when they seek to become mothers through assisted reproductive technologies and adoption. Despite the enormous potential for technologies and adoption to sever the links between biology and the family, opening the door for different kinds of kinship, the sheer cost of both assisted reproduction and adoption make them accessible to a fairly select group. Furthermore, the medical establishment and the legal system still assume heterosexual couples make the best parents.

In these complicated times, all single mothers are asked to prove their ability to govern themselves as subjects of freedom—freedom from any kind of dependency—in order to qualify as "normal." We can usefully ask the same set of questions about the acceptance of single mothers as Nikolas Rose asks about the governance of all subjects under neoliberalism: "How have we come to define ourselves in terms of a certain notion of freedom? How has freedom provided the rationale for all manner of coercive interventions into the lives of those seen as unfree or threats to freedom: the poor, the homeless, the mad, the risky, or those at risk?" (16). I would add to his list of questions: What spaces of freedom are produced for single mothers who want to maintain alternative family formations? Is it possible to operate outside the state regulation of maternal bodies in a manner that is not purely self-serving?

This book takes on these questions in all their complexity, never dismissive of the practical, everyday realities of single mothers and never sanguine about the effects of an acceptance based on autonomy. At this point in history, the valorization of self-reliant single mothering dominates, and thus the single-mother family presents a fairly limited challenge to the nuclear family even though the possibilities are vast and the stories of single mothers inspiring. Autonomy grants single mothers a kind of respect; however, the respect is most quickly earned if single mothers operate as if they were a nuclear family, temporarily minus the live-in dad. This principle guides both policy—with its sometimes-explicit endorsement of marriage—and media representations, which give little attention to alternative forms of family. As such, the endorsement of single mothers usually ignores possibilities for alternative family formations—such as extended families and community child care—that have been common at different historical moments for some ethnic and indigenous populations.

Still, there *are* other possibilities, generated in a space somewhere between the state and the individual. Self-reliance does not always mean solitude; it can encompass community groups, churches, support networks, extended families, and friends. Sometimes this sounds suspiciously like the solutions proposed by neoliberalism. At other times, however, it's a more organic, grassroots response, as offered by the women of the Rebecca Project, who have combined personal responsibility with solidarity and mainstream legislative lobbying. Community support for single mothers may also emerge from a history of well-founded suspicion of state regulation. In Chicago's Humboldt Park neighborhood, the Puerto Rican Cultural Center's program for single mothers is part of the struggle for collective self-determination, based on the fact that Puerto Rico is a colony of the United States. In the Rio Grande Valley of Texas, undocumented single moms help form neighborhood associations premised on the belief that undocumented people are entitled to basic human rights that the state denies them because they don't have legal papers. Across spaces, I found what feminist political theorist Wendy Brown calls the struggle for "collective self-legislation," the "desire to participate in shaping the conditions and terms of life," which "remain a vital element—if also an evidently ambivalent and anxious one—of much agitation under the sign of progressive politics" (4).

The critical question is this: Can the conditions under which certain single mothers are accepted be turned, reimagined, reconceived, and transformed so that all single mothers—indeed all mothers—are supported in caring for themselves and their children, thus leading to the growth of family structures that represent true alternatives to the traditional nuclear family and its predictable gendered and sexual roles?

In part, this book is an attempt to make sense of my own experience as a single mom in academia, where the pressure to demonstrate self-sufficiency has been intense. Seeking alternatives, I've returned to some of the activist communities where I lived and worked before becoming a mother, to the Puerto Rican Cultural Center in Chicago and to Proyecto Libertad, an immigrant rights' group on the Texas-Mexican border. I have sought out other groups, including the Rebecca Project. I have studied corporate America's attention to mothers' issues—including the corporate university—and examined television and film for their representations. I have probed policy realms—welfare, immigration, medical, and legal—to understand what rules govern our lives and what agency might be wrested from within those structures. In short, I have tried to capture the complexity of single mothers' lives, both represented and real, without claiming that this picture is in any way exhaustive.

This book blends the personal, the practical, and the political as it addresses readers inside and outside of academia. It is shaped partially by frustration with my primary academic field—cultural studies—due to both its institutional disregard of child-care issues and its theoretical dismissal of mothering, something I'll address again later in this chapter. Yet cultural studies has also been very useful in helping me formulate a methodology for analyzing the current conditions that shape single mothering. Perhaps most importantly, this work is guided by cultural studies' desire to participate in social change, a desire that means one never knows ahead of time the answers to the questions one is asking. To intervene in the present conditions is to see how power is articulated across sites, how it insinuates itself into everyday life, and how people make do in conditions not of their own making.

The three major sections of the book derive from some of the most important governing concepts in cultural studies: everyday life, spaces, and ethics. Within each of these sections, other "keywords" play an important role: care of the self, community, mobility, organizing, choice, and bodies. I'm drawing loosely on Raymond Williams's influential *Keywords in Cultural Studies*. Williams's book historicized and contextualized terms that were shaping cultural studies in Britain in the 1960s, and his book continues to help define the field. Similarly, each of my keywords represents issues critical to cultural studies; however, my discussion of these issues also shows how cultural studies has failed to treat mothering as an issue worthy of research and writing. Our lack of attention to mothering perpetuates the division between private and public, a division visible in the still vaunted category of the "public intellectual," a role Williams occupied and which still informs the academic left's attempt to define its spokespeople. This tradition can be traced (although this isn't the only source) to Gramsci's notion of the organic intellectual.

The dominant class has its intellectuals, its naturalized leaders, says Gramsci, who emerge from generation to generation as part of the process through which hegemony is maintained. The business entrepreneur, for example, is an organic intellectual, an "organizer of the masses of men" (301), who works to maintain capitalism. Hegemony is sustained primarily through two interlocking systems: the class division between manual and mental labor and the schools, which reproduce the class division, allowing only certain people access to the status of intellectual. There is nothing intrinsic that defines an intellectual; rather, the role is the product of particular social and historical relations, which reproduce themselves until and unless marginalized groups can develop their own intellectuals, thus interrupting the class division. For Gramsci, all men have the potential to become intellectuals: "All men are intellectuals, one could therefore say, but not all men have in society the function of intellectuals" (304).

Gramsci suggests that one must rise above physical labor to become an intellectual, which virtually ensures that mothers, as mothers, will never become organic intellectuals. The domestic sphere is not perceived to be a site of intellectual activity. The organic-as-public intellectual is completely divorced from domestic work, which is implicitly posited as the most manual, the least stimulating of labor. It's not that women can't become intellectuals but rather that they won't in their capacity as mothers. Yet many of the skills Gramsci describes are skills that mothers practice daily, most importantly the skill of organizing. What we organize, however, seems not to circulate with value in public. Child care, cooking, laundry, lawn mowing, and bottle cleaning are not part of civil society, the educational system, or obvious realms of governance.

Gramsci's model still seems operative in many left intellectual circles. Yet in mainstream society, perhaps times have changed. In the United States at the turn of the twenty-first century, single mothers have emerged as entrepreneurs and exemplars of how to succeed, writing self-help books and starring in films and television shows. This emergence qualifies them to speak on behalf of other single mothers, showing them how to distance themselves from state aid and other forms of dependency. Yet this is not the kind of domestic intellectual who will define a strong alternative to hegemonic forms of family, for her rhetoric risks mimicking the rhetoric of choice and self-sufficiency that governs liberal capitalism and liberal feminism. What will enable us to articulate an oppositional position, where single mothers are supported in sustaining truly different family formations, where boys and girls can be raised to challenge gendered and sexual norms and where marriage does not become the most expedient solution to exhaustion?

The answer lies in organizing outside one's immediate interests, in the social project of the Rebecca Project, for example. Although the group does not escape the rhetoric of personal responsibility, their insistence on reciprocity and commitment represents more of a possibility that they will articulate an oppositional politics than Single Mothers by Choice, whose focus on the individual can be easily absorbed into mainstream conceptions of family. To be a domestic intellectual is not to transcend the domestic, defined as a realm of giving and bodily interdependence, but to connect that realm to other sites. Domestic intellectuals give value to the work of mothering—to the pure organicity of birth, diaper changing, nursing; they are organic intellectuals who do not rank intellectual over bodily labor but rather live out their convergence.

There are many kinds of domestic intellectuals, and I am definitely not excluding some single mothers, such as those in SMC, because they seem less explicitly oppositional than those in the Rebecca Project. Precisely because organic intellectuals do not rise above their class but remain part of it and the larger social spheres that define it, contradictions are to be expected. There is, as I shall argue throughout this book, the practical matter of everyday survival that sometimes makes appeals to choice and autonomy a necessity. Yet I will also look throughout this book for domestic intellectuals who carve out positions of collaboration that make "choice" a less autonomous endeavor. Ideally, the domestic intellectual does not seek an individual position of esteem that lifts her above other single mothers; rather, organizing produces a collective position of resistance to the pressures of assimilation to the nuclear family. The domestic intellectual does not act as a mediator authorized to speak on behalf of single mothers who remain behind, "mired" in the work of raising children. Rather, the domestic intellectual moves from home to school to library to park to Congress to the streets, mapping paths, expanding single mothers' access to one another and to other sources of assistance.

The domestic intellectual is not a luminary. She may or may not attract media attention. She operates within the mundane and everyday routines of domestic life. She is an organizer and as such she provides insights into how to valorize organizing in other realms, such as the academy (where organizing is routinely devalued in comparison to publishing and other individual acts). To use Foucault's terms, the domestic intellectual is a specific intellectual, one who has "gotten used to working, not in the modality of the 'universal,' 'exemplary,' the 'just-and-true-for- all,' but within specific sectors, at the precise points where their own conditions of life or work situate them" (1972, 126). It's interesting that Foucault positions specific intellectuals at different points, not just the academy, where it is perhaps too easy to adopt the mode of the "universal" intellectual. Domestic intellectuals act as an antidote to universal claims, connecting rather than transcending places of life and work.

The domestic intellectual speaks frankly out of personal experience—another realm often demeaned in cultural studies. Drawing here on feminist practice, I write out of a personal desire to express some of the difficulties and joys of single mothering, to share my own experiences and those of women I've interviewed, and in the process to present something useful to single moms. My keywords also represent some of the most operative terms in the contemporary organization of the lives of single mothers in the United States. They serve as a vocabulary for thinking about the agency of single mothers, insofar as they define both how single mothers are viewed and governed and how we might think about ourselves and the possibilities for reshaping our lives. I hope the nonacademic reader finds that the theory woven throughout the chapters derives as often from the interviews and situations as it does from academia.

"Academia" can't be homogenized, and I'm sure there will be various academic readers who object to my impure methodological approach. In this respect, this is truly a cultural studies project, for the field does not respect disciplinary boundaries as it pursues the best tools for the project at hand: "The choice of research practices depends upon the questions that are asked, and the questions depend on their context" (Grossberg, Nelson, and Treichler 2). I am reluctant to identify the disciplines represented here because I have in fact drawn on whatever resources seem most useful for understanding the history and current state of single mothering in the United States. In doing so, I am abdicating any claims to be an "expert" in any discipline, for such disciplinary policing actually works against a full understanding of the many forces shaping single mothering today.

Freedom from Marriage?

Single mothering emerges as a state of possible freedom: freedom from marriage, freedom from the stigma of "out of wedlock" births, freedom to have different sexual partners, freedom to raise children in alternative fashion. Yet the question remains: How free are most single mothers to pursue these possibilities? Some of that freedom is impeded by the privileges that marriage continues to confer.

Marriage in the United States has been based on the same political and moral values that shaped the country, as Nancy Cott argues in her history of the institution: "Political and legal authorities endorsed and aimed to perpetuate nationally a *particular* marriage model: lifelong, faithful monogamy, formed by the mutual consent of a man and a woman, bearing the impress of the Christian religion and the English common law in its expectations for the husband to be the family head and economic provider, his wife the dependent partner" (3). These are public as well as private roles, and Cott describes the many ways the legal system shapes citizenship in relation to gender, sexuality, and race. Although marriage ostensibly represented the freedom to choose a partner in a ceremony validated through a social contract, it was, like other forms of contract, not as free for some as for others. The legal doctrine of coverture basically "turned the married pair legally into one person," says Cott, "enlarging" the husband while the wife gave up her legal rights: "He became the one full citizen in the household, his authority over and responsibility for his dependents contributing to his citizenship capacity" (12). As Carole Pateman argues, marriage was constitutive of liberal society, dispersing patriarchy across public and private, two separate but complementary realms. A sexual contract was the basis for the social contract guaranteeing fathers' rights: "The original pact is a sexual as well as a social contract: it is sexual in the sense of patriarchal—that is, the contract establishes men's political right over women—and also sexual in the sense of establishing orderly access by men to women's bodies" (2). Marriage became the means for controlling the products of sexual desire—babies—making those products the property of men.

Marriage also determined citizenship by excluding racial categories of people deemed "unworthy" of belonging to the nation: slaves had no access to legal marriage, and it wasn't until 1967, in the case of *Loving v. Virginia,* that the U.S. Supreme Court struck down race-based state laws restricting marital freedom (sixteen states still considered marriage across race lines a crime; Cott 4). Immigration quotas and policies have also been used to regulate which "outsiders" may gain citizenship through marriage, a practice that continues to the present. And of course the current debates about gay marriage testify to the ongoing exclusionary powers of the law based on the desire to determine what constitutes a proper family.

Throughout much of U.S. history, bearing children outside marriage has carried heavy penalties for women and their children. Because marriage was the basis for citizenship, the "bastard" had no "recognized legal relations with his or her parents, particularly not those of inheritance, maintenance, and custody. Nor did the illicit couple have any rights or duties toward their spurious issue" (Grossberg 197). Illegitimate children were used to enforce proper sexual conduct, and mothers have suffered the consequences of violating this conduct. Hence Nathaniel Hawthorne's rendering of Hester Prynne and the real stories of single moms that have been told throughout the twentieth century. Said one unmarried mother living in Pittsburgh in the post–World War II years: "I fear no hell after death, for I've had mine here on earth. Let no man or girl deceive herself—hell hath no punishment like the treatment people give a 'fallen woman.' The heartache, tortured thoughts, recriminations, fear, loneliness could not be put on paper. Neither can the scorn, insult, and actual hate of self-righteous and ignorant people" (qtd. in Solinger 2001, 33).

Until the 1930s, all single mothers, regardless of race, were considered "ruined" due to a biological defect, says Rickie Solinger: "Illegitimacy occurred at the intersection of negative sociological and biological conditions and was an expression of an inhering, unchanging, and unchangeable 'physical' defect" (16). After World War II, it became possible for women who got pregnant outside marriage to redeem themselves—but only if they gave the baby up for adoption. The explanatory emphasis in terms of white single pregnancy shifted from biological defect to psychological neuroses, in part, says Solinger, because the number of single mothers was increasing—it simply became unrealistic to claim they were all ruined women.[1] Because the problem was psychological rather than biological, single mothers could be cured of their illness. By admitting they were sick and agreeing to give up their babies, white unwed mothers could be made marriageable again and assume their proper roles as mothers (Solinger 86). By contrast, black unwed mothers in the postwar years continued to be portrayed as biologically unfit, "unrestrained, wanton breeders, on the one hand, or as calculating breeders for profit on the other" (9). It was a Catch-22: their sexuality was seemingly uncontrollable, intrinsic, not a choice—yet their decision to keep their babies indicated too much choice, a savvy cunning deployed to subvert the state. They were not considered eligible for psychological treatment, nor were they pressured to put up their babies for adoption. The "white public" resented money going to black welfare mothers. "In the mother-blaming mode of the postwar decades, many analysts identified the black single mother's alleged hypersexuality and immorality, her resulting children, and the public expense as traceable to the source: the Negro woman who gave birth, as it were, to black America, with all its 'defects'" (49).

In the mid-1960s, the nuclear family assumed normative force through the writings of social scientists including Daniel Moynihan, Nathan Glazer, and Oscar Lewis, all of whom, in varying ways, blamed black and Latino families for inherent psychological and moral deficiencies that trapped them in a cycle of dependency. Most to blame, especially in Moynihan's report, "The Negro Family: A Case for National Action," were "dominating" black women, who, by working for wages *and* rearing families on their own, had emasculated black men, causing their lack of motivation and turn to criminal activities. Black and Latina single mothers were both disempowered and terribly powerful, and the very traits of hard work and family loyalty that should have received praise were demonized (Feldstein 143). Oscar Lewis's book *La Vida* on Puerto Ricans was more sympathetic in that he identified the structural conditions of migration and capitalism as reasons for poverty, but he also tended to blame Puerto Ricans generally for failure to assimilate, and especially husbands and fathers for abandoning their families (Pérez 58).

This brief history of marriage serves as a reminder that the nuclear family is a socially constructed norm that often precludes one from thinking about other kinds of families and other ways of taking care of kin, both biological and non-biological. The nuclear family/children as property model is an Anglo norm that should not be used to gauge the validity of "family." It wasn't always so and it needn't continue to be so, even though policy decisions continue to be based, in many ways, on the traditional family. One has only to look at Native American and African American communities to find alternatives. Patricia Hill Collins describes the practice of "othermothers"—"women who assist bloodmothers by sharing mothering responsibilities," which she traces historically: "The centrality of women in African-American extended families reflects a continuation of both West African cultural values and functional adaptations to race and gender oppression" (219). The importance of women does not necessarily indicate the absence of husbands and fathers, as they may play significant roles in family life without living in the home, or while living in the home without being as powerful as the women. Nevertheless, the absence of men is due in part, as Collins suggests, to racism and poverty—hence her nod to "functional adaptations." Shared child-raising practices contribute to a people's self-reliance, says Collins: "Black women's relationships with children and other vulnerable community members is not intended to dominate or control. Rather, its purpose is to bring people along, to—in the words of late nineteenth century Black feminists—'uplift the race'—so that vulnerable members of the community will be able to attain the self-reliance and independence essential for resistance" (233).

In other ways, marriage as the only acceptable way to have and raise children began to lose its normative hold in the 1960s. Beginning around 1965, the rate of formal marriage began dropping while the divorce rate rose. The number of unmarried-couple households recorded by the Census Bureau multiplied almost ten times from 1960 to 1998 (Cott 203). The women's liberation and gay rights' movements challenged sexual norms, leading for perhaps a relatively brief period in the 1960s and early 1970s to an increasing acceptance of sexual experimentation even within marriage. *Roe v. Wade* was a landmark decision in the feminist battle for women to control their reproductive fates. No-fault divorce was first adopted in California in 1969; by 1985, every state had some version of it. The 1964 Civil Rights Act included "sex" as an unwarranted basis for discrimination and helped feminists dismantle sex distinctions in employment and education. Although women continue to be paid less than men for comparable labor, increasing financial independence for some women allowed them to choose single mothering more readily. There was less pressure for women who got pregnant "out of wedlock" to give up their babies for adoption. Groups such as the National Welfare Rights Organization and the Sisterhood of Black Single Mothers organized on behalf of single mothers. Solinger identifies the mid-1970s as the period in which the term "single mother" gained currency, replacing "unwed mother" and indicating a newfound respect and acceptance for mothers of different income levels. This acceptance was reflected in Supreme Court decisions, the creation of educational support programs for young mothers, and sympathetic mainstream media coverage.[2] It was a relatively brief moment of acceptance, however; at the same time, there was growing resentment about the expansion of social programs. With Ronald Reagan's rise to power came a renewed demonization of the single mother as the source of social problems.[3] The very category of "choice" that had been deployed to liberate women from the articulation of marriage and morality was turned against single mothers who couldn't show their financial independence. I'll elaborate more on the demonization of dependency later in this introduction.

Nevertheless, by the mid-1970s, the denunciation of single mothers was by no means automatic, and, increasingly, people lived in families that did not fit the Ozzie and Harriet ideal. The proportion of adults who declined to marry at all rose between 1972 and 1998 from 15 percent to 23 percent. By the end of the century, people living alone comprised one-quarter of all households. Half of all marriages now end in divorce. More than one-third of all babies are now born to unmarried mothers, compared to 5 percent in 1960. Rates of single mothering have increased most rapidly among nonteenage white women: "White women's rate of unmarried childbearing more than doubled after 1980. Black women's rate moved up only 2 percent during the same years, so that where their rate had been 4 or 5 times that of whites in 1960, in the late 1990s it was only about twice as high. As a result of both non-marriage and divorce among women with children, one fifth of family-based households of whites were female-headed in the 1990s, as were almost three fifths of black families and almost one third of Hispanic families" (Cott 204).

For many mothers, marriage is no longer a prerequisite of good citizenship, not even when there are children involved. Single moms aren't immediate objects of shame and exclusion. The sexual contract is not intrinsically necessary for liberal society to function, notes Wendy Brown: "As women are no longer required to enter a sexual contract—subordination in marriage—for survival or societal recognition (although these both continue to be enhanced by heterosexual marriage), liberal political orders no longer need refer to an imaginary social contract for their legitimacy" (137). Capitalism doesn't need the nuclear family or marriage in order to thrive.

Perhaps because of the growing acceptance of single-parent families, however, there is an ongoing conservative push to restore the "sanctity" of marriage. In 1996, Congress passed and President Bill Clinton signed the Defense of Marriage Act, which defined marriage as the legal union between a man and a woman. Much of the congressional debate on the bill revealed a bipartisan consensus on the proper way to raise children. As Senator Robert Byrd, Democrat of West Virginia, said, "If same-sex marriage is accepted, America will have said that children do not need a mother and a father, two mothers or two fathers will be just as good. This would be a catastrophe." Eight years later, after the state of Massachusetts legalized gay marriage, President Bush called for a constitutional amendment defining marriage as the union between a man and a woman, hoping to keep other potentially renegade states in line. "Ages of experience have taught humanity that the commitment of a husband and wife to love and to serve one another promotes the welfare of children and the stability of society," Bush said in a February 2004 press conference.

Furthermore, marriage continues to carry with it considerable material benefits: "A 1996 report from the U.S. General Accounting Office found more than *one thousand* places in the corpus of federal law where legal marriage conferred a distinctive status, right, or benefit" (Cott 2). In *The Trouble with Normal,* Michael Warner cites some of the entitlements marriage confers, including a variety of state income tax advantages, rights relating to inheritance, award of child custody in divorce proceedings, the right to spousal support, the right to postdivorce property division, and more (117–118). Not surprisingly, then, while one in two marriages end in divorce, the national rate of remarriage is high. These continued rights suggest that the legacy of gender subordination that historically defined marriage as an institution *does* still matter in terms of a liberal discourse that organizes jurisprudence, public policy, and public consciousness. In other words, you can be a single mom with no particular stigma attached, but the legal system and economic and public policy will still work against you, making marriage seem like the most attractive option for ensuring the long-term well-being of yourself and your children.

Given this conflicted and generally exclusionary history, it is not surprising that some academic theorists, especially in queer studies, express considerable reservation about relying on marriage as a venue for inclusion. Inclusion in what? Heteronormative privilege? As Michael Warner argues, "as long as people marry, the state will continue to regulate the sexual lives of those who do not marry. It will continue to refuse to recognize our intimate relations—including cohabiting partnerships—as having the same rights or validity as a married couple" (1999, 96). As Judith Butler rightly asks, why should marriage be seen as the only way of securing kinship? Both Warner and Butler take issue with gay and lesbian activists who argue for the right to marriage, arguing that to subject oneself to the state's regulation will produce new exclusionary effects. For Warner, an appeal to marriage flies in the face of a queer politics that resists normalization: "Marriage, in short, would make for good gays—the kind who would not challenge the norms of straight culture, who would not flaunt sexuality, and who would not insist on living differently from ordinary folk" (113). As Butler puts it,

In the case of gay marriage or of affiliative legal alliances, we see how various sexual practices and relationships that fall outside the purview of the sanctifying law become illegible or, worse, untenable, and how new hierarchies emerge within public discourse. These hierarchies not only enforce the distinction between legitimate and illegitimate queer lives, but they produce tacit distinctions among forms of illegitimacy. The stable pair who would marry if only they could are cast as currently illegitimate, but eligible for a future legitimacy, whereas the sexual agents who function outside the purview of the marriage bond and its recognized, if illegitimate, alternative form now constitute sexual possibilities that will never be eligible for a translation into legitimacy. (3)

In the same fashion, single mothers who make it clear that they want some day to remarry are "eligible for future legitimacy" and thus granted temporary respect and even admiration. By contrast, single mothers who work to construct alternative and long-standing family formations and who construct a political and social identity around single mothering as a preferred status represent a less legitimate, although perhaps not completely illegitimate, position. Again, this legitimacy rests on their ability to demonstrate lack of need.

Cultural Studies and Domesticity

Could it be, then, that single mothers are queer? If so, why do academic theorists, such as Warner and Berlant, who are so eager to embrace the margins, offer so little in the way of material support or even intellectual acknowledgment of single moms? In Warner's chapter on marriage, for example, considerable attention is paid to alternative forms of intimacy that queer culture embraces outside heterosexual culture, but there is no sense that children are part of this queer counterpublic. He says, "Between tricks and lovers and exes and friends and fuckbuddies and bar friends and bar friends' tricks and tricks' bar friends and gal pals and companions 'in the life,' queers have an astonishing range of intimacies" (116). There are clearly no children among this "welter of intimacies" that are constructed outside of traditional frameworks of social obligations.

In general, cultural studies has failed to take seriously the politics of domesticity, family, parenting, and children, perhaps because domesticity seem so irrevocably bourgeois, so linked to property, containment, and essentialized identities—so unable to be rearticulated to something more in line with the perceived politics of cultural studies. Often, this disregard is implicit. Occasionally, it becomes explicit. Responding to a proposal by the American Association of University Professors that professors with newborn babies should be granted more time to achieve tenure, cultural studies scholar Cary Nelson told the *Chronicle of Higher Education* that the proposal "has an odd echo of Republican family values, that nothing matters more than the raising of your family. I'm not amongst those who idealize children" (Wilson, November 9, 2001). The *Chronicle* also sponsored an online forum on the AAUP proposal, and although some people were supportive, many more wrote in to say how tired they were of "children and breeders getting all the consideration all the time."

By not theorizing issues of home spaces and their bodies, cultural studies misses the opportunity to rearticulate conservative invocations of family and to build discursive support for alternative families, including single mothers, gay and lesbian parents, and parents of children with disabilities, as well as for heterosexual couples who want to raise their children in a less nuclear fashion. Indeed, our silence on issues of domesticity threatens to cede the territory of the family to the right, as conservative politicians and intellectuals capture the media limelight on matters of marriage, children, and families.

An important exception to this tendency is Lawrence Grossberg's new book, *Caught in the Crossfire: Kids, Politics, and America's Future,* which appeared just as *Single Mother* was entering production. One of Grossberg's objectives in describing the current conditions structuring the lives of youth in the United States is to "take seriously the particular set of alliances and interests that I call the New Right, to treat it with respect and to begin to understand its thoughts and appeals for significant portions of the American public" (xiii).[4]

Some important work has been done in relation to the home, especially in media studies by scholars such as Janice Radway, Lynn Spigel, David Morley, Roger Silverstone, and Ellen Seiter. Cultural studies has been fascinated with youth culture, yet "youth" seems to begin at adolescence, when youth *leave* the home. It seems fair to say that the majority of articles and books produced on space deal with spaces other than the home. The 1990s was characterized by a publishing explosion on globalization, diaspora, migration, citizenship, geography, cities, public policy, citizenship, civil society, sex in public, public intellectuals, and so on. Since

1990, *Cultural Studies* and *Public Culture*[5] have published only a handful of articles on domesticity, and articles specifically focused on mothering and children are even fewer.[6] Work on various public spheres is often articulated to/through theories of citizenship, to a politics of civil society and public policy, again to the exclusion of the home as a site where citizenship is also formed. Domesticity did not figure, for example, in the debates on policy studies in cultural studies in the early and mid-1990s, mainly instigated by Australian cultural studies scholars such as Tony Bennett, Stuart Cunningham, Ian Hunter, Tom O'Regan, and John Frow.

The turn to spatial analysis in cultural studies thus happens almost always in relation to public formations—museums, cities, nations, hospitals, and schools—via theorists such as LeFebvre, Foucault, and Deleuze and critical geographers such as Mike Davis, David Harvey, Edward Soja, and Doreen Massey. Also important in this context is the work on globalization, migration, and diaspora by scholars such as Arjun Appadurai, Paul Gilroy, George Yudice, Alberto Moreiras, Saskia Sassen, Michael Hardt and Antonio Negri,[7] and many others. In most of this work, home in the domestic and familial sense rarely enters into the discussion, especially in the context of parenting and child-care issues. Rather, the focus is on mobility across and between nations; as David Morley comments, "In recent years much has been made of the idea of postmodernity. Images abound of our supposedly de-territorialised culture of 'homelessness': images of exile, diaspora, time-space compression, migrancy, and 'nomadology.' The concept of home often remains as the uninterrogated anchor or alter ego of all this hyper-mobility" (3). As an example of the focus on mobility, Morley cites the founding statement of the journal *Public Culture,* in which editors Appadurai and Carol Breckenridge describe the late twentieth century as "an increasingly cosmopolitan world" (qtd. in Morley 9).

The tendency to devalue the domestic can also be seen in cultural studies' critique of neoliberalism as a form of privatization, which implicitly positions the home, again, as a site of bourgeois privilege to be counteracted with a revitalized politics of the public sphere. Henry Giroux, for example, argues that "within the increasing corporatization of everyday life, market values replace social values, and people appear more and more willing to retreat into the safe, privatized enclaves of the family, religion, and consumption" (2001, xi). It's interesting here to note the conflation of family, religion, and consumption, all of which are articulated to an interiorized notion of home, which is seemingly impervious to public debate and progressive change. Similarly, Michael Warner and Lauren Berlant argue that "ideologies and institutions of intimacy" are offered as "the only (fantasy) zone in which a future might be thought and willed, the only (imaginary) place where good citizens might be produced away from the confusing and unsettling distractions and contradictions of capitalism and politics. Indeed, one of the unforeseen paradoxes of national-capitalist privatization has been that citizens have been led through heterosexual culture to identify both themselves *and their politics* with privacy" (193).

This is tricky territory. Although it is certainly important to critique the privatization of public services and sites, I would argue that it is not necessary in the process to either ignore or demean the home (an "institution of intimacy") and to suggest that it is only in "public" where progressive politics occur. It is important, as feminists have argued, to challenge the assumption that "home" is private, to show its material connections to other spaces. The above critiques of neoliberalism seem to cede the home to the right because they offer no alternative conceptions and exhibit no desire to rearticulate the home. How, for example, might queer politics open up the home to diverse practices? What might those diverse practices be? How would mothering and child care change? What are the mundane details of everyday life that would remain largely domestic, in the material space of the home, and how would those practices redefine public discourses of caring? How are citizens shaped in home spaces in ways that might not collude with neoliberalism?

Similarly, an emphasis on policy in the rapidly developing field of disabilities studies has too often elided the home, say Rayna Rapp and Faye Ginsberg. They argue that disabilities studies has not acknowledged the "intimate arena of kinship as a site where contemporary social dramas around changing understandings and practices of reproduction and disability are often first played out" (535). One of their main points is that caretaking of disabled children requires extended support networks and thus reveals the limits of the "gendered nuclear family model" (540). In the same special issue of *Public Culture*, Veena Das and Renu Addlakha show that the strategies used by Indian families in Punjab and Delhi to cope with relatives with various disabilities had a powerful impact on their public identities, and that one should not assume that citizenship is constituted at public sites that act unidirectionally on the home. Das and Addlakha argue for "(1)displacing citizenship from its conventional association with publics defined through civility and (2) displacing domesticity from its conventional place in particularistic loyalties" (530).

Cultural studies has always cited as one of its defining features a concern for its own conditions of practice. Incessantly self-reflexive, cultural studies has produced many articles and talks on the question of how to define itself in relation to existing disciplines, how to fully acknowledge the institution without becoming too embedded in it. Several prominent scholars in the field have written extensively about the need to support graduate student unionization. Yet despite all this talk about institutional conditions, little attention had been paid to child-care issues—to providing child care at conferences, working for better maternal-leave policies and more child-care centers on campuses, and incorporating children in social events. As a field and a practice, cultural studies has not provided material support for alternative forms of family and parenting within the academy, thus implicitly endorsing the nuclear family as the most viable and practical form for raising children.

Despite the fact that much recent cultural studies theory has led away from analyzing the home, there is nothing intrinsic to the theories that precludes such analysis. In fact, I hope to show in much of this book that the theories of space, migration, and mobility can be very useful in illuminating the conditions shaping single mothering. In turn, single mothers offer cultural studies critical insights into and thus possibilities for redefining the neoliberal agenda.

Liberalism/Neoliberalism

Neoliberalism insofar as it suggests a new political and economic phase of government may be a misnomer. As some critics note, neoliberalism is more accurately seen as an intensification of liberalism, with its foundations in free-market economics, rational individualism, and property accumulation. There have been brief periods in the United States of a limited welfare state, extending from the New Deal of the 1930s to the Great Society of the 1960s, but since then, there has been a steady and growing consensus about the need to dismantle even that commitment to social programs. Democrats and Republicans alike agree, notes Lisa Duggan, on the "neoliberal agenda of shrinking public institutions, expanding private profit-making prerogatives, and undercutting democratic practices and noncommercial cultures" (xv). Through the practices of deregulation, flexible labor, and privatization, the gap between rich and poor has widened around the world, obviously to the benefit of Western creditors and corporations. As the state withdraws, neoliberals exhort "civil society (the 'voluntary' sector) and 'the family' to take up significant roles in the provision of social safety nets" (Duggan 10). These intertwined impulses of neoliberalism—the demonization of dependency and the insistence on autonomy—are powerful forces determining the subject positions available to single mothers.

It wasn't always so. Early forms of assistance to single mothers who couldn't support their children were actually meant to encourage them to stay home—although only if they had not chosen to be single mothers— widows, for example, or women abandoned by their husbands. These women were considered worthy recipients of the various forms of public assistance that began in the early 1900s—assistance that positioned the state as the replacement for the absent father. The Mothers' Pension Program, for example, was instituted in 1921, based on the belief that mothers' most important service was mothering, not semiskilled labor. Only certain mothers qualified, notes welfare scholar Mimi Abramovitz: "Only women with permanently absent husbands due to death, long-term imprisonment, and incurable insanity were routinely eligible in all states. Such eligibility rules distinguished among women according to their marital status and denied aid to other husbandless women viewed as departing from prescribed wife and mother roles" (201). Although standards were gradually broadened to include some divorced mothers by 1931, widows still headed over 80 percent of the more than 60,000 families receiving aid nationwide.

Making aid contingent on morality continued in the implementation of the Aid to Dependent Children (ADC) program that was part of the landmark 1935 Social Security Act. Says Abramovitz: "The ADC program perpetuated the mother's pension philosophy that maternal employment negatively effected child development and that 'deserving' women belonged in the home. Like its forerunner, ADC subsidized mothers to reproduce the labor force and maintain the non-working members of the population, but made receipt of a grant highly conditional upon compliance with the family ethic" (318). Although the act didn't contain any specific "suitable home" provisions in the manner of the Mothers' Pension program, "the preliminary legislative debates, the congressional committee reports, and an early version of the bill implicitly granted states permission to evaluate ADC applicants' moral character" (318). Supervision of the "morals" of recipients included questions about sexuality, home visits, and requirements for proof of paternity before aid could be received. Suitable home rules were often used to deny aid to black women, especially in the South, where state officials wanted to ensure a low-wage labor pool (Amott 288).

State supervision was most intense for those mothers who seemingly *chose* to have their babies, or, once pregnant, chose to keep their babies rather than give them up for adoption. The choice rendered them suspect. Public aid was given reluctantly, only with surveillance and stipulations. When single mothers were very young, or very poor, or in other conditions when "choice" seemed like an unlikely possibility, the dependency of the single mother—her need, in other words, for some kind of state support—was explained by shaming her sexuality rather than by examining the conditions that caused some women to become pregnant, such as lack of access to birth control and sexual education. This burden fell particularly heavily on women of color.

We arrive at the 1960s and the birth of the culture of poverty theory, which appealed to many people across the political spectrum. The 1960s saw a renewed commitment to social welfare, but this very commitment produced public resentment against its recipients. The culture of poverty theory "appealed because it suggested that black unwed mothers achieved or deserved their fate. As a consequence, it suggested American culture was absolved of any responsibility for both black illegitimacy and the problems it caused black girls and women in the community in general" (Solinger 83). Through the push toward "welfare reform" in the 1990s, the unregulated sexuality of single mothers on welfare was cited as reason for their failure to make the "right choice" and then targeted as the cause of poverty.

Since sexuality represents the irrational choice that leads to dependency, single mothers are told to pursue the seemingly rational alternative of paid labor that will lead to self-sufficiency and thus remove them from the realm of scrutiny and shame. At least if you work, goes the reasoning, you are not asking the state/taxpayers to be responsible for your bad choices. The 1996 Personal Responsibility Act was hailed and criticized as the bill that "ended welfare as we know it," but Congress has been passing welfare-to-work laws since the 1960s. In 1967, Congress established the Work Incentive Program, which "disqualified adults and older out-of-school children from AFDC payments if they refused to accept employment or participate in training programs" (Trattner 330). Richard Nixon further pushed the welfare-to-work agenda, proposing a plan that "was coupled with an elaborate system of penalties and incentives designed to force recipients to work. "In the final analysis," he said, "we cannot talk our way out of poverty; we cannot legislate our way out of poverty, but this nation can work its way out of poverty. What America needs now is not more welfare but more workfare" (qtd. in Trattner 339). Several decades passed before Congress passed another significant poverty bill—the Family Support Act (FSA) of 1988. According to feminist legal critic Martha Fineman, "The FSA's primary objective was to link poverty with the lack of a work ethic, thereby attaching welfare recipients to a new workfare scheme. This was accomplished in two ways: first, by mandating that the single mother work (or train for work); and second, by establishing a system for substituting support from fathers for state support . . . thus transforming a child's primary source of support from public to private hands" (110).

In the last two decades, the cheap labor pool created through denial of benefits to black women has increasingly included immigrant women, both undocumented and documented, as Grace Chang says in *Disposable Domestics*. Welfare reform is linked to immigration policy in an insidious manner, leaving the most vulnerable of women—single immigrant mothers, many of whom are undocumented, without recourse to public assistance for their children: almost half of the projected $54 billion savings in welfare cuts from the 1996 act was achieved by restrictions on immigrants. The assumption underlying welfare and immigration policy is that poor women of color are less valuable as mothers to their own children than as domestic, factory, and field workers.

The alternative to work, built into both welfare and immigration policy, has been marriage, which acts as both a moralizing and a privatizing force. As welfare scholar Gwendolyn Mink argues, by making it so difficult to survive on reduced payments and by instituting new requirements for establishing the paternity of the father and collecting payments from him, the Temporary Assistance to Needy Families program introduces a new level of assault on the "intimate associational rights" of poor women. She summarizes the TANF provisions:

Under the paternity establishment provision, a mother must disclose the identity of her child's biological father or must permit the government to examine her sex life so that it can discover the DNA paternal match for her child. Under the child support enforcement provision, a mother must help government locate her child's biological father so that the government can collect reimbursement from him for the mother's TANF benefit. A mandatory minimum sanction against families in which mothers do not cooperate in establishing paternity or collecting child support enforces government's determination that a biological reproductive nexus constitutes a social family. (69)

Other elements of TANF encourage marriage: states get a "performance bonus" if the percentage of children living in married families increases, and they can use TANF funds to encourage marriage classes and counseling. States receive a bonus if the "illegitimacy" rate drops without an increase in abortion rates. Abstinence is also encouraged; a provision of the 1996 PRA pays states to "teach groups which are most likely to bear children out-of-wedlock" that "sexual activity outside the context of marriage is likely to have harmful psychological and physical effects" and that one should "attain self-sufficiency before engaging in sexual activity" (qtd. in Mink 70).

Given the troubling history of welfare's intervention in the lives of poor women, we might ask: At what cost do we turn to the state for assistance? Wendy Brown argues that the right's attack on "big government" since the mid-1970s has led the left to uncritically defend the welfare state: "As the Right attacked the state for sustained welfare chiselers and being larded with bureaucratic fat, liberals and leftists jettisoned two decades of 'Marxist theories of the state' for a defense of the state as that which affords individuals 'protection against the worst abuses of the market' and other structures of social inequality" (15). Brown cites the work of several prominent progressives, specifically a book called *The Mean Season: The Attack on the Welfare State,* authored by "'democratic socialists' Fred Block, Richard Cloward, Barbara Ehrenreich, and Frances Fox Piven. The back cover says 'our boldest social thinkers argue for (the welfare state's) real, hard-won accomplishments. More than a defense of the welfare states, economic efficiency and fairness, *The Mean Season* is a reaffirmation of those decent, humane values so much under attack in Reagan's America'" (qtd. in Brown 15). Clearly skeptical about the complicity of liberal humanism with liberal policies, Brown asks rhetorically: "What kind of attachments to unfreedom can be discerned in contemporary political formations ostensibly concerned with emancipation? What kinds of injuries enacted by late modern democracies are recapitulated in the very oppositional projects of its subjects?" (xii).

A good question. However, Brown runs the risk here of dismissing the everyday lives of single mothers for whom welfare assistance can provide the means for leaving an abusive partner, for feeding one's children, and for eventually freeing oneself from the state. As the organizers of the Rebecca Project demonstrate, single mothers emerge *from within* the prevailing economic and social conditions; one cannot transcend or reject them.

The Self-Regulating Mom

The neoliberal alternative to dependency is personal responsibility, which has indeed been used to remove the stigma from single mothers who can demonstrate self-sufficiency. It would seem that the self-supporting single mom, through no singular power of her own even though it is represented as such, puts more pressure on the low-income single mother to distance herself from dependency in order to gain respect. In fact, ethnographers of poor women say that their interviewees' main goal is to become self-reliant: "In the long run, the goal of most mothers was to earn enough to eliminate the need for any government welfare program and to minimize their dependence on family, friends, boyfriends, side-jobs, and agencies" (Edin and Lein 64).

I would like to avoid creating a binary of middle-class versus welfare moms along the lines of self-sufficient versus dependent. In reality, single mothers' lives are much more complicated than this, and the desire for self-reliance emerges in different contexts not completely determined by governmental imperatives. Yet even when self-reliance seems to be a purely individual endeavor, I argue that we should not dismiss it, as academics are wont to do in relation to anything that hints of an "autonomous self." Nikolas Rose writes about the poststructuralistic critique of the enlightened, reasoned individual:

> At the very moment when this image of the human being is pronounced passé by social theorists, regulatory practices seek to govern individuals in a way more tied to their "selfhood" than ever before, and the ideas of identity and its cognates have acquired an increased salience in so many

of the practices in which human beings engage. In political life, in work, in conjugal and domestic arrangements, in consumption, marketing, and advertising, in television and cinema, in the legal complex and the practices of the police, and in the apparatuses of medicine and health, human beings are addressed, represented and acted upon as if they were selves of a particular type: suffused with an individualized subjectivity, motivated by anxieties and aspirations concerning their self-fulfillment, committed to finding their true identities and maximizing their authentic expression in their life-styles. (1996, 169–170)

Herein lies the dilemma. The appeals to an "individualized subjectivity" are disseminated at so many sites of governance that it comes to seem like the only option. President Bush, for example, exhorts single mothers to work in order to be free, and this coincides with the self-help tendency to focus on internal motivation, as if that were distinct from social conditions. It seems especially dangerous to extol the powers of the self at a time when social support is steadily dwindling, replaced by the neoliberal version of the self-regulating subject.

Yet I'm reluctant to dismiss this popular discourse. In part, my reluctance stems from the recognition that there is simply no outside—although one can criticize the reliance on the self, one cannot dismiss the fact that millions of people believe in it. Hence, in order to change that belief, one must first engage with it—go through it rather than around it. As well, I'm aware of the fact that appeals to the self will have different effects in different situations. When it comes to mothering, an appeal to the self actually counters the conservative tendencies to essentialize the selfless mother. I want to laugh when I read the following bit of advice from Andrea Engber and Leah Klungness in their popular guide, *The Complete Single Mother: Reassuring Answers to Your Most Challenging Concerns* (129), but I also understand where the advice comes from and, in some ways, I draw some comfort from it. Don't worry about what anyone else thinks about single mothers, they say: "The only expectations that you should strive to meet are the ones that you create for yourself . . . when you allow other people's views to alter your opinion of yourself, you risk losing the ability to care for yourself" (130). The authors prescribe a series of feel-good exercises: pat yourself on the back, tape affirming notes to the refrigerator, walk around the house reciting nice things about yourself (130). The same language of self-affirmation appears in a March 13, 2005, *New York Times* article on the phenomenon of "parent coaches," the new class of entrepreneurs who give advice to stressed-out parents on how to handle their unruly kids. One such coach, Mary Scribner, advises Marcia, a single mother of a troubled seventeen-year-old daughter, to "take time for self-care," and when this seems to work in helping Marcia stay calm during an argument with her daughter, Scribner says, "Give yourself a pat on the back, Mom" (Belluck A23).

Although the advice seems rather pathetic, it is also an implicit critique of the lack of material and emotional support for mothering: if no one else will encourage you, then you must do it for yourself. The more systemic solution would be to address the policies and structures that make single mothers feel like they have to compliment themselves, but I also think we cannot dismiss the simple but important question: What is to be done in the meantime? The conditions of single mothering—indeed of all mothering—require a different lens through which to view various aspects of self-help. How are single mothers to survive in a world that grants them respect only if they are autonomous beings? How does the appeal to a singular self constitute a subject able to speak, act, and care for oneself? What can be accomplished if you believe yourself to be empowered and "normal"? How is the self assembled across a number of discourses (economic, cultural, political) that prompt single mothers to this belief? Does the appeal to individual freedom and choice necessarily preclude support and community? Or, given the general lack of support for parenting outside the nuclear family, is the appeal to self a necessary component for single mothers to begin building a support community that extends beyond the home?

Choice becomes the word a single mother uses to convince herself and perhaps others that she is in control of her life, when there are so many things that feel out of control. The endless details of everyday life can be managed but rarely set aside completely, as my journal entry illustrates:

SEPTEMBER 19, 2001

Constant striving against chaos. The obsession with details, multiple events coalescing in one's mind—pick up the glass, carry it to the sink, use that napkin to wipe up some dog hair on the kitchen floor, write my undergrad class assignment on one computer while Alex is doing homework on the other computer, switching back and forth between my assignment and the internet site from which he needs information. Take the dog for a walk, first meet Alex in the garage where he's getting his scooter, but remember the cardboard box that the pizza came in for the garbage can so the kitchen doesn't stink like leftover pepperoni. Wash dishes while I'm talking on the phone, grade papers while I'm sitting at the stoplight, read an article while I'm walking to pick up Alex at school. It's all part of maintaining, organizing.

A single mother knows she would benefit from a support network, extended family, or community, and she may look about for something that resembles any of those formations. They are hard to find. In the meantime, the life you are trying to manage is making you extremely tired, and the self is dissolving into a series of harried fragments.

What's encouraging, then, is to see these harried lives and concerns increasingly represented by the mainstream media. On television and Internet sites, in film, self-help books, and romance novels, through media coverage of celebrities and in advertising, single mothers are encouraged to see themselves as autonomous agents but also as people deserving of certain rewards and desires. In Part I of this book, "Everyday Life," I analyze these media texts as a set of guidelines for both single moms and others who are curious about this newly valorized identity group. Yet there is still a gap between the representation and the reality. To illustrate this gap and to situate the analysis within the space of a particular home, I also describe in "Everyday Life" how television shapes some of my own experiences as a single mom of a young boy.

Spaces of Community

The increasing pressure on single moms to reject dependency and prove autonomy illustrates the paucity of options available within the terms of liberalism. As Nancy Fraser and Linda Gordon argue, what is missing in the "dominant understanding of civil citizenship," which opposes the individual enterprise of contract law to the stigmatized dependency of charity, is "a public language capable of expressing ideas that escape those dichotomous oppositions, especially the ideas of solidarity, non-contractual reciprocity, and interdependence that are central to any humane social citizenship" (125–126). Yet some communities *have* developed such a language of reciprocity and solidarity, devising hybrid ways of living that combine independence and solidarity.

We can't assume that self-reliance and community are antithetical terms. In the second part of this book, "Spaces," I show how self-reliance can be articulated through group identity and community formation and thus represent an alternative to isolated notions of the self *and* to the demonization of dependency. This is not to say these efforts escape the terms of liberal governance but rather that activists are savvy pragmatists, able to create both practical solutions and long-term hope. Who has the luxury of purism? In the different spaces to which I turn, single mothers work as organizers, cobbling together whatever strategies work for raising their children.

What extends across all the sites studied in this book, from media texts to corporate America to community projects, is the desire for personal agency, what academic critics might dismiss as complicity with liberalism's emphasis on the individual. Yet empowerment becomes complicated by the formation of a community that exceeds the individual. And while the appeal to governmental policy realms may seem like an uncritical concession to the powers of the state, this move also becomes more complicated when seen in the context of everyday life. In Part II, I analyze this complex mixture of strategies and conditions as they play out in the three spaces—the corporate university, the Puerto Rican Cultural Center, and the Rio Grande Valley in Texas, all spaces I occupy and have occupied as an academic, activist, and single mother.

I want to be clear that I'm not nostalgic for community as a response to government or capitalism. And I'm trying hard not to romanticize community, although admittedly at times that is difficult to resist. My longing is due to the conditions of the space in which I work, given the highly individuated and isolating work practices of academia, where few colleagues or administrators have recognized child raising as worthy work. It thus comes as little surprise that single mothers don't really feel part of the academic community. Community formation depends on a shared recognition that mothering is indeed work, something that exists for the both the Puerto Ricans and the mothers of the Rebecca Project.

Undocumented legal status complicates the creation of community, as single mothers avoid making their presence more visible and often live alone or perhaps with a few close relatives or friends. Along the U.S.-Mexican border, Proyecto Libertad has had some success in organizing neighborhood associations, but in my interviews with undocumented women, one sentence, in slight variation, recurred: "I have to do this on my own." Some women come to this position after failed marriages with abusive husbands—husbands they often have married to gain legal status, as immigration policy makes marriage the most expedient route to legality and thus to safe and sustainable work. Other women simply decide that they would rather live on their own than risk partnership with men who may exploit their undocumented status, even if that means piecing together odd jobs at less-than-minimum wage: selling Mary Kay cosmetics, cleaning hotel bathrooms, and waiting tables at strip clubs. They become entrepreneurs, savvy about how to negotiate the potential of the "American dream" even as they see its unfairness.

Working across these spaces, it becomes clear that the category "single mother" is highly diverse. Indeed, in certain spaces, such as the Rio Grande Valley, single mothers might not even claim that identity with any kind of recognition that it signifies in a wider, political sense. Yet it also becomes clear that some single mothers are operating as domestic intellectuals, and that political power may be garnered through forming alliances across a fluid and heterogeneous identity category. Because we must work through policy realms, via activist strategies, the category "single mother," deployed strategically, can do important work toward increasing the agency of all single mothers, perhaps even all mothers.

Identity Politics?

Who counts as a single mom? Some cases are clear, others not so clear. The forty-something woman who decides she wants a child and gets inseminated with donor sperm is obviously a single mom. What about the divorced mom who shares physical custody with her ex-husband? The twenty-something woman who lives with her father's baby but doesn't get married? And what's to be gained and lost by drawing lines? How, indeed, politically efficacious a category is "single mom"?

How one becomes a single mom shapes life as a single mom. In the last part of the book, "Ethics," I examine three ways in which moms become single—divorce, assisted reproductive technologies, and adoption—analyzing the legal, medical, and social scientific discourses that shape these options. What are the ethics of these practices? Foucault asks, "What is ethics, if not the practice of freedom, the conscious practice of freedom?" (1997, 284). It's true that all these options represent choices of single moms to free themselves from reliance on a husband and father for their children. It's also true that the freedom to choose removes mothering, to some degree, from the realm of essentialism that has kept women and their children defined by predictable gendered and sexual roles. New reproductive technologies hold considerable potential for reformulating the family, for disarticulating kinship from biology. The parent is joined by others in the act of reproduction—perhaps a surrogate mother, a sperm donor, the doctor doing the insemination. As anthropologist Marilyn Strathern notes, "making visible the detachment of the procreative act from the way the family produces a child adds new possibilities to the conceptualization of intimacy in relationships. However minimal the role of those involved, dispersed conception may provide a model for relations that can take on a kinship character even where they cannot take on a family one" (1995, 353). The problem for many single mothers who conceive via assisted reproduction, however, is that no network remains after the act of conception.

Pure choice is an illusion, always shaped by structures and institutions. Single mothers by divorce are often held to the contradictory expectations of the judicial system, expected, for example, to both support their children financially and to spend many hours at home providing a stable environment. Much sociological and popular literature on divorce sounds a warning about the effects on children; there is particular concern about sons' ability to develop "normally" when single mothers raise them—a topic I explore in chapter 5, "Mothers and Sons." Furthermore, choice is limited by the fact that many single mothers cannot afford new reproductive technologies or adoption. Insurance policies in many states discriminate against single mothers, assuming that only couples suffer from infertility. Infertility clinics prefer couples, and many adoption agencies still discriminate against single moms, especially lesbians. Increasingly, single women are pursuing transnational adoptions, which further complicates the category of choice: the mothers who are forced to give up their babies due to poverty and war can hardly be said to have made that choice.

Because of these differences in privilege, it is critical, as many feminists have written in respect to the category "woman," to keep in mind the heterogeneity of the category "single mom." It should be a capacious and flexible category that nevertheless coheres around mutual issues. Problems arise when the category becomes exclusive, as in the rhetoric of Single Mothers by Choice, whose set of criteria for who counts as a single mom is designed to set them off from the stigma of welfare. They engage in a politics of exclusion and moralism, creating categories of "others" in a manner that plays into the politics of worthy and unworthy subjects.

The task of both theorizing and living the identity of "single mom" is a difficult one. On the one hand, as I demonstrate throughout this book, marriage is still the norm in many instances and locations. Even when there is no stigma attached to single mothering, material privilege accrues to the married couple. Hence, resistance to this category is necessary. We need to present clear alternatives in the interest of revealing the norm and how it works to discriminate, to make life harder for those who choose, to whatever degree, to live on the margins. Resistance can produce pride, solidarity, cohesiveness, as we have seen over and over again in the various articulations of identity politics. These feelings are especially important when life continues to be difficult; identity groups provide inspiration, ideas, resources, and companionship.

Yet identity politics often ventures into the territory of resentment that Wendy Brown identifies in *States of Injury*. Identity remains indebted to the very structures it critiques, such that some perverse kind of thrill, some martyrdom is gained through the retention of the problematic category: "Politicized identity, premised on exclusion and fueled by the humiliation and suffering imposed by its historically structured impotence in the context of a discourse of sovereign individuals, is as likely to seek generalized political paralysis, to feast on generalized political impotence, as it is to seek its own or collective liberation through empowerment" (70–71). The danger lies in positing single mothers as victims of patriarchy in order to make claims for social change. In this line of arguing, it is only by virtue of being a victim that a subject can claim agency. The victim needs her oppressor in order to consolidate her identity, in order to continually make claims on the very institution that has defined her identity in the first place. We see this tendency in the work of Martha Fineman, who has written extensively on how legal policy shapes mothering: "Single motherhood as a social phenomenon should be viewed by feminists as a practice resistive to patriarchal ideology. . . . As such, the existence of single motherhood as an ever-expanding practice threatens the logic and hold of the dominant ideology" (125). The single mother then is faced with the difficult prospect of retaining her status as victim in order to represent a political position of always potential but never quite realized transgression.

However, being a transgressor may be, in terms of everyday life, very difficult. A celebration of transgression may well transcend the details of everyday life—and thus offer no effective alternative to the conservative idealization of mothers. That position, like many associated with aggressive identity politics, turns potential allies into oppressors, and it relies on the retention of the oppressor/oppressed binary for the formation of identity. It thus offers limited possibilities for effecting material change. Identity should be a category you pass through on your way to a less restrictive life, one more defined by the freedom to raise children in a loving, shared environment. This desire for something more expansive than "single mom" as an identity is better for single moms in the long run, who must address the question: What will be my identity after my child grows up?

An alternative politics would make everyday life in all its mundane details visible and show how both governmental and feminist rhetoric often ignore everyday complexities. We need to recognize single mothers in their positivity, their singularity, apart from any relation to an Other (everyone who's not a single mom should pity us). This entails recognizing the specific conditions of single mothering, not to set her apart from everyone else but to show that there is nothing essentially true about mothering—it's constituted through the cumulative practices of everyday life, in which anyone can share.

PART I

Keyword: Everyday Life

Alex giggles his dark curly hair is almost shoulder length. He's got on a Garfield the Cat shirt and a saggy cloth diaper. We're unloading groceries from their plastic bags in the kitchen. He has developed his own game: he takes an item out of the bag, announces its name, and finds some place in the kitchen to deposit it. He can't reach many of the shelves and cupboards. "Bananas" go not in the fruit bowl but on the shelf beneath the bowl. I follow behind, putting items in their proper places. Then he becomes wise to my corrections. "Loops!" he says for Fruit Loops, and puts them in the refrigerator with a sly smile. I smile back and patiently take them out and put them in the pantry. "Ice cream!" goes in the towel drawer. "Milk!" in the dog's dish. Then he wanders farther from the kitchen, returning for new items, delighted with himself: cheese in the toy box, bread in the bathroom sink, a box of graham crackers on top of the hamster cage. He's a little *bricoleur*, moving randomly yet with some reason throughout the house, redefining its places in his own small way. The bags finally empty, Alex smiles, "All done!" Yep, I say: thanks for the help! I set him up with magic markers and paper, and sneak around to the different rooms, gradually returning the items to the kitchen. I retrace his paths, further producing in my movement our domestic routine—closely intertwined, random, with few rules, yet still managed, to keep disorder just at bay.

Alex is a tactician, as most children are, defying the strategists who attempt to contain them, rein them in, impose a rationality on the wonderful spontaneity of their lives. In his *The Practice of Everyday Life*, Michel de Certeau divides the world into these two camps: tacticians and strategists. Tacticians are the weak, the marginal, the mobile, the insurgent, whose unpredictable and mainly unintentional movements through time and space make brief but ultimately unsuccessful incursions on the spaces of the strategists, occupiers of the institutions of rational capitalism and property. "A tactic is determined by the absence of power just as a strategy is organized by the postulation of power," says de Certeau (38). Does that make me the strategist in this situation? I guess I am more powerful, putting things back in their proper places, installing some order within the home. I've become complicit with the larger mandate of parenting: socialization of your children into the world of rules, conformity, and rationality.

Or have I? That's the problem with de Certeau's bifurcation of the world into tacticians and strategists: you can never acquire a stable place or you've gone over to the side of power. But what about stability for your kids? They require a place, stasis, property—all those things that indicate complicity but that you couldn't raise a child without. And having a stable place doesn't mean pleasure is negated. In fact, finding more room for pleasure within life's everyday routines requires careful planning, constructing the places from which spontaneity can arise. The question for single mothers is how to create and maintain these spaces and times for play, how to carve joyful moments out of everyday routines, how to truly appreciate them when they happen, when the very work of managing by yourself threatens to erase the possibilities for pleasure. Perhaps I wanted to cut the game off immediately, just save time and put the groceries immediately in their place. But not really. I wanted to hold on to the pleasure of disorder even in the midst of exhaustion. The pleasure that erupts within the everyday work of mothers is not transcendent, for it is out of these very conditions of work that we find joy. It must be so, for otherwise there would be no time at all for play. How do we maximize pleasure, given the fact that, as Roger Silverstone writes in his book on television and the everyday, "everyday life is a continuous achievement, more or less ritualized, more or less taken for granted, more or less fragile, in the face of the unknown, the unexpected or the catastrophic" (165). In the rituals and routines, in the constant organization and negotiation between work and play, exhaustion and euphoria, single mothers as domestic intellectuals make everyday life happen for their children.

Everyday Life and Cultural Studies

The "everyday" and "everyday life" have been critical concepts in cultural studies for several generations, perhaps beginning, in a slightly different phrasing, with Raymond Williams's insistence that "culture is ordinary" (1958). Elaborated through de Certeau, Lefebvre, Bourdieu, and media scholars like David Morley and Charlotte Brunsdon throughout the 1970s and '80s, this work helped cultural studies scholars develop a material approach to culture that did not rely on the Marxist tenet that production is all-determining. Everyday life situates consumption not in some abstract theory but rather in the material spaces where and when people watch television, cook, shop, listen to music, and so on. In its attention to the routine, a politics of the everyday allows us to deploy Foucault's teachings on the microphysics of power as manifested in the body's movements through time and space. It does not disdain routine and habit but rather sees them as constitutive of everyday life (Felski). It is also attentive to how power operates differently in different sites, unpredictably and complexly. It tries to discern the relationship between the macro and the micro, what Anthony Giddens termed "structuration," the idea that it's only through the repetition of individual acts that structures are reproduced. The question is: How much control do people exercise over those acts and their effects? De Certeau is not as interested in what people consciously do so much as what inevitably happens as people go about their lives: "People have to make do with what they have" (18).

Other theorists of the everyday have been more invested in people's somewhat conscious transformations of the materials at hand, although not without attention to larger social forces. I would place here, for example, Janice Radway's study of women romance readers; as she says:

> To know, then, why people do what they do, read romances, for instance, it becomes necessary to discover the constructions they place on their behavior, the interpretations they make of their actions. A good cultural analysis of the romance ought to specify not only how the women understand the novels themselves but also how they comprehend the act of picking up a book in the first place. The analytic forces must shift from the text itself, taken in isolation, to the complex social event of reading where a woman actively attributes sense to lexical signs in a silent process carried on in the context of her ordinary life. (8)

Here we see another important element of the study of everyday life: the act of interpreting a cultural text must be situated, even decentered, in order to understand its effects within a complex daily routine. The act of picking up a book—of finding the time to read given the demands of housework and child care—is just as important as the content of the book. Noting the "veritable dailiness" of television, Silverstone sets out to answer how it is "that such a technology and medium has found its way so profoundly and intimately into the fabric of our daily lives?" (2). Focusing on media's imbrication within everyday life shows the complexity of the home's relationship with other sites; consumers use television even as they are positioned by it—both by its place within the home (the bedroom, the living room, the kitchen) and by its textual representations. Also, "everyday life" offers an alternative to various theories that assume mass media's unidirectional effect on hapless consumers because it shows how the consumption of television is shaped by other practices.

Studies of the media, especially television, have constituted the major body of work in cultural studies—perhaps the only body—that takes seriously the domestic sphere. Within that body of work, a few of these scholars, including Silverstone, consider the labor of parenting and the lives of children. Cultural studies' general dismissal of the domestic is curious, given its investment in the everyday as a governing concept. What's more everyday than parenting? It may be that the everyday lives of mothers and children is simply *too* everyday: diaper changing and bottles, play dates and snacks, soccer practice and trumpet lessons. What's there to theorize? The unfortunate assumption is that mothering doesn't provide enough material for analysis, that it can't give rise to the theories of the everyday that something like wandering the city might. Unfortunately, the elision of mothering reinforces larger cultural beliefs that mothering is not a creative or intellectual activity. The absence also points to a curious distance between cultural studies and key feminist texts on mothering such as Adrienne Rich's *Of Woman Born,* an elaboration of the relationship between the everyday life of mothering and the institutions that shape it.

I hope to show in much of this book how important it is, given cultural studies' interest in political engagement, to take seriously the everyday lives of mothers and children, in particular single mothers. Family issues are of central concern to conservatives, and without an alternative to their platform, cultural studies cedes critical political territory. How do mothers make do, in conditions not of their own making? An ethical politics of mothering and the family emerges from the everyday lives of single mothers, and this book aims to make those practices visible, to connect the micro to the macro and vice versa, thus contributing to the conditions in which domestic work and pleasure are valued and shared. The

"Spaces" section describes the everyday practices of single mothers at universities, on the border, and in a Puerto Rican community in Chicago.

Despite their lip service to the value of families, politicians rarely address the details of everyday life. Recall George Bush's praise of single mothers, which I cited in the introduction as an example of the shift from the demonization of single mothers to their celebration. Yet this celebration relies on abstracting mothers from their everyday lives at home, for it is only through ignoring the fact that domestic labor is in fact labor, albeit uncompensated, that Bush can proclaim paid work to be the moral alternative to welfare. The elision of the everyday is the ethics—or lack of ethics—of neoliberalism. As Elizabeth Walden argues in "Cultural Studies and the Ethics of Everyday Life," "The right's most powerful ideological tool, neo-liberalism, precludes ethical debate by being represented as part of a process of rationalization pure and simple, inevitable and incontrovertible. The right, then, eludes the ethical both by slipping beneath it, with its moralism, and by transcending it, appealing to the rationalism implicit in an economistic world-view" (2002). When it pushes for welfare reform, the right slips beneath the ethical by erasing the nittygritty work of raising kids. Its answer is to rise above the quotidian details of child care and transportation, favoring a reductive belief in the transformative effects of paid work. The assumption that economics provides the only basis for rational decisions and that the only moral choice is work is what Simon Duncan and Rosalind Edwards, in their analysis of welfare legislation in Britain, call "the rationality mistake," or "the idea that people act as rational economic men, coupled with the normative stance that it is paid work which is the most moral activity on offer" (289). In their critique of British welfare reform, which assumes that getting a job will get women off welfare, Duncan and Edwards argue that life is much more complicated: "What these pictures of economic rationality gloss over is the fact that lone mothers are indeed mothers who socially negotiate particular understandings about what constitutes 'good' motherhood within particular cultural and neighbourhood settings. This negotiation and understanding proceeds in different ways to the process assumed in the model of individual economic rationality" (118).

The question for feminist cultural studies becomes how to counter this view of economic rationality with a careful rendering of everyday life—without celebrating everyday life as transcendent of economic forces. Duncan and Edwards argue that welfare "reform" will not work if it ignores all the factors that mothers must take into account when considering whether to enter the workforce. These factors include money-related questions such as whether wages and benefits (if provided) will offset the costs of child care and transportation, as well as noneconomic factors such as how their children are doing in day care or school, the emotional stress of putting children into a new place, the desire to spend more time with children when they're young—all factors that middle- and upper-class moms can consider without the stigma of "welfare mom" attached. U.S. studies also have shown that "rational economic assumptions" don't account for everyday life. Kathryn Edin and Laura Lein found in their study of 397 low-income single mothers in Chicago, San Antonio, Boston, and Charleston that "welfare-reliant mothers were able to cover only three-fifths of their budgets with welfare, food stamps, and benefits from other means-tested programs in the early 1990s. Wage-reliant mothers could cover about two-thirds of their monthly budgets with wages from their main jobs" (224). In order to survive, both groups had to draw on alternative sources, such as supplemental work, and not report the wages, which would be deducted from their welfare payments. The difference, concluded Edin and Lein, is that wage-reliant mothers had much less time to do extra work than welfare mothers and thus were generally worse off.[1]

Too Rational?

For de Certeau, it's not just economics that imposes a rational order on everyday life. Almost everywhere you turn, order is being imposed: city planning, science, medicine, education—all try to regulate the body's movements in punishing and predictable ways. Capitalism tells us you can master these spaces, and that doing so proves your "success"—your ability to become autonomous through rational decision making. For critics of this "invasion" of everyday life by rational structures, then, the objective seems to be to reveal people's general inability to see what pawns we've become.

Yet for de Certeau, the body resists, and this resistance is captured in a poetics that eludes rationality. Institutions oppose creativity; the body somehow expresses it, but not intentionally. De Certeau speaks of the "reminiscences of bodies lodged in ordinary language and marking its path, like white pebbles dropped through the forest of signs. An amorous experience, ultimately. Incised into the prose of the passage from day to day, without any possible commentary or translation, the poetic sounds of fragments remain" (163). This is actually a wonderful description of single mothering. It is in fact an amorous experience; you fall in love with your child. Yet you also lose touch with your own body, its pleasures become a kind of memory lodged in the routine of the everyday. There are times to remember it—occasional love making, when you find someone who understands, and other moments of stolen pleasures. But mainly you find your pleasures through your child's. His body is my body, I strive to feel what he feels, a practice that begins in infancy when he can't talk but continues throughout childhood when things are still hard to explain and into preadolescence when desire becomes inexplicable. Of course this is all wonderful and moving and powerful: the opportunity to become one with another person. Yet it is also exhausting and cannot be continued for many years without a cost to the mother's body and soul. To alleviate this burden, you need support; if you don't have it, you must become an organizer extraordinaire, constantly maneuvering routines in order to have a little time for pleasure at the end of the day. And here's where de Certeau's theory breaks down again: single mothers must be rational to manage everyday life. There is no easy divide separating pleasure and bodies from rationality.

The positing of the everyday as simultaneously the repository of the rational forces of capitalism *and* the possible site of resistance has kept the "everyday" from being a really useful category for cultural studies, argues Tony Bennett. He finds in de Certeau, Henri Lefebvre, and other theorists a tendency to figure the everyday as

> the source of a tension between, on the one hand, the oppressive stultification arising from the routinisation of everyday life that is dictated by the invasion of system and, on the other hand, the sources of renewal—provided they can be identified and tapped into—derived from the residues of a pre-modern period in which everyday life was inherently authentic and whose traces have been carried organically from the past into the present. It is this fracture within everyday life that allows its analysis to serve as a privileged locus for engaging with the dynamics of the everyday. (2004, 26)

How does one tap into these authentic residues, or perhaps, better stated: Who gets to do the tapping? It would seem the only way is for critics to position themselves as somehow outside the everyday, so that they can act as the agents of defamiliarization, able to show how the everyday has become defined by rationality. Yet how does the critic break free of the everyday that is so all-determining for everyone else? This "radical politics" is rather ineffective, suggests Bennett, for it rests largely on a false claim of transcendence from the quotidian; it becomes a purely critical move, even as it harkens back nostalgically to "the subterranean history of the body," a desire expressed in both de Certeau and Lefebvre (Bennett 2004, 29). The critic of the everyday thus gets to have his cake and eat it too, to claim freedom from *his* body in the ability to see how *other* bodies move through space and at the same time to disdain rational self-reflexivity in favor of a nonrational bodily and creative practice. One wonders what were the everyday conditions in which de Certeau wrote: did he care for a child in between writing the paragraphs of *The Practice of Everyday Life*? Surely the rational planning and management of everyday life done by most women facilitates the intellectual production of many male writers and critics.

It is certainly tempting to adopt the position of the tactician, always operating outside power, as a transgressive and insurgent force. Who wouldn't want to count herself among the "unrecognized producers, poets of their own affairs, trailblazers in the functionalist rationality"? (de Certeau 34). Yet in this formulation, the everyday has to exceed rationality, routines, and normativity. Its resistance lies in its transcendence. By contrast, says Rita Felski, the everyday must "make peace with the ordinariness of everyday life" (31). This entails seeing that routines, while they may sometimes be "personally constraining and socially detrimental," says Felski, can also produce comfort and security rather than being the source of alienation and dehumanization. When applied to housework and child care, Felski's words seem right: the endless routine of diapers and dishes is in fact personally constraining, especially when done all alone. Yet that routine also produces the comfort of knowing you're providing for your child's security and well-being. Out of these everyday conditions emerges the recognition for a new kind of family, one in which single mothers could be supported in expanding possibilities for comfort, security, and even creativity within these same routines—in which other people will also someday participate.

The Critique of Transgression

The everyday, in other words, need not be celebratory in order to present an alternative to an abstract politics, whether that be George Bush's abstraction of mothers from everyday life or feminist critics who sometimes argue that single mothering inherently transgresses patriarchy. I addressed this tendency in the introduction and argued that a transgressive politics articulated mainly for the sake of resistance may not address such mundane chores as cleaning hamster cages; it may transcend the details of everyday life—and thus offer no effective alternative to the conservative idealization of mothers that also divorces mothering from work.

Domestic intellectuals are defined by the everyday; they don't rise above but remain firmly within, and it's the movement within that allows possibilities for rearticulation. As Bennett argues, everyday life is not a homogeneous force but a complex and shifting ensemble of forces, and this complexity is what gives rise to agency: "There is sufficient potential for the dissonance and clash within the multiplicity of powers that are at play in the everyday to suggest that everyday life is more pertinently viewed as the source and site of incessantly transformative social mechanisms than of a seamless structure of habit and repetition that has to be transcended in some general way" (2004, 32). In this formulation, no one is either purely victimized by everyday life, unable to see their place within it, nor able to step outside it in order to better comment on what needs to change. This strikes me as an accurate description of single mothering: it's impossible not to feel, as you go through everyday routines, the conditions shaping your body's movements. The very need to organize, plan, and move through the day is one of incessant self-reflexivity. What de Certeau or Lefebvre might call "defamiliarization" is actually a very familiar, everyday practice.

But how does one connect these familiar practices to the larger structures that shape them? One important way is through an analysis of popular media representations, which are produced through an interaction of political and economic forces and everyday reception. In terms of single mothers, media representations have become an influential, legitimating, and perhaps normalizing force. They have helped bring single mothers into the national imaginary as respectable "family" people; as David Morley argues, television historically has helped construct the national family, contributing greatly to perceptions of who belongs and who doesn't (107). Single mothers are an attractive marketing demographic; on any evening, commercials during prime time feature apparent single mothers: a woman and her son rent a washer and dryer from the Rent-a-Center; another single mother and her children get a house from Habitat for Humanity, and Whirlpool furnishes the kitchen appliances. This normalization works within a neoliberal insistence on the self-regulating subject, as I will argue shortly. However, popular media's representation of the single mother also works against neoliberalism because it makes visible the details and struggles of everyday life. Hence, media consumption illustrates the power of the theoretical lens of the everyday, to show how change occurs within those very routines. It's possible that the media can defamiliarize those routines, perhaps creating sympathy and support for single moms.

Finally, I'll turn to television's embeddedness in everyday life—the everyday life I share with my son, as a specific attempt to show how television defines and is defined by domestic routines. Television's "veritable dailiness," in Roger Silverstone's phrasing, fits well within a single mom's life—it's cheap, convenient, doesn't require a babysitter (in fact, sometimes functions as a babysitter), allows you to get other work done while enjoying some distraction. Increasingly, as it represents single moms as hard-working, good mothers, it even makes you feed good, as if you belong, if not to the nation, then to some imagined community of people who care about their kids. Yet this imagined community is also a rather poor substitute for social interaction and support, and in that sense, television's tendency to isolate one within the home intersects with other forces that compel self-reliance.

1

Representing the Single Mom (and Watching TV with Alex)

In March 2004, ABC's *Extreme Makeover: Home Edition* featured Contessa Mendoza, a single mother of three children, owner of a small, dilapidated home in California. Mendoza is introduced as a twenty-seven-year-old social worker who put herself through college while raising her daughter, graduated with honors, got a full-time job, and took in two foster sons in addition to providing a temporary home to other foster kids. In her application video, Contessa says "I've given my entire life to the kids. As a social worker, I'd probably never see the money to be able to do what ABC could do for me."

What the home-makeover crew did for her was truly amazing. With blueprints and bulldozer, the crew virtually tore down the house and built it up from scratch, adding a second floor, transforming the backyard into a nature preserve/campground, and tailoring each room to fit the personality of its inhabitant. Ten-year-old Analicia's room became a Disney-inspired sea-world fantasy, including a huge aquarium filled with exotic fish; eighteen-year-old Angel's a hip-hop hangout with expensive sound equipment; and twelve-year-old Tony's a planetarium with a computer to operate a telescope on the roof. Contessa's bedroom became a plush boudoir and her bathroom got a whirlpool. Said the crew leader, "We need to take care of Contessa because she has been taking care of everyone else. That's her life. Now we need to make her feel pampered."

The Mendoza story was sponsored by Sears, which advertised its tools and appliances for home improvement throughout the show: "Shop at Sears: Ideas for the Good Life." At the end of the seven-day makeover, the exhausted but exuberant crew planted a U.S. flag atop the house and awaited the family's return from their trip to Disneyland. Contessa Mendoza, a "real" mother, becomes a televisual hero, her life underwritten by

Sears. In the intersections of reality and television, she represents to viewers what it takes for the single mother to become the desiring, desirable, and desired subject. Her home is transformed and she is treated exactly as her name suggests she deserves—as a countess.

Contessa joins a growing list of single mothers who have become the darlings of national television and Hollywood. Single mothers on screen now represent the acceptance of some nontraditional households precisely because real single moms can choose—choose to have or raise a baby on their own and to consume, for both themselves and their children. These representations help legitimate the single mom within the routines of everyday life, making her part of the national family, moving her from the margins to the mainstream.[1] The film version of Dr. Seuss's *The Cat in the Hat,* released in 2003, featured a sexy and enterprising single mom, whereas in the 1957 book, the reader sees only the mother's leg entering the house at the end of the day of trouble. We assume she's married, but who knows? In the film, there's no ambiguity. The mom's status as single plays a big role in the plot, for it's when she can't immediately return to take care of the kids because of work obligations that the cat shows up, ready to wreak havoc. Despite her house literally falling down all around her, however, the mom resists the advances of the handsome next-door neighbor (who turns out to be a jerk). The final image shows a very happy mom jumping up and down on the couch with her two happy children.

The freedom to choose not to marry is clearly connected to the freedom to spend, and as heads of households, single mothers may be even more attractive than single women without kids or married women: they have kids to support but they don't have to run any purchases by a husband. As the authors of *The Complete Single Mother* boast, "Single mothers represent a growing $174 billion marketplace. Marketers are watching the rise in single mother household incomes and are now targeting this growing pool of women who make decisions on their own" (10). The valorization extends across other media: in films, romance novels, advice books, and Internet sites, the single mother is represented as the Horatio Alger of the new millennium. Television shows in the last decade featuring single moms in addition to those already mentioned include *Ally McBeal, Philly, Frasier, The Practice, Once and Again, Resurrection Boulevard, Monk, Six Feet Under, CSI,* and *Desperate Housewives.* Celebrity single moms contribute to the legitimation: Jodi Foster, Madonna, J. K. Rowling (author of the Harry Potter series), Angelina

Jolie, Rosie O'Donnell, and other celebrities graced the covers of glossy magazines during their time as single moms.

This single mom is palatable because she constantly demonstrates her self-sufficiency, distancing herself from the welfare mom. Contessa Mendoza apparently never received governmental support, or if she did, it wasn't part of her story. The perfect liberal subject, she governs herself. For help, she looks to advice books and Internet support groups, fitting into the self-help movement, which, as Heidi Marie Rimke says, constructs citizens who are "rendered entirely responsible for their failures as well as their successes, their despair as well as their happiness. Indeed, this is the social subject of a liberal governance" (63). She is the domestic intellectual of the sort that Gramsci might call the entrepreneur, the organic intellectual with considerable directive, technical, and organizing skills across spheres, including the economic realm. Single mothers are household managers as well as business entrepreneurs, showing the intersections rather than the exclusion of those realms.

Despite its complicity with liberalism, the media valorization is not all bad. As I argue in the introduction, there is a complex conjuncture here that draws on liberal feminism as much as it does on neoliberalism, reliant as they both are on "choice." Furthermore, the demonstration of self-sufficiency produces some unexpected effects, effects that contradict elements of neoliberalism. For example, popular culture often renders visible the details of everyday life—such as domestic labor—that neoliberalism tries to erase, laying the foundation for admiration, empathy, and maybe even material support. In their emphasis on choice as a conscious process of holding life together, the texts cumulatively present a set of rules for how to mother, and in doing so, remove mothering from an essentialist realm. If mothering is constituted through the repetitive practices of everyday life rather than residing in some inner calling—some biological imperative—then anyone can become a mother. Successful self-governance exempts one from the judgment of others. More often, it is the critics of these moms, represented as characters on the shows, who end up looking ignorant or mean spirited or even anti-family. All of this is a far cry from the mother-blaming mode of Quayle–Murphy Brown. The shift from stigma to celebration could have multiple and unpredictable effects that exceed and even contradict liberalism's emphasis on autonomy.

Furthermore, there are rewards for all this hard work: single mothers indulge in small pleasures and feel free to express their desires. In fact, popular culture is producing a rather significant rewriting of the narrative of self-sacrificing motherhood—again a major shift from a decade ago. This valorization of self-care is not unlike what Foucault called "care of the self" as it was practiced in Greco-Roman times (at least by some people, that is—men). As he describes it, care of the self included attention to the most mundane of bodily needs, such as eating, gargling, and sleeping, as well as reflection on those practices. With the growing influence of Christianity and other forces, this care of the self "became somewhat suspect . . . being concerned with oneself was readily denounced as a form of self-love, a form of selfishness or self-interest in contradiction with the interest to be shown in others" (1997, 284). Self-renunciation, says Foucault, became "the condition for salvation. . . . 'Know thyself' has obscured 'take care of yourself' because our morality, a morality of asceticism, insists that the self is that which one can reject" (1997, 228).

We might say, then, that media single mothers are trying to return us to the care of the self, rejecting the idea that the best mother is the one who proves herself a good mother through a renunciation of herself. This attention to the self further removes mothering from essentialism, from the very idea that there is some internal mothering core. Through caring for themselves, mothers become better mothers for, as Foucault points out, the "postulate of this whole morality was that a person who took proper care of himself would, by the same token, be able to conduct himself properly in relation to others and for others" (287). Care of the self is a practice of freedom, says Foucault, which makes it an ethical practice. What is ethics, asks Foucault, "if not the practice of freedom, the conscious practice of freedom?" (1997, 284).

Foucault's valorization of these self-practices as indicators of freedom merges interestingly with the liberal subject, who is also expected to care for herself and thus prove her independence. This is also, however, where Foucault's elaboration seems woefully inadequate, even complicit with neoliberalism. Freedom is all well and good, but how does one get some while working an eight-hour shift, making a mad dash to the day-care center or the after-school program, then beginning another work shift at home: dinner, dishes, laundry, homework. With few exceptions, popular culture doesn't present structural alternatives such as proposals for better child care or family leave policies or support networks that would lessen the burden of self-sufficiency. As such, the presence of televisual single moms in millions of living rooms across the country may not represent a significant challenge to most people's beliefs about families as autonomous units where women still do the majority of the domestic work.

Working Hard for No Money

Feminists have been arguing for years that mothering should count as productive labor and that, in terms of marriage, husbands should shoulder more of the domestic workload. Yet women still do the bulk of household labor; according to one study, mothers on average spend thirty-one hours a week on child care and housework, which amounts to 80 percent of the total (Williams, *Unbending Gender,* 2000, 2). This statistic is premised on two parents; obviously, single mothers do 100 percent of the work, much more than thirty-one hours.

All this work doesn't count for anything outside the home. It doesn't qualify women for social security credits, unemployment benefits, or workers' compensation. It does not count in the gross national product, even though some studies have estimated that in order to fully compensate a mother for one year's work—child rearing, cooking, cleaning, managing household finances, and so on—one would need to pay her $100,000 (Crittenden 8). By contrast, the work of raising children has been recognized in many European countries; in France and Belgium, for example, about 95 percent of preelementary-school-age children are in publicly funded child care centers (Williams, *Unbending Gender,* 2000, 49). In France, all single mothers receive regular payments until their children reach three years of age, and all families receive a family allowance for each child beyond their firstborn (Folbre 132).

What role might television and film play in valorizing mothers' work, bringing into that very domestic sphere representations of women working, alongside the women who are actually working? Perhaps more people need to see that household work is in fact work—perhaps the sight would create the feeling of the effects on the body of this endless juggling act. One might think that popular culture would not be particularly eager to represent the tedium of this work, but actually, a fair number of single-mom texts spend some time showing the daily routine. Episodes of *Judging Amy,* for example, almost always contain the harried morning scene when Amy is making breakfast and packing lunch for her daughter Lauren while simultaneously scurrying around the kitchen, making coffee, burning toast, unplugging the kitchen drain, and stuffing papers in her briefcase. Single moms also do chores that husbands would normally do: Lorelei of *The Gilmore Girls* cleans leaves out of her gutters. Halle Berry in the film *Monster's Ball* struggles to keep her car running so she can get to her minimum-wage job.

The juggling act between home and work is perhaps more likely to be represented in relation to single moms than to married mothers on television and in film, because that's one strand of the narrative that defines their lives and shows their admirable self-sufficiency, their ability to do what usually requires two parents. Take, for example, the 2002 film *Maid in Manhattan,* starring Jennifer Lopez as Marisa Ventura, a single mom who works as a maid in Manhattan. Of course, J-Lo is hardly the everyday hotel maid, but the film actually goes some distance in representing her struggles to raise a son and work a job amid larger structural issues of racism and sexism. In the opening moments, for example, Marisa is running late. Her ten-year-old son is dawdling and she is scrambling, gathering their things—his backpack, his lunch, telling him in a loving but harried way to hurry. Their apartment is a mess. They rush to catch one bus, then transfer, then catch another. On the bus, her son worries that his father won't show up for a long-awaited weekend fishing trip. She assures him he will. The bus drops him off at school and Marisa catches another bus to her job, practically running when she gets off in order not to be late, grabbing a cup of coffee and a pastry from a stand on the street. Then the father cancels the camping trip, and she must take her son to work with her on the weekend. We see the difficulties of single mothering, her determination to make their lives better, even if that means being pleasant to racist white guests, and her connection to her "people"—working class, Latina, and black, in her camaraderie with fellow employees. This is not the lone masculine subject wandering the city that we find in de Certeau's depiction of everyday life, which seems curiously removed from work obligations.

Recent films have been just as likely to focus on the working-class single mom as her middle-class counterpart. In 2002, single-mom films included two gut-wrenching depictions of low-income single mothers whose lives are marked by tragedy. In *In the Bedroom* Marisa Tomei plays a working-class single mother of two young boys, whom she supports by working in a convenience store. In *Monster's Ball,* Halle Barry is a waitress, mother of a preadolescent son, living on the verge of eviction and utter poverty. In the last decade, *As Good as It Gets, Jerry McGuire,*

Erin Brockovich, Tumbleweed, Where the Heart Is, Anywhere but Here, Kindergarten Cop, Riding in Cars with Boys, Monster's Ball, In the Bedroom, and *Gas, Food, Lodging* all featured single mothers who hold low-paying service jobs. Not all of these moms have "chosen" to become single moms. Indeed, for many, it was not a choice—fathers of their children left them, or they divorced because their husbands were losers. But choice is still a critical category that distances these moms from welfare: the choice to hold things together for your children, to rise above poverty and other adverse circumstances. In *Maid in Manhattan,* for example, Marisa just keeps working harder, and eventually she is rewarded with a promotion to manager and, at last (but only after achieving her own financial success), a handsome, wealthy husband.

Many films don't have Cinderella endings. Everyday routines are numbingly routine. In Allison Anders's independent film *Gas, Food, Lodging* (1991), Nora is a burned-out waitress and single mom of two teenage daughters. She has been having an affair with a married man, and he's trying to talk her into resuming it, but she says she has to be a good role model for her daughters. "Wouldn't you be a good role model if they saw you enjoying yourself?" he asks. And she answers: "Women are lonely in the '90s. It's our new phase. We'll live. I've been lonelier." Nora's life is joyless, and even when she meets an unattached man who shows interest in her, she seems to have lost the capacity to fully feel pleasure because she has had to learn to protect herself, to maintain a distance from men who are always on the verge of leaving. She is isolated and lonely; the family lives in a mobile home; Nora seems to have no other friends.

Learning to Mother

Films and television shows are like advice books, teaching a set of mothering skills, showing that "mother's instinct" is a myth. It's acceptable to say you don't have all the answers. Says Kate, the single mother in the television show *8 Simple Rules,* when she finds out that her two teenage daughters have defied her and sneaked out to a party to be with their boyfriends, "I'm just making this up as I go along." Some people who aren't biological mothers may be better at times than the mothers in dealing with unhappy babies or children's issues. During a *Friends* episode, single-mom Rachel has just come home from the hospital with newborn Emma. In her apartment with her friends Phoebe and Monica, Rachel gazes adoringly at her sleeping baby. "I can't get enough of her. Right now I miss her, I actually miss her." Against the advice of her friends, Rachel picks up Emma, who wakes up and immediately begins to cry. The crying continues for hours, and nothing works: Phoebe and Monica read aloud from baby advice books, making suggestions, all to no avail, and Rachel, desperately rocking Emma, says, "What am I going to do? I can't even comfort my own baby. I'm the worst mother ever. . . . Anybody else is welcome to try!" Monica offers to hold Emma, and Rachel leaves the room to go to the bathroom, during which time Monica gets Emma to sleep by singing a little ditty about a bouncing baby. Rachel returns, surprised and grateful, not in the least threatened by Monica's "super-aunt" skills. At the end of the episode, Rachel is sitting on the couch with the baby monitor, apparently ready to get up the minute Emma starts crying. When Emma cries, however, Monica rushes to comfort her. Even the child-hating Samantha on *Sex and the City* learns to take care of Miranda's baby. She first expresses her own ambivalence: "I hate it when friends with babies expect you to turn into a Norman Rockwell painting." But then she arrives to care for Brady. "Here I am, Mary Fuckin' Poppins," she says to the baby. Disaster looms, however, when the vibrating baby chair breaks, and Brady starts screaming again. After a moment of panic, Samantha improvises, and when Miranda returns, she finds Brady curled up peacefully against her vibrator. This articulation of a sexual toy and child care is another challenge to essentialisms about mothering.

If single mothering highlights the ways mothering is learned rather than instinctual, there is still a code of appropriate behavior to be mastered. However, it is a code that is seemingly self-imposed rather than state mandated; freed from the gaze of the state and the taxpayers, single mothers assume the burden of their own inspection. In a special documentary on special mothers on the Oxygen cable channel, one woman talks about her decision to become pregnant by artificial insemination after realizing she wasn't going to meet "Mr. Right." She finds herself wondering about the demands of raising a child by herself: "It's a lot of pressure—but it's pressure from myself. I feel like I need to be a good mom." Similarly, in her capacity as a family-law judge, Amy often hears cases that prompt her self-reflection upon dilemmas she has encountered in raising her own daughter; she considers both the similarities and differences in the situations of less privileged women and herself. While the other mothers come before the scrutiny of the judicial system, Amy, representing a more middle-class norm, judges herself, in relation to them—hence, one could argue, the show's title, which also invites viewers, single moms and others, to understand the complexities of single mothering rather than judging it. Amy is often vexed about her mothering—self-scrutiny is not an easy state of being. As Nikolas Rose describes the self-regulating subject:

> The individual is to adopt a new relation to his or her self in the every-day world, in which the self itself is to be an object of knowledge and autonomy . . . to be achieved through a continual enterprise of self-improvement through the application of a rational knowledge and technique. To live as an autonomous individual is to have learned these knowledgeable techniques for understanding and practicing upon yourself. Hence the norm of autonomy produces an intense and continuous self-scrutiny, self-dissatisfaction and self-evaluation in terms of the vocabularies and explanations of expertise. (1999, 93)

The question thus arises: Is a "norm of autonomy" really "freedom"? Perhaps to a degree, insofar as demonstrating one's freedom is an option that low-income women don't often have. But it's not really freedom. The language of expertise adopted by authors of single-mother self-help books demonstrates the constant *work* of living freely. "If you are a single mother, it is up to you as an individual to carve out your own success," says the author of *The Single Mother's Book: A Practical Guide to Managing Your Children, Career, Home, Finances, and Everything Else* (Anderson xv). Later, she elaborates: "There is a freedom that comes with single parenthood . . . doing things your way. With freedom comes responsibility. . . . The choices that you make through time will define you" (8).

Foucault might say that middle-class single moms are "governed at a distance." I'm using here his notion of governmentality, a way to think about neoliberalism's reliance on a dispersed, decentralized form of power. For him, "governmentality implies the whole relationship of the self to itself," which covers "the whole range of practices that constitute, define, organize, and instrumentalize the strategies that individuals in their freedom can use in dealing with each other" (1997, 300). Media technologies enact this form of governance. Governing at a distance through, for example, mothering manuals, is still a form of governance—just less obviously so, and perhaps more insidiously so, a means by which single mothers come to constantly evaluate themselves. Experts try to convince us that self-evaluation can serve as a way to build self-confidence, precisely by convincing yourself that what other people think about single mothers shouldn't matter. It's a cliché but one that in everyday life may be helpful. "One of the big messages contained in this book is that the real expert on living successfully as a single mother is you," say Engber and Klungness in *The Complete Single Mother* (129).

From Home Management to Business Success

The single mom is an enterprising figure, constantly organizing, plotting, and strategizing about ways to maximize her time and opportunities in order to make life better for herself and her children. These skills apply not just to the household but to the business world as well, making the single mother a desirable employee. She is what Nikolas Rose would call the "enterprising self," a self that will "project itself a future, and seek to shape itself in order to become that which it wishes to be" (1996, 154). Enterprise is a form of self-governance that ostensibly distances the middle-class single mother from the welfare mom, making the former ethical in her ability to manage herself and her household and the latter unethical in her laziness and irresponsibility. Enterprise, says Rose, "designates a form of rule that is intrinsically 'ethical': good government is to be grounded in the ways in which persons govern themselves" (1996, 154). The household, once posited as outside direct governance, becomes a site where one can prove one's citizenship through self-governance. Once perceived as a haven from the economic world, the household is now increasingly linked to financialization, argues Randy Martin in his *The Financialization of Daily Life:* "Financial self-management leaves no corner of the home untouched . . . the oikos of economics returns to its original residence where home organizes both labor and its reproduction" (xx).

In his treatment of financial management via the Internet, Martin doesn't speak to the issue of single mothers (unfortunately reproducing a nuclear-family norm), but it would seem single mothers are the paradigmatic example of the increasing permeability of boundaries between the home and finance. Single mothers comprise a significant audience for the growing genre of financial self-help books, many of those directed at women who currently or will some day live alone. Financial independence is equated with freedom from dependence on men, and although "feminism" is rarely mentioned, liberal feminism is the unstated political agenda that drives the claims made in books such as Joan Perry's *A Girl Needs Cash: How to Take Charge of Your Financial Life:*

> The freedom we enjoy today came in stages: from education to the vote to control of our health to increased employment opportunities to more power in our relationships. . . . Today's generation of women has greater freedom and opportunity than previous ones. But have we made the new freedom work for us? The truth is, regardless of age, occupation, marital status, or future promise, we must all go to the next level and actively develop our financial well being. (5)

Freedom is work, work that women must do on their own. Don't fall prey to the white knight myth, "a belief system that prevents us from moving forward and controlling our own destinies" (63), says Perry.

It's a short step from household manager to small-business woman. One of the first filmic examples of this was *Baby Boom* (1987), in which Diane Keaton plays a Manhattan yuppie named J. C. Wyatt, a market consultant on the fast track at a company called Food Chain. A Harvard graduate who professes no interest in any kind of domestic life, J. C. is about to receive a promotion because she doesn't present any of the problems other women do—in fact, her boss says he "doesn't look at her as a woman." Then, much to her surprise, a long-lost cousin dies in a car crash and leaves her in charge of his eighteen-month old child, Elizabeth. J. C. is angered and perplexed; she can't figure out how to diaper or even hold the baby, and she decides to put her up for adoption. In the course of a week, however, J. C. falls in love with Elizabeth and decides to keep her. She determines to have it all, bringing Elizabeth to work when one nanny after another fails. J. C.'s bosses lose faith, demoting her. Finally, J. C. has had it with the juggling routine. She buys a sixty-acre estate with a rundown house in rural Vermont and leaves the city behind.

Life on the farm turns out to be harder than J. C. anticipated, however, as one thing after another goes wrong with the old house and she finds herself isolated and critical of the country folk. The house needs a new roof, a new heater, and a new water line, and finally, she screams at the taciturn plumber, "I need to work, I need people, I need a social life. I need sex!" Desperate and bored, she begins making her own baby apple sauce, packages it creatively, calls it Country Baby, a gourmet baby product, and sells it at the local stores. Sales take off. Using her business acumen, she transforms it into a hugely profitable line and becomes the darling of the business media. The magazine *Entrepreneur* carries a feature: "Baby Boom!" It helps that at the same moment, J. C. meets the local vet, played by Sam Shepard, and her cry for sex is met.

Rewriting the Script of Sacrifice

Because the single mother evaluates herself and manages her own life, she needn't fear being judged by others, at least as much as a low-income or undocumented mother must worry about surveillance by the state (are your children left alone while you're at work? Do you have legal working papers?). The combination of hard work and self-assessment produces a sense that single moms are "free" to do things that other moms aren't. For one, the single mother is allowed to complain and even to feel ambivalent about the ways mothering keeps her from doing other things that would fulfill her. Mothering isn't all it takes to be happy. There are single mothers on television and film saying things that mothers think but are never allowed to say for fear of being labeled a "bad mom." Lorelei Gilmore sighs in exasperation at her nineteen-year-old daughter's nonstop chatter upon her return from college; when Rory goes in her bedroom for a moment, Lorelei shuts the door and puts a chair underneath the handle. She also continually orders take-out food, shamelessly proclaiming her ineptitude in the kitchen. In the 2000 film *Riding in Cars with Boys*, Drew Barrymore's single mother sacrifices much of her youth to take care of her son, frequently expressing her ambivalence. Then, when he's twenty and still needs her, she asks him, "Isn't this job ever done?"

No one should have to demonstrate they deserve time for pleasure, but mothers are often in that position due to pressures to sacrifice their needs for children and partner. Sexual desire gets subsumed within the couple. By contrast, single moms are allowed to express sexual desire and revel in their desirability in ways that violate the societal taboo on sexual mothers. Single moms are hot. That's the wonderful discovery that Hugh Grant's character makes in the 2002 film *About a Boy*. He even fabricates a young son so he can attend the single-parent support group, which for him works as a convenient pickup spot. In the opening sequence of Austin Power's *Goldmember*, Gwyneth Paltrow appears, riding a motorcycle, dodging bullets fired at her from a helicopter. She's dressed in tight black leather pants and jacket. She screeches to a stop after Austin Powers blows up the helicopter, takes off her helmet and shakes out her long blonde hair. "I'm Dixie Normous," she says. "I may just be a small-town FBI agent slash single mother, but I'm still tough and sexy." Austin Powers responds, "Shall we shag now or shag later?" and she says, "Oh, Austin, behave."

The representation of the sexual single mom extends to Latino popular culture, which has in general been slower to embrace nontraditional families.[2] Telemundo caused a stir in 2003 when it featured a single mom on its reality dating show *La Cenicienta* (*The Cinderella*). The twist was that the show's producers didn't reveal the fact that the beautiful twenty-four-year-old Minerva Ruvalcaba was divorced and a mother of a 2 1/2-year-old girl until the final round. Among Latinos, said the show's producer, Nely Galan, "that's the scarlet letter—if you have a kid you're used merchandise. . . . I want to change the way men see single mothers."(qtd. in Navarro). In the opening season of the ABC television show *George Lopez*, a comedy featuring a Latino family, George and his wife Angie struggle to deal with their thirteen-year-old daughter's desire to date. They find out she has lied to them and gone to a party with a boy they don't like, at the home of a boy whose parents are gone. George and his friend Ernie, who is single, burst into the party; the kids are busted. George leaves with his daughter and asks Ernie to chaperone until the other parents arrive. As soon as George leaves, Ernie asks the kids, "OK, who among you has a hot single mom?" At least half of the twenty kids in the room raise their hands.

I want to be careful not to homogenize the rather wide-ranging set of representations on sex and the single mom. To eroticize a single mom may not do much to create the conditions in which she can pursue sexual pleasure. *About a Boy*, for example, doesn't really encourage single moms to care for their sexual selves—it's more about one man's shallow pursuit of pleasure. Grant plays a lazy, self-centered dilettante who realizes that single mothers are not only attractive, they're vulnerable, horny, and flatter his ego. It's easy to be the good guy because their children's fathers have likely dumped them and they're desperate for some company, some relief from the tedium of round-the-clock child care. He gets to swoop in as the savior until he gets bored. Because Grant looks so superficial, however, the film represents the obstacles single mothers face in finding sexual partners.

Other texts, especially the self-help books for single moms, offer more practical advice about sex. Masturbation is suggested as a great stress buster that doesn't require a partner. As hip single mama Ariel Gore puts it in *Breeder: Real-Life Stories from the New Generation of Mothers,* "It's a good thing we don't take ourselves too seriously or we might just lose it in motherhood's chaos when the vibrator stops working" (2001, xiv). Masturbation is also a good way to resist the urge to date someone just because you're desperate for an orgasm, say the authors of *The Complete Single Mother:* "Masturbation may be frequent at times like these, which is perfectly normal. . . . After all, you're single, not dead" (336). The point being as well that you'll be in a better position to have a good relationship with someone if you go into it already happy and fulfilled on your own. Care of the self leads outward, to other relationships. Potentially, at least.

The range of texts works cumulatively to normalize mothers' desires, to bring sex into the everyday. It's now even acceptable for the televisual *pregnant* sexy mom to say she wants sex, even to desire it outside of any relationship, a significant shift given the long-standing taboo on eroticizing pregnancy. One episode of *Sex and the City,* for example, focuses on the fact that, as the very pregnant Miranda puts it, she "has never been hornier." She finally asks Steve, her baby's father, to have sex with her but insists: "This doesn't mean we're a couple. This is a mercy fuck." She jumps on top of Steve, he grunts and she maneuvers, and the scene shifts to the narrator, Carrie, who comments that Miranda had multiple orgasms that night. When *Friends'* Rachel is pregnant and single, driven by raging hormones, she tells her friend Joey, "I have all of these feelings, and I don't know what to do with them. I can't date like a normal person, which is fine because I don't need a relationship. All I really want is one great night—just sex, no strings attached, no relationship. Just someone I feel comfortable with, who knows what he's doing. Just one great night. Is that really so hard to find?"

Impediments to sexual desire are represented as exactly that—impediments that should be cleared for the single mom to function as a better mom. In *As Good as It Gets,* Helen Hunt plays a beleaguered waitress named Carol whose young son suffers from asthma. Between frequent trips to the E.R. and her job as a waitress (where she's harassed by Jack Nicholson, playing a misogynistic, homophobic writer), Carol manages to get a date with a handsome young man. She brings him home to their cramped apartment, where her mother is caring for her son in the bedroom. Carol and her date fall onto the couch in a passionate embrace, but they're interrupted by her son's coughing fit, as only a curtain separates the bedroom from the living room. Carol jumps off the couch to check on him, and returns moments later to resume their make-out session. Her date, however, recoils when he rubs up against a blob of spit-up on her shoulder. "What?" she says. "It's only a little vomit." And he says, on his way out the door, "A little too much of the everyday."

This is also another huge issue that single moms face: How do you have sex when your child is around? On an episode of *Sex and the City,* Miranda meets an old lover at a party. She's reluctant to tell him she has had a baby, but finally she does. He pauses, obviously disconcerted. She says, "Oh, let's just fuck our brains out," and convinces him to return to her apartment. But when they start making love, Brady starts crying. Miranda screams, "Mommy's coming!" It's too weird for her lover. Deflated, he leaves. Miranda walks dejectedly into the bedroom, looks down at her baby in exasperation, then smiles as she gazes at him.

Sex has to be managed, just like other aspects of everyday life. The National Organization of Single Mothers features on its Web site eight guides, including "The Single Mother's Guide to Sex and Dating," next to similarly packaged guides for child care, money matters, child support, custody and visitation, raising boys, and so on. If managed successfully (i.e., if your child does not walk in on you having sex), then having sex does not impede one's ability to be a good mother—in fact, it is one area of life that needs to be developed in order to care for the self. *The Mother's Guide to Sex: Enjoying Your Sexuality through All Stages of Motherhood* includes a chapter, "Sex and the Single Mom," that describes the reluctance many single mothers feel to pursue relationships that might make it difficult to put their kids first, and urges single mothers to find outlets for sexual desire that will, in turn, make them happier and more responsive to their children (Semans and Winks 249).

Do you tell your child about your boyfriend? Amy of *Judging Amy* begins dating someone fairly regularly but still finds it hard to tell her eleven-year-old daughter, Lauren. Why is it so hard, she asks herself? Indeed, there's one perfect opportunity, when Lauren asks her why she doesn't go out on dates, and Amy is about to tell her, and then chickens out. Amy's fears aren't irrational or overprotective, though—she has had previous boyfriends who haven't worked out, and she doesn't want to introduce her daughter to someone who might not be around for long. Amy starts to doubt her ability to form long-term relationships. Her self-questioning provides real single mothers some relief from the loneliness of self-surveillance. Even though she remains in the mode of self-inspection, viewers understand why she asks the questions: Am I too worried about protecting my child? Is it easier to have boyfriends without having them get involved with my child? What if they leave? What if they don't want to make love on the couch? What if my boyfriend doesn't like my kid? What if my kid doesn't like my boyfriend?

Poverty can make the pursuit of desire even more difficult. In *Monster's Ball,* Leticia loves her overweight son but is also disgusted by him. The child's appetite has consumed the single mom. Tyrell is grossly overweight—189 pounds. Leticia berates him frequently and loses her temper completely when she finds him sneaking an ice cream bar. She forces him into the bathroom to stand on the scale, slaps him, shoves him until he falls down, and screams at him for being fat. Leticia knows that you can't be a fat black man in America because avoiding racism means making yourself less visibly "other." All this happens on the night that Ty's father is being electrocuted for killing a man. Soon after, Ty is hit by a car and dies, and Leticia is more empty than ever. She turns, unknowingly, to Hank, her husband's executioner, first for comfort, then for sexual fulfillment. Hank is sympathetic but uncomfortable, for at this point he realizes his connection to Leticia's husband, although she doesn't. "I'm not sure what you want me to do," he says. And Leticia replies, "I want you to make me feel better. Make me feel good." She offers him her breasts and starts pulling off her clothes. In guttural tones, she keeps repeating, "Make me feel good. I wanna feel good." They fuck, hard and quick, without much feeling. He apparently climaxes, but she doesn't. She makes herself reach orgasm by rubbing herself on him. "I needed you so much," she says. The lines between the mother's needs and the child's desires, the mother's desires and the child's needs, are complicated and interwoven, unable to be adequately disarticulated, yet sexual hunger remains.

Is Self-Love the Solution?

Many of these texts illustrate, to different degrees, that although single moms have earned the right to care for themselves, it is often difficult to find the time and space. Yet the representations stop short of proposing alternatives that extend beyond the individual's initiative. Advice books recognize that single moms need support, but usually leave it up to the single mom to organize her own network. Take the initiative to build a support network, says Stacy M. DeBroff, author of *The Mom Book:* "It becomes even more critical—and more difficult—for you as a single parent to meet with other adults on a regular basis. Finding sympathetic parents in similar situations makes coping more manageable" (295). OK, but how do you find the time to construct a support network, make phone calls, and organize regular meetings when you don't have enough time in the first place to get out and meet people, and you're tired of organizing, since every day is an exercise in multitasking? Even writers who are more skeptical about the powers of the individual see few other options when it comes to mothering. Novelist Anne Lamott writes in *Operating Instructions,* a journal of her first year as a single mother, "I naively believe that self-love is 80 percent of the solution, that it helps beyond words to take yourself through the day as you would your most beloved mental-patient relative, with great humor and lots of small treats" (53).

If single mothering is to become a sustained alternative to the nuclear family—that is to say, if these representational moms are to function as domestic intellectuals who define lives extending beyond the autonomous household—then the importance of support networks must be represented. These networks would include extended family, friends, and community groups, and they would be buttressed by good employer policies on maternity and family leave time, child care, and benefits for kids. Too often, popular culture solves the struggles of the single mom—and seemingly rewards her—by finding her a handsome husband. Not surprisingly, romance novels featuring single moms nearly always have them married by the end. By the series-ending finales of both *Friends* and *Sex and the City,* Rachel and Ross had reunited, vowing to stay together forever, and Miranda was readying to marry her son's father. Other televisual single moms, like Amy and Lorelei, are still resisting marriage, though potential partners always lurk in the background. Their resistance, however, is facilitated by the fact that they have strong support in the form of family and friends. Amy lives with her mother, and Lorelei's parents and close friends all pitch in. The many films' conclusions are too varied to homogenize; while some, like *Maid in Manhattan,* rely on the predictable closure at the altar, many mothers do remain on their own, although it's not at all clear that's what they want. What is often missing from these texts is a clear sense of the social, of what would really need to change in order for the majority of single mothers to have the ability to choose to remain single, to raise their children in alternative family formations, and to care for themselves.

Yet representations have multiple and sometimes unpredictable effects. They don't function in isolation, and the cumulative effect *may* be to produce a kind of imagined community for single mothers watching and reading, getting advice from each other. This strategy characterizes many mothering guidebooks; the authors of *The Complete Single Mother*, for example, construct their book around questions from single mothers that they've gathered in their counseling practices over the years. The book reads like a collaborative effort at sharing advice, especially because both authors are single mothers. It is full of lists and charts and sources, very practical stuff mixed in with more philosophical musings, from money matters to spirituality to sex. Online sites for single mothers often feature chatrooms and listservs that create virtual communities.

It's impossible to ascertain what work texts actually do in the complex social world without entering that world. Once you do, you can see that texts sometimes have little relation to reality, even though they can still provide some comfort amid the routinized chaos of everyday life.

Watching T.V. with Alex

Television helps provide a sense of security, continuity, connectedness. It's reliable, steadfast. Even if you turn it off in anger or disgust and stomp away, it simply awaits your return. It provides, according to Roger Silverstone, a kind of ontological security: "Our individual and collective ability to trust is a consequence of upbringing . . . but it is something which has to be sustained in the routinised activities of daily life, activities that require constant attention and sophisticated, albeit taken for granted, skills" (6). Integrated into the everyday routines of mothers and children, the television assumes a comforting presence, perhaps especially so in times of uncertainty.

I worry about Alex's sense of stability after separation from his father, the transitions between households. He was three when we split up, which maybe is a good age for this to happen. He won't remember any of this—us living together, growing apart. He'll only remember our two separate households, going back and forth between them. Mainly living here, working out a sense of order and stability in this place that has become very crucial for me to maintain as home. I almost never go out at night, don't want to find a babysitter now and introduce another new element in his life, leave him at night when he seems most fragile. I rush home after class rather than going to the library to pick him up from Carol's house so that we can make it home in time for his favorite show, *Kratt's Creatures.*

He loves animals. He has a collection of dozens, maybe several hundred plastic creatures of various sizes and species. He likes to organize them. We build a zoo that nearly covers the living room floor. Wooden blocks and plastic alphabet squares make up the haphazard fences. Each animal joins his species, even though the sizes and colors are incongruous at times: a little pink pig from some Fisher Price farm alongside a carefully crafted wild boar, a realistic gorilla next to a plastic wind-up monkey. But they're friends, all friends organized by Alex the zookeeper. After he has them all in cages, we count, and count again, writing down the numbers: 9 cows, 17 monkeys, 12 zebras, 27 elephants, and so on. The final number on the page must add up to the number of animals he's already counted by pointing to them individually on the floor. If there's a difference, we start over. I wonder if this is his way of ordering and managing his world. Would he do this even if his father and I lived in the same house? Perhaps. Maybe not. This is the dilemma for the single mom: How much of my child's identity is a product of these transitions, this living arrangement? How much can he say about what he feels? How much should I try to help him articulate feelings without naming something that he doesn't even feel?

The zoo stays up for days, accumulating crumbs and dog hair. If Sally knocks down a fence, Alex notices it: "Sally, you dumb dog!" And he repairs it carefully. We tiptoe over and around it. I step on the sharp nose of an anteater and swear. "Shit!" repeats Alex cheerfully.

It's time for *Kratt's Creatures,* an animal show on PBS. The two funny Kratt brothers go exploring around the world. Today they find a three-toed sloth hanging in a tree in Australia, and I curl up on the couch behind Alex, happy for the chance to close my eyes. "Sloth," says Alex, enjoying the feel of the name. "Sloth."

Our own pets. First, there's Binky the Rabbit. Maybe Alex was too young. Kept dropping him on the floor, chasing him around. Feeling bad, I let him run free in the basement. Rabbit poop everywhere. Then he got big. And mean. He'd hide under the steps and nip at my ankles when I went down to do the laundry. I started wearing my snow boots to go downstairs.

Then there was the first hamster, Amos. He took too many rides in the automated car. Got traumatized and lost all his hair. But then we bought him some special vitamins and he recovered. Alex had lost interest,

though, and Amos sat in his cage on the bookshelf for a few years, interrupted only by my cleanings of the cage when the stench became too powerful to ignore. Everyday life is about cleaning up shit.

Sammy Sosa the exotic goldfish had a short life. The expensive setup—
the aquarium, plastic plants, the complicated pump. All that money and it
was still really loud. I couldn't stand the gurgling. Surely he'll be OK for a
few hours, I thought that night, desperate for some sleep. Unplugged. Float-
ing at the top in the morning. He's sleeping, honey, I said in a panic, thinking I could rush out and buy another. But already at 3 1/2, too smart for me.
"He's dead, Mommy." And we buried Sammy Sosa in the backyard.

The ant farm. The cricket cage. The jar of slugs. The butterfly net. The
terrarium with worms. The two female rats we got so they wouldn't mate
who turned out to be pregnant when we bought them. Twenty-six baby rats
munching Cap'n Crunch cereal. And most importantly, Sally, the Chow-
Chow puppy. Weeks of negotiations first. I didn't think Alex at four was
ready to take care of a dog. One huge argument: "I'm ready for a dog. I'm
just not ready for you," he exclaimed. So I gave in. We loved her from the
start but never had time to train her. She never has learned to respond to the
"come" command. Regularly escaping from the backyard, racing around
the neighborhood, enjoying the game of us approaching, letting us get
within inches, then scurrying off, curling tail wagging and purple tongue
hanging. Furry.

TV guarantees a continuity across the miles when you move away from
family and friends. We had to reconstitute an imagined family in State College, rebuild home across the miles, through the airwaves. I feel even more
the intensity of creating a stable, firm sense of home in this new place,
when so much has been left behind, and we're moving even farther away
from my parents and Alex's father.

I dread telling Alex we have to move from Champaign-Urbana, away
from the only world he's ever known. His best friends who are like brothers, their parents who have cared for him like their own. Away from the
Chicago Cubs and his hero Sammy Sosa. Every time we play baseball in the
backyard, Alex is Sammy, slugging the ball over the fence. A good baseball
player myself, I chase it down. State College is a long way from Wrigley
Field. It's football country. But it's a job, and academic jobs in English
aren't to be turned down in exchange for geographical continuity. I need the
economic security of a tenure-track position.

To my dismay, there's no way to get the Cubs in State College—WGN is
not on the cable tier. I have to buy a satellite dish (that seems like something

an English professor shouldn't do). It's going to cost $35 a month and there's nothing else in this package I really want. But it means we can keep watching the Cubs, along with Si and Gabe and my parents in Iowa and his dad in Minneapolis. Thank god for superstations, uniting Sosa fans from the Dominican Republic to Iowa. Alex can keep watching his hero. Even if the Cubs keep losing as they've been prone to do. They haven't been in the World Series since 1945, when my dad was eight.

Television is simultaneously stabilizing and destabilizing, bringing into the home images of the outside world. It occupies a liminal space between public and private. In terms of children, this raises the question of how television foregrounds disjunctures between the home and other sites. TV has the potential to either make what's going on at home seem weird and different or to seem everyday and "normal." This is another reason it's important to have more single moms on television—it lessens the stigma, the sense of outsiderness that can come from being a child of a single parent if you live in an area where nuclear families are still the norm.

Married couples and nuclear families populate children's television, although there are some exceptions. On *The Rugrats,* Chuckie lives with his father, who's a single dad. Arnold of *Hey Arnold* lives with his grandparents. It's not that unusual to see a movie on the Disney channel where the parents are divorced, although sometimes the plot involves the kids getting them back together. For the first three years that we live in State College, Alex has no other close friends whose parents are divorced—all come from white suburban families. Perfectly pleasant.

Their mothers are nice to me, but I wonder what they really think. I don't dress like any of the other moms in State College: that's quite obvious at his elementary school, where I've volunteered frequently. The only one to wear short skirts, high-heeled boots, red lipstick, a bright red coat, a nose ring. I'm always having a bad-hair day, unable to keep the curls in order and the ends neatly trimmed. The other mothers frown at my bad example. How does the proper bourgeois mom dress? I think of Sherry,[3] mother of three, including Alex's friend Andrew. Active member of the Parent Teacher Organization. Volunteers in the classrooms of all her children. Perfect house. Every time I pick up Alex or return her son, she's cleaning or telling me what she's about to clean. Every holiday features a new set of decorations: perfect plastic pumpkins, cheerful Easter bunnies, perky Leprechauns. Like her house, her body is in perfect order: minimal makeup, no split ends, no tight pants. Pleasant. Sensible shoes. Nicely tailored pants and a pretty blouse. Like all the other mothers who wait for their children to emerge from the classrooms at the end of the day, she has a smile plastered on her face, a smile that becomes a little more forced when she says "hello" to me. Funny thing is that I want her to like me—her and the handful of other mothers whose sons Alex has befriended. This is especially important to me the first year that we're here, when Alex is in third grade, and I want him to adjust, have lots of play dates. Plus, I need to build a network of child-care support for after-school meetings and events. And the moms are friendly enough—a group of four women who dress like Sherry—but they're never too friendly. It is always me who calls them, to either ask if Alex can come over or if their son can come to our house to play. Sometimes I worry: Will there be a day when they decide I'm too different, that they would rather their son not be around our house? I put the books of erotica on my shelves in a less obvious spot. I hope the moms don't "google" my name and find out the title of my first book—*At Home with Pornography: Women, Sex, and Everyday Life.*

Despite the changing representations in popular media, people here are still scared of sex and mothers, and people are especially scared of sex and single mothers. They think you're trying to steal their husbands. They think you're setting a bad example for the kids. They think if you wear sexy clothes, then (oh, my God) perhaps you actually enjoy having sex, and that would be a desire not fit for a proper mom, especially one without a husband. I get this feeling even, or perhaps especially, around my colleagues. It may seem like I'm exaggerating, but my friends have occasionally shared rumors they've heard about me. It ranges from rather vague comments such as "they just don't get you—the single mom and the way you dress and the cultural studies" to more direct insults, people who thought I was downright slutty. That one hurt but it made me laugh as well, given the fact that I had no social life. Said another colleague, in my defense, "The dirty secret about Jane is that there is no dirty secret. She's a good mom."

Television plays an important role in establishing household routines, schedules, and traditions. Routines aren't necessarily bad; they can produce moments of relaxation and pleasure. Silverstone describes TV's role as an everyday object: "The screen provides the focus of our daily rituals and the frame for the limited transcendence—the suspension of disbelief—which marks our excursions from the profane routines of the daily grind into the sacred routines of schedules and programmes" (19).

SEPTEMBER 15, 2000

Alex is fascinated by Regis. One night we are planning to watch the millionaire show on our basement television when it begins at 8 P.M. Alex runs upstairs to get something and responds to my call that the show is beginning with "I'm coming, Regis! I'm coming!" As the show begins, with Regis and the current contestant walking onto stage, Alex says, "Watch—they're going to shake hands." And indeed they do. He imitates Regis at different points in the day: "Is that your final answer, Mommy?" And he is fascinated by the various strategies Regis employs to delay telling contestants whether their answer is correct or not. "You said the Rolling Stones." Long delay. Seconds pass. "And Rolling Stones is the right answer! You've won $32,000!" The next contestant chooses to "use a lifeline" and call his mother. "Your mother?" says Regis. "We all go back to our mothers, don't we?" But then Regis cuts through the seeming homage to women by saying sarcastically, once the contestant's mother answers, that he needs his "mommy's" help. And then, flustered, she is in fact unable to help—can't even muster a response before the 30 seconds expire. It's the first commercial break. Alex wants dessert, and I race upstairs to make a s'more in the microwave. Graham crackers, marshmallows, and Hershey bar are all in the graham cracker box. Pull a small plate out of the cupboard. Put half of a graham cracker and three squares of chocolate on the plate. Microwave for 11 seconds. Add two marshmallows. Watch them puff up until they almost explode. Place the other graham cracker square on top and squish down. Put some water in the kettle to boil for coffee. Total time: 2 1/2 minutes. Race back down the stairs in time for the show. Time-space compression. Next commercial break: the water is boiling. Race upstairs, grind the coffee, pour it in the filter. Too fast. Water goes over the top of the filter and washes some grinds into the cup. Oh, well. I drink it anyway.

MARCH 22, 2001

Mealtime in front of the TV. Often *The Simpsons*. It didn't used to be this way—I can't even remember exactly when I gave up on the dinner table. This feels better. Diverts attention from the inadequacy of my cooking. We rarely eat anything home cooked, unless quesadillas count. When we shop for groceries, Alex takes off on his own, headed for the frozen food section: "I'll get dinner for Tuesday and Wednesday nights," he calls over his shoulder, returning with bean burritos and potato skins. I know that I could save money by cooking more from scratch, but I simply can't find the time or the desire. "What's in the microwave for dinner?" he'll sometimes say. "My mom doesn't cook," I overheard him tell a friend matter-of-factly one day as they were headed out the door, walking up the street to his friend's house around dinner time. My role model is Lorelei Gilmore, who regularly jokes about her inability to cook. On one episode, she announces that she is organizing the kitchen, which turns out to mean that she has delegated a drawer to take-out menus and is alphabetizing them. There's a gradual lowering of standards—the single mother doesn't have to prove her worth through her cooking talents. Good thing, take-out. Sometimes going to the grocery store seems like too much. Here's what I wrote in my journal at the end of one especially busy semester when Alex was in fourth grade:

WEDNESDAY, MAY 2

This is what it means to gradually come undone. To be grocery shopping at the Giant and suddenly to think "I can't do this anymore." To have to convince myself I can—I can get just one more thing—the lunchable so Alex has something for lunch tomorrow, the tortillas and cheese so I can make some quesadillas for dinner, the marshmallows I promised him so we can make s'mores tonight. I don't even look at the cost of things as I toss them quickly into the basket and push toward the check-out lane. I wanted a basket instead of a cart; somehow a cart seems too permanent, as if I plan to really stay in this town, shopping at the Giant forever.

To come slowly undone, to un-become. Un-becoming. To feel like I'm going to do something crazy in the supermarket—weave wildly through the aisles or just sit down in the midst of the shoppers for a good cry. But of course I don't. I finish my shopping, drive home, unload the bags, turn on NPR, and greet Alex at the door with a smile. "How was your day, hon?" And there, in the house, in front of the TV, things gradually seem sane again.

The everyday is sometimes taken for granted, but sometimes feels almost unbearably present. The list of chores hangs in the air, palpable, visible. As Silverstone says: "Our everyday lives are the expression, in their taken-for-grantedness, as well as their self-consciousness, of our capacity to hold a line against the generalised anxiety and the threat of chaos that is the *sine qua non* of social life" (165). I have this sense—of feeling very self-conscious about the taken-for-grantedness of everyday life. The threat of chaos is the feeling that if you're not constantly working, things will pile up. The dishes will flow over the sink, the laundry will flow over the washer, the grass will grow so high the mower won't cut through it. No one else will do it if I don't. Chaos is a very mundane possibility, yet for that very ordinariness, more terrifying. It makes me extremely aware of my body's movements as it goes through the evening routines that will make the next day manageable. Now I'm walking up the stairs with a handful of dishes, snacks from the evening activities in the basement. Now I'm putting them in the sink and running some water over them so they won't be too hard to wash tomorrow. The disciplining of the body, as Foucault described, though he never mentioned the home as perhaps the paradigmatic place where bodies are broken down into their utilitarian parts. A hand reaches to grind the coffee while another reaches to push the toast down. A back bends, arms reach, gathering up Alex's homework, putting it in his backpack, while eyes glance around the room for things forgotten. Legs walk, back bends, arms reach, filling the dog's bowl with water. Checking to see if the back door is locked. Writing a check for school lunch. Walking, bending, looking around, lifting, moving. Supervising tooth brushing and face washing. Turning on the closet light. Reading him a book. Filling my own bathtub.

It's 9:15 at night; Alex is in bed but not yet asleep. I sink into a hot tub gratefully, moaning because my whole body aches from last night's soccer practice. My left big toe is surely sprained. I've walked all over campus today, to classes, to a student protest, back to pick up Alex and his two friends, then another game of soccer, make dinner, do homework, supervise trumpet practice, take the dog for a walk. A game of 2-square in the basement. And finally a hot bath. And then an eight-year-old voice: "Mom, my left arm hurts. Are you in the tub?" Yes, honey. "Oh. Just tell me what I can do about it." Give me five minutes and I'll get you an aspirin, hon. "OK." I slide under the bubbles, hoping against hope that he'll go to sleep. Is that a little voice I hear, I wonder, but I block it out. I emerge, start caressing my body with soap, eyes closed. Pitter patter. I look up and there he is, saying, "I was talking to you, and you didn't answer. But now I see—you were getting your hair wet." And he patters back to bed. "I wanted to tell you one thing, and then I'll go to sleep," he calls from his bed. OK. "Remember that episode of *The Simpsons,* when Homer's friend tells him, "Homer, the best thing I can say about you is that you're the stupidest man in the world. And Homer says, 'Well, I didn't do too bad.'" I laugh. "Good night, Mommy." Good night, hon.

Television isn't an escape, it's a time and place of working stuff out, producing meanings that reshape the home, our sense of family, of belonging in the small and large sense of that word. There may be an identity we strive for even as we recognize the gap between reality and representation. "Everyday life," says Silverstone, "becomes then the site for, and the product of, the working out of significance. The meanings that we produce, the representations that we reject or appropriate, the identities we attempt to secure, the rituals which we accept, are all both found and created within a shared, often disputed and always a highly differentiated social space" (164–165).

It's Tuesday. Embarrassing that I think on Tuesday morning—"it's Tuesday." That means *Judging Amy* is on tonight. I check the TV guide that came with the Sunday newspaper—is it a new episode—if so, there's a little "n" next to the title. Yes! A new show. This is so pathetic. If Alex is in bed by 9, I can take a bath and do some dishes, maybe grade a paper before 10. Maybe just let myself sink into the couch. I like Amy—she's more confident and assertive than I. But she has some of the same insecurities. Why don't relationships work out? She leaves one man at the altar (good, I didn't really like him). She starts dating another one, and he's much cuter, but he's also a bit of a jerk. She bursts into his office and confronts him: "Are you scared to date me because I'm a single mom?" He looks surprised but maybe he's not. Some guys are scared or just not interested in the complications. Stay away from them, for they will resent your closeness to your child. Eventually, Amy walks away from this guy even though she loves him because she realizes he's a mess. I like her resolve. It's probably because she has lots of support. Her confidence comes from never being alone. She lives with her mother and daughter, and the rest of the family is always around. Almost every episode, the whole family gathers around the table—grandmother Maxine, mother Amy, daughter Lauren, uncle and aunt and their toddler, cousin, and often a close friend or two. There's some home-cooked meal on the table that gets passed around, and the adults drink wine. There's usually some interesting conversation going on, and Lauren listens attentively, often asking questions. It's not the nuclear family but it's still the family, sharing the labor of meals and dishes, coming together and talking about their days. This extended family also means Amy can go out for dates at the drop of a hat, sometimes sleep over at her boyfriend's house. One night my boyfriend is over, after Alex goes to bed, watching the show with me, and the episode begins with Amy on her boyfriend's couch. What are they doing at his house? my boyfriend asks, and I explain that she has a live-in babysitter. We laugh, but I feel a little uneasy as well. I know he'll resent it when I ask him to go home later rather than letting him spend the night. I don't want him here when Alex wakes up, especially because he hasn't shown much interest in getting to know him.

How to satisfy my desires and meet my child's needs? I can't disentangle them. This week I'm teaching Foucault's care of the self in my graduate seminar, and it strikes me that the very notion assumes that you can first distinguish your "self" from your child's "self." This differentiation is especially hard for single moms because the requirements of caring completely for another person are so all-consuming. It's not just a question of time, but of how you come to think about THE WORLD (small as it has become). My boyfriend asks me sometimes, "But what do *you* want? What would make *you* happy?" And while I appreciate the spirit of the question, I try to explain that it's not an easy one to answer, and it's not even one I really want to try to answer, because it makes me resent feeling guilty about thinking of my desires as contingent on Alex's needs. I want to hold on to the belief that seeing the world relationally is a good thing. The question is: Can you take care of yourself while still acknowledging this interdependence? Is it possible to see that your needs and desires are always intertwined with your child's, but not so completely interwoven that you can't disarticulate them, even partially, at times? It's a delicate balancing act, one bound to make you feel uncertain and insecure—it's that self-inspection thing that's not really freedom at all. You're a bad mom if you don't love them enough, or if you love them too much. As a single mom, you're especially subject to accusations of overprotection. Colleagues who would never ask me to dinner have taken the liberty of telling me that Alex and I are too close. How do they know, I wonder? And what does that mean to them? Surely such smart people wouldn't resort to such stereotypical ideas about mothers and sons.

Household technologies as they've developed over the years have been gendered, and the television remote control belongs to the man. Perhaps that's changing, and perhaps it should change more quickly in nontraditional households. Being the single mother of a son, I should be able to raise him outside the expected socialization pattern. And in some ways, that's true. He'll still sit on the couch with me to watch a Friday night movie. But it's usually a guy film. We've seen all the James Bond films, although I can't watch the violent scenes, and I'm occasionally distracted, so I miss some of the plot turns and Alex fills me in. At eleven, twelve, thirteen, he is a boy, and it seems still so true that boys have a greater affinity to the traditional masculine genres. Am I reproducing gender roles in this seemingly nonconventional family? I can make a left-handed hook shot and star at second base for the English department softball team, but I can't stand to see a fistfight on screen. Now the screen is not just for television and movies but also the GameCube. Finally, after years of resisting, on the Christmas right before he turned 12, I conceded and bought him one.

This isn't so bad. We buy *Simpsons Road Rage,* and the only violence there is crashing into buildings and people. I do a lot of that, and Alex always wins. But the games become increasingly violent; there's little choice at the store. The new James Bond movie is out and now there's a video game. I let him buy it, but when I see it, I'm appalled. The game positions kids as snipers, looking down the barrel of the gun, stalking their next victims. No way, I say, we're taking this back. A long exchange about how many of his friends have it, he'll play it at their house anyway, but that doesn't matter to me, because what matters is that in this house, I can't have that kind of violence. OK. He seems persuaded, somewhat reflective. A few days later, his friend is over, and they're playing another game, not quite as bad but still a variation on the same theme. "Let's go get a movie," I say. We're wandering around Blockbuster, and although I really didn't plan this, I suggest Michael Moore's *Bowling for Columbine.* "He's funny," I say, and they agree. We start watching, and it's not really funny. We get to the beginning of the description of the Columbine shooting, and they are both looking rather ashen. Can we turn it off? asks Alex. Sure, I say, upset myself but glad they've seen this. We go outside and play basketball. I feel good, like perhaps they'll take a break from the guns. But it's short-lived. Searching on the Internet an hour or two later, they come up with the idea to buy rubber-band guns. They arrive a few days later, and Alex has three friends over for a game of two-on-two rubber-band gun fighting. I hear their shouts as they race around the yard: "You're hit!" "I got you!" And I really don't know where the play will lead.

Television allows me time to be with Alex while also accomplishing small tasks—pay the bills, grade a paper, prepare for tomorrow's class, fold the laundry. I watch for any references to single moms on TV, and over the years, I accumulate quite a few notes. The problem is tracking them down again when I need them. They're folded into old notebooks, scribbled on the back of napkins stuffed into a folder, penciled into the margin of a library book. My brain hurts from trying to remember where everything is and how it fits together. When Alex was four and I was trying to write my dissertation, I wrote this in my journal:

Got up at 6 A.M. today with A.—he refused to go back to sleep. Groaned, crawled out of bed, made bagels, made a zoo, did an art project with lizards and glue, made it until *Mister Rogers* at 7:30, crawled onto the couch and tried to doze through *Sesame Street* until 8:30—then two hours of suggestions, both of us getting bored. He torments pet rabbit Binky for awhile. Feel so sorry for the poor thing, I've let it run free in the basement. Finally picking up Silas and Gabe at 10:45 for 2 1/2 hours of madness, fights, trashing K-Mart then our house, where I try to clean the basement so they can play down there, but then basement sink overflows with Binky poop and pee; why did we buy that stupid rabbit after all. Desperate for coffee, load them all in the car, buckle the car seats, check to make sure I have diapers for Gabe and head off to Espresso Royale, bribing them all the while with promises of hot chocolate and cookies even though they're already wise to the mother's pursuit of coffee. Find a parking place close to Espresso but realize I have no change. Coffee seems more important than another parking ticket at this point, so gather the three and finally we are ordering, three hot chocolates, one double espresso, three brownies, and they're sitting down, marshmallows in their puffy winter coats, which we need to unpeal, and soon the table is covered with crumbs and chocolates, and Silas and Alex are teasing Gabe, and people are starting to get annoyed, and I realize they think this isn't an appropriate place to bring kids. Coats back on, out the door, a $5 ticket on the window of the car. Finally, Alex is at Carol's and I sit down for two hours to concentrate on domesticity, and porn—I work best when I write for forty-five minutes, then get up and do laundry. Then write for thirty minutes, go for a jog—it's hard to find time to exercise. Try to leave for a jog with a particular idea in my head that I can work out while running. Jot that down when I get home, on to a new idea that I can ponder while taking a bath. Run to the store before picking up Alex because he's going to be too tired to shop. I can't keep all these domestic thoughts and duties from intruding into any ideas I have about my diss. I pick up Tony Bennett's *Outside Literature* and I think about that pile of dirty dishes, dirty laundry, the empty frig.

Eight years later, I'm trying to finish this book, and my thought processes haven't changed much:

And here's what I'm thinking: it's 2:38 P.M. and I've promised to send this chapter and three others to an interested editor by 4 P.M. this afternoon. I'm also thinking: I wonder if Alex is nervous about his basketball tryouts, which start in about an hour. I remember to call the mother of his friend, to inquire as to whether she has found Alex's case of GameCube discs—all the games he owns, which are worth about $350 and which he lost at a weekend sleepover. I think: I wonder what we're going to have for dinner. I haven't eaten much today because I'm trying to get these chapters done. I even dug a bag of barbecue potato chips out of the trash—I threw them away unopened because they seemed too unhealthy for Alex, and I only bought them for his sleepover party of a week ago. I think I should walk the poor dog, who hasn't peed since 8 this morning and who occasionally wonders into the computer room to look balefully at me. I hear a city leaf-sucking truck go by and I think: I should really rake some leaves. I should write the check for $440 to the plumber who so kindly came out to my house ten days ago on an emergency call as the water heater started to leak all over the basement. Not sure I have enough money in my checking account to cover that amount. I wonder if he takes credit cards. I should figure out what I'm going to say in my two classes tomorrow. I make a cup of tea and eat a Milky Way candy bar left over from Halloween. And I think: I need a wife. Maybe then I'd have time to think and figure out: how does one write creatively?

Can the utter love for your child produce creativity? There's de Certeau's celebration of bodies yet his erasure of mothers. The interdependency of bodies, mother and child, is potentially ecstatic, countering the tedium. Yet in itself, repeatedly, care of others can drain one of creativity. One night I rent the movie *Sylvia,* starring Gwyneth Paltrow as the writer Sylvia Plath. It's far too depressing for me to keep watching this Friday night on the basement couch after Alex goes to bed, but I do anyway. Depressing to see how Sylvia's husband, the poet Ted Hughes, loses interest in being a husband after their two children are born, choosing his writing over his family. And how Sylvia has no time to write, turns increasingly bitter and contributes to Ted's alienation. He leaves, and Sylvia becomes a single mom. Kate Moses, a writer and editor of the "Mothers Who Think" column on Salon.com, imagines in her fictionalized account of Sylvia Plath's life what it must have been like for the writer after her husband left her a single mother with a toddler and a baby. Moses describes Plath's struggle to write in the midst of a brutal London winter when both children were sick:

When did she become so porous? . . . She cannot remember when, exactly, her body and her needs so completely shaped themselves to her children's, when motherhood overflowed its banks and carried her, willingly, deep into its current. When did she change into a nightgown, pleating it into a thick tube between her hands, like stockings, and dropping it over her head in one efficient move? When did she gather the puzzles, the diapers, the bottles, the cups and plates? When did she collect the heap of new poems, loose sheets hastily plucked off the bedclothes and weighted beneath a candlestick on the bedside table, and shove them into a drawer of her desk, dismissing the idea that she might try to work while the children rested—impossible—in unison? (121–122)

Plath thinks of her every movement in terms of its efficiency, to the point where her movements become automatic. She can't even remember them. She gives up on the possibility of writing; creativity is lost. One can't help but think that Plath's isolation, her loss of creative time, her inability to care for herself, contributed to her suicide just a few months later. Kate Moses, herself a single mother for a time, recovers Plath's everyday routine through her book and turns Plath's bodily connection to her children into a creative practice. I suppose herein lies the hope for carving creative moments out of repetitive tasks. Single moms can't hold onto the hope for uninterrupted time to write. We must embrace the particular kind of disjointed, fragmented, distracted thinking that emerges from domesticity. It's worth a try, I think, turning off the television, turning off the lights, locking the doors, checking to see if Alex is soundly sleeping, and crawling into bed.

PART II

Keyword: Spaces

When Carmel Sullivan-Boss's marriage fell apart after seventeen years, she lost her husband, her hopes for their happy future with a young son, and her house. Forced to relocate to Los Angeles to look for work, she found herself overcome with fear that she wouldn't be able to take care of her seven-year-old son. "It wasn't just about money," she writes. "It was the loneliness. It was not understanding my place in the world anymore, not knowing where I belonged. For the first time in my adult life, I felt utterly powerless and alone" (32).

In the midst of these "postdivorce blues," Sullivan-Boss had an idea: she could live with another single mother. She looked for a house big enough for two families and when she found one, she posted a notice: "Single mom seeks same to pool resources and share a house with a garden. Let's work together to create a safe environment for our children" (32). She received eighteen responses, and while meeting with the women, she realized that she could match them up with each other in addition to finding her own roommate. She then thought: if eighteen single mothers responded to her poster in her neighborhood, how many others were there in Los Angeles? California? The United States? And she devised the perfect way to connect them—through www.co-abode.org, a Web site that matches up single moms who want to share housing and resources. Now, the group has more than 16,000 members across the country, many of whom recount how joining households has transformed their lives.

The mother's home is the place she will spend the vast majority of her time; it is the place that will both provide her children comfort and security and at times seem like an island removed from the rest of the world. It is a concrete place, with a roof that leaks and paint that chips, and it is a place of immaterial feelings—of love and frustration and exhaustion. The recognition of this intertwining, of the physical and the emotional, is what led Sullivan-Boss to challenge one of the primary structures that undergirds the nuclear family: the private dwelling built for a couple and their children. Creating an actual space where single mothers help each other take care of themselves and their children goes beyond the "care of the self" described in the last chapter, for it recognizes that in fact single mothers can't fully care for themselves on their own, and that this is a spatial problematic. Sharing a space means that everyday tasks such as grocery shopping, meal preparation, cleaning, and child care can much more easily be shared than they could if friends and family are dropping by. A communal house produces the conditions of reciprocity and community that, as I argue throughout this book, are necessary if single mothering is to be sustained as a truly alternative practice to the nuclear family.

Co-abode does not completely escape the pressure to prove one's self-sufficiency that so dominates discourse on single mothering. The group makes no mention of governmental support, for example. It is fitting that Sullivan-Boss has a chapter describing co-abode.org in the quintessential self-help book *Chicken Soup for the Single Parent's Soul* (published in 2005, it seems to be the latest in the best-selling series of "Chicken Soup for the fill-in-the-blank").[1] Yet Sullivan-Boss also goes some distance toward redefining autonomy and creating a material space for communal child raising. By working with the materials at hand—a poster and a Web site—she becomes a domestic intellectual, providing solutions for others in her class.

Domestic intellectuals challenge the division between public and private spheres that has worked so powerfully to isolate the home since the Industrial Revolution in the United States. Although many women of color never had the luxury of staying at home to care for their children, the social and material construction of a space set apart from the turmoil of the public world of work and leisure continues to have material effects in the lives of all men and women. Domestic intellectuals, working in the tradition of feminists, recognize the ongoing power of public/private while at the same time redefining it, connecting the home to other sites. They retain the materiality of the home, in all its significance, for single mothers, as well as the value of the labor done there, without drawing boundaries around the home, setting it off, as conservatives are prone to do, as if it had no connection to the rest of the world. In their frequent valuing of the public intellectual, some cultural-studies scholars are also guilty of retaining a public/private dichotomy, implying that the public sphere is the realm where politics and social change happens, while the private sphere remains either explicitly conservative (family values) are just obscured (see introduction).

Domestic intellectuals are specific intellectuals, as I argued in chapter one, drawing on Foucault's notion that intellectuals work from the "precise points where their own conditions of life or work situate them." To borrow another idea from Foucault, domestic intellectuals exercise a kind of biopower, a force generated by the body in response to disciplinary forces. Resistance derives from the conditions of discipline. The authors of the blockbuster book *Empire,* Antonio Negri and Michael Hardt, call this maternal labor "biopower from below." In a rare departure from globalization scholarship's dismissal of the domestic, Hardt and Negri describe "maternal work" as a kind of "biopolitical production" that entails "the creation of life," the "production and reproduction of affects," all of which present "an enormous potential for autonomous circuits of valorization, and perhaps for liberation" (198). Maternal biopower cuts through and across all those binaries characteristic of private and public, encompassing both the material and the immaterial, economy and culture. This section was cut from *Empire,* however, suggesting once again that in these circles, domestic labor is placed on the back burner.

Still, it's instructive to consider the possibilities of articulating maternal biopower to "autonomous circuits of valorization," a phrase that suggests a freedom from containment in the home. How do mothers transform maternal labor into biopower? How do we deploy beyond the home this life force derived both from attention to material bodies and to immaterial feelings of well-being and love, this force that is both corporeal and intangible? How do we create the spaces where the needs of mothers' and children's bodies are accommodated? Where mothers can nurse without embarrassment? Where children can play and be cared for? How do we break down the very coherence of the domestic, expanding the identity of mothering and parenting to encompass multiple activities and people across sites? These conditions are necessary for mothers to emerge as domestic intellectuals who can live alternative lives, going beyond the mandate of self-sufficiency to build communities and networks of support.

In this section, I look for these possibilities of dispersed reciprocity, of collaboration and community, in three spaces: the U.S. research university, with a focus on my place of work, Pennsylvania State University; a Puerto Rican community center in Chicago; and the Rio Grande Valley of

South Texas. Single mothers' identities take shape differently in each of these complex spaces. A spatial approach is radically deessentializing, showing that there is nothing universal about the home or any mothering practice and thus hopefully leading to ideas for social change, for new spatial practices that increase single mothers' mobilities and agencies.

Women's homes in these different locations are defined through their interactions with other spaces; as feminist geographer Doreen Massey argues, every place is defined through its connections to other sites:

> Instead, then, of thinking of places as areas with boundaries around, they can be imagined as articulated moments in networks of social relations and understandings, but where a large proportion of those relations, experiences, and understandings are constructed on a far larger scale than what we happen to define for that moment as the place itself, whether that be a street, or a region or even continent. And this in turn allows a sense of place which is extroverted, which includes a consciousness of its links with the wider world, which integrates in a positive way the global and the local. (154–155)

Home is always a product of its relation to other sites. This insight is critical to understanding how the conditions of single mothering can be improved, and it must be made conscious, to use Massey's term. I'm speaking here of what has become a truism of geography and spatial studies—the intertwining of local, regional, national, and global spaces. This configuration of spaces has often excluded the home in the pursuit of more cosmopolitan spaces and movements. The home in its very privateness and interiority seems to be a site unavailable for scrutiny. Yet as the upcoming chapters show, homes *are* "extroverted"; they are shaped by and reshape other sites in discernible and important ways. Single mothers act within these spaces—they engage in what Michel de Certeau called spatial practices—their movements through and between spaces are what define them, in both intentional and unintentional ways.

Across spaces I examined, then, I looked for answers to the following questions. First, is the home seen and valued as a site of productive labor? Second, is the home connected to other sites in a manner that shows how difficult it is for single mothers to get around, from home to work to child care to leisure? How is this mobility shaped by national and global factors, such as immigration policy? Third, how can attention to mobility across sites lead to the development of communities, composed of people who traverse various sites without regard to notions of private and public? How is the creation of community contingent on hybrid practices that are both complicit with and resistant to capitalism? In other words, what kinds of legal and economic policies do domestic intellectuals have to engage with in order to redefine the spaces of single mothering? In addition to "spaces," key words that emerge in each of these chapters include "mobility," "organizing," and "community."

I begin with the university, incorporating in this institutional analysis my own experiences going through graduate school and assistant professorship as a single mother at two public research universities. Overall, academia is a lonely place for single mothers, relying as it does on highly individuated work practices. Furthermore, only recently has academia begun to implement policies that recognize child care as a work-related issue; it still lags behind corporate America in its attention to work-family matters. Rarely do spaces such as classroom buildings and conference halls accommodate children. When administrators and educators do attend to child care—for example in the pages of the *Chronicle of Higher Education*—they often assume a heterosexual couple and thus the policies suggested may have limited effects for single parents. In short, there is at this point little in place structurally that would encourage communal spaces for academic single mothers.

I travel from the university to the U.S.-Mexican border for chapter three. Here, the undocumented mothers I interviewed said repeatedly that their dream is simply to own a home where they can raise their children. Their mobility is severely limited by their legal status; they live in fear of deportation and separation from their children. Immigration activists are trying to help these mothers and other undocumented people build communities through attention to immediate, everyday issues, such as the right to work permits and drivers' licenses. As with academia, where changes must proceed (albeit skeptically) through agitation for better child-care policies, here change is happening through policies that allow undocumented women opportunities for acquiring legal status.

Chapter four details the efforts of the Puerto Rican Cultural Center in Chicago, where organizers have been working for more than thirty years to build a community that resists and responds to the effects of the U.S. colonization of Puerto Rico. The needs of single mothers are met most directly in the Family Learning Center (FLC), a space where the young women finish their high school degrees as their children are cared for in an on-site center. The FLC is one of many spaces that Puerto Rican activists have constructed to create a community that valorizes Latina identity, rejecting dependence on welfare and replacing that with communal support. To survive, the community needs to retain control of its neighborhood, and thus has battled gentrification, quite successfully, in collaboration with the City of Chicago. Activists subvert the profit imperative of capitalism to create hybrid spaces that can survive in this economy, at this point in time. Finally, this is a global movement, built in recognition that the local organizing efforts are shaped by the long history of U.S. colonization of Puerto Rico and the equally long history of resistance.

Cumulatively, these chapters reveal the complexity of the category "single mother," a complexity demonstrated in part through differences in mobility. It should prompt those of us in the relatively privileged space of the university to ask how our mobility is contingent on the immobility of others. This notion of constructing space through attention to different degrees of mobility is what Doreen Massey calls a "power geometry": "Different social groups have distinct relationships to this anyway differentiated mobility: some people are more in charge of it than others; some initiate flows and movement, others don't; some are more on the receiving end of it than others; some are effectively imprisoned in it" (149).

As I interviewed other single mothers on the border and in Chicago, I was acutely aware of these differences in mobility. I could purchase an airplane ticket and fly to Texas, rent a car, and drive around the Valley without fear of deportation. I could drive to Chicago in the summer when Alex went to visit his father and interview teenage mothers who had to take two or three buses to get to the school, lugging child, diapers, bottles, and books. The ability to move freely between sites of home, work, leisure, and child care is one important indication of the agency of single mothers, and I was constantly aware of my own agency in relation to the other mothers, attentive to the possibilities that my mobility was contingent, albeit indirectly, on others' lack of mobility.

This question of mobility is also complicated, obviously, by the fact that I was collecting stories in order to write this book, a book that will further my career. While my desire to put together these stories far exceeds my career goals, I cannot totally divorce the act of interviewing and narrating women's lives from the academic practice of putting these stories into a theoretical framework and an argument that then becomes a book for sale to (mainly) other academics. Furthermore, friendships are formed, especially around the commonalities of single mothering. This is the dilemma described by anthropologist Ruth Behar in *Translated*

Woman, the story of her relationship with a Mexican street peddler named Esperanza: "Working to put feminist principles that challenge neutrality and objectivity into practice, feminist ethnographers have found themselves caught inside webs of betrayal they themselves have spun; with stark clarity, they realize that they are seeking out intimacy and friendship with subjects on whose backs, ultimately, the books will be written upon which their productivity as scholars in the academic marketplace will be assessed" (297).

Can the subaltern speak, as Gayatri Spivak so famously put it? Representation is always an act of translation, not only of language but also of practices and values. How do we avoid the distortion of lives when there is no alternative to narrative reconstructions, no outside to language? Like Behar, I've decided to let the single mothers tell their own stories, as much as possible, without interrupting their narratives with my own commentary. In the case of the undocumented women in Texas, I have translated their stories from Spanish to English and recorded them here as faithfully as possible. I have also used pseudonyms to protect them, given their legal status. In the chapter on the Family Learning Center in Chicago, translation of language was not an issue, as all the women I interviewed speak English. I was attentive, however, to my position as an Anglo academic, especially because I had worked as an activist in the same community twelve years earlier and knew that Puerto Rican organizers expected a high degree of self-reflexivity on the part of Anglo supporters, an expectation with which I agree.

Anthropology has in recent years acknowledged its history of colonizing "informants" as exotic subjects and argued that fieldwork can be done not only in "foreign" locations but also in one's backyard, even in one's kitchen. Drawing on those insights, I have made my own story part of the overall picture and distanced myself from any pretense at objectively representing other women's lives. Furthermore, I've returned to places where I've worked as a journalist and activist; my friends in Texas and in Chicago put me in touch with single mothers, and I gained their trust because of a commitment to their struggles that preceded my academic work. The movement back and forth between academia, the border, and Chicago over the last fifteen years has partly constituted my own identity and thus the way I write the stories of other single mothers. As James Clifford describes fieldwork in the age of postmodern anthropology where ethnographers eschew objectivity, "the materiality of travel, in and out of the field, becomes more apparent, indeed constitutive of the object/site of study" (67). In the process of weaving together our stories, I've looked both for differences and commonalities, thus avoiding the construction of a category of "Others" that can be demonized and/or pitied in various discourses.[2] There are common social conditions that produce common concerns that I have addressed throughout this book— the pressure for self-sufficiency, the fear of failing your child, anxiety about resources and support, the risk of being judged for your sexuality, and so on.

I travel as an activist and mother more than as an academic. I travel with more than a touch of nostalgia for the sense of belonging these other spaces foster and with more than a fleeting thought of returning to the border or Chicago to live some day. The university is not a space conducive to the work of domestic intellectuals; rather, it is a space of intellectual purism where praxis matters very little. By contrast, in Chicago and on the border, activists strive—although they don't always succeed—to figure out what works, in those locations, for both immediate improvement in the lives of mothers and their children and for long-term structural changes. Their activism acknowledges the material site of the home without opposing it to a "public sphere."

2

The Corporate University

Critiques of the corporate university abound. These are sobering accounts of the increasing entanglement of universities with private corporations, the pressures on faculty to secure outside grants and then compromise their research in order to retain them, the dominance of the Nike swoosh on school apparel and sports scoreboards, the shrinking budgets for the humanities, the disappearance of collaborative learning and debate as students become career-driven consumers. No longer, it would seem, does the university stand in opposition to the market; it's just another place where, as Henry Giroux puts it, "market values replace social values, and people appear more and more willing to retreat into the safe, privatized enclaves of the family, religion, and consumption" (2001, xi).

For a moment, I'm convinced. I feel sad, wishing I'd started my career when the university was truly a site where democracy was practiced, where students and faculty were free to say what they wanted, where social issues were hotly debated without fear of offending some corporate funder, where communities of scholars form because of a shared commitment to certain causes and beliefs. But I only feel sad for a moment, and not even that, really, because I can't help but wonder: Did this "public sphere" ever really exist? If so, did it recognize that a community of scholars is not produced simply because a university exists? As the feminist critique of Habermas has aptly put it: the so-called public sphere has relied on the exclusion of all but the bourgeois male and preserved the hierarchies of labor that keep women at home, caring for children, so that men can go out and drink coffee. I can't muster much nostalgia for the liberal university, given the dishes piled up in the sink, the papers waiting to be graded, the deadline for this book looming, and the prospect of a lonely weekend when colleagues who critique the private (the familial) retreat to their individual enclaves.

Perhaps, as a colleague of mine has written in a slightly different context, the corporate university should actually become more corporate (Nealon). Thumbing through the annual issue of *Working Mother* dedicated to reviewing the most "mother-friendly" corporations, I'm struck by the way mothers' work is made visible and by the policies that seek to make mothers' lives more manageable—things I've never even heard of, like a lactation room where breast-feeding mothers can go to pump milk. By the year 2001, writes labor and industrial relations scholar Robert Drago, "67 of the corporations listed in the *Working Mother* magazine's top 100 U.S. companies for working mothers had on-site or near-site child care facilities, and 8 of the top 10 companies offered this benefit" (62). By contrast, few universities offer on-site child care, and if they do, it is woefully inadequate for meeting the needs of faculty, staff, and students. Unions have begun pressuring corporations to commit resources to child care; for example, the United Automobile Workers successfully negotiated with Ford Motor Company for a package of thirty Family Service and Learning Centers that include after-school care for preteens, tutoring for teens, museum trips for retirees, and five state-of-the-art, twenty-four-hour on-site child-care facilities across the country. In announcing the centers, Ford connected caring to profits, saying that by producing a more "stable work force," it will surpass G.M. as the world's largest auto maker, bringing the discourse of caring in line with the discourse of excellence (Greenhouse).

Excellence is the mantra of the corporate university, a point made in Bill Readings's oft-cited book on corporate academia, *The University in Ruins*. According to him, excellence is a contentless quantifying category used to gauge efficiency and profit. Yet if excellence leads to on-site child care, I'll take it, since it's already here when it comes to measuring my c.v. What matters when it comes to tenure and promotion is not so much the argument or the eloquence but the numbers: how many articles in excellent journals, how many books published with excellent presses, how much money from outside sources. Those lefties who want the public sphere back might acknowledge that corporations with family-friendly work policies have made it easier for women to "go out" in public. In fact, academics on the left are perhaps singularly negligent in providing child care at talks, conferences, and other events. If these are indeed public events, they are public only for the academic with no children or with a spouse at home to care for them.

In fact, in these purportedly progressive academic circles, any attempt to talk about the work of child care often meets with charges of whining and even bourgeois privilege. For example, in the fall of 2001, the American Association of University Professors (AAUP) issued a series of recommendations concerning parenting and child care in the academy, including perhaps the most controversial one: professors with newborn babies should be granted more time—up to two years longer than other candidates—to achieve tenure. The proposal sparked a lively discussion in an online forum sponsored by the *Chronicle of Higher Education,* and although some people expressed their support for the policy, many more argued that academics with children should stop complaining about a personal decision and take responsibility for their private affairs. Even Professor Cary Nelson, who has written extensively about academic labor issues, disdained the proposal as having "an odd echo of Republican family values," as I mentioned in the introduction in relation to cultural studies' disregard of child-care issues. The following is a representative sampling of contributions to the *Chronicle*'s online forum on the AAUP proposal.

From Jill Carroll, a lecturer at Rice University: "People should take responsibility for the life decisions they make—and the implications of those decisions, career and otherwise—and not expect everyone else to make up the difference for them. . . . The AAUP proposal and the entire discussion of it here is a veiled rendition of the 'for the children rhetoric' we hear all the time. I, for one, am tired of children and breeders getting all the consideration all the time."

From Manuel D'Espana, University of New Mexico: "The argument that raising a child is the responsibility of the village is a weak one, since few parents are willing to listen to the village, or accept the village's judgments toward their children. The argument that the presence of healthy children has a positive effect on a society is also weak. Many things have a positive effect on society."

We see in these comments a blend of seemingly contradictory sentiments that characterize the academy and partially explain why this institution has been slower than much of corporate America to implement policies that address the intersections of work and family. First, those academics most interested in labor issues—scholars on the left such as Nelson—view the domestic sphere as a bourgeois, private site with no significance to the ideally public sphere of academic labor. This view intersects with a seemingly conservative endorsement of self-sufficiency and autonomy (we all makes choices, and no one should get special treatment), especially, again, in relation to family matters. These sentiments play out in a work environment that positions scholars, at least in the humanities, to see the products of their labor as largely disconnected from any collaborative effort, and where publication (and tenure and promotion) are competitive ventures; in corporate speak, this is the pursuit of excellence. In contrast to activist groups working together to accomplish something, where people have something to gain, both individually and collectively, from shared work, academics generally guard their time and their space as their own. Domestic issues reside only in the home, which is cut off from work and assumes no public value. The details of juggling child care and housework while pursuing an academic career are not given institutional sanction but are rather rendered invisible. Hence, to speak the details in an effort to make the case that child care is work that shapes academic production becomes an individual endeavor, again privatizing the work. Under these conditions, domestic intellectuals don't really have a place to intervene. The university continues to valorize the public intellectual without acknowledging that domestic work makes possible the public visibility of scholars.

A certain irony arises in the academy: the same scholars who might bemoan the corporate turn at universities because of the emphasis on individual motive, accounting, and excellence rather than collaborative learning and public debate implicitly endorse the work environments of individuated labor and self-sufficiency when they disdain or ignore the domestic sphere. This liberal model does not recognize its complicity with the conservative endorsement of self-reliance because it assumes that all professors—men, women, couples, and single parents—have equal autonomy and mobility. The result is an academic work climate in which to seek help as a parent renders one vulnerable to charges of failure to recognize middle-class privileges or of not making the grade as a serious scholar. The colleague who brings a child to a meeting or a dinner runs the risk of appearing needy, unable to keep her private affairs sufficiently private. The scholar who turns down speaking engagements or fellowships because extended child care is too hard to find or because moving your child for a year would be too unsettling for the family may not be able to meet the professional criteria of tenure. The professor who does not pursue competitive job offers because she can't imagine moving her child will not get the raises that colleagues who play the game of offer and counteroffer will receive.

The default mode is simply to rely on one's spouse for help in the domestic sphere, which means that the effects of limited child-care support in academia fall particularly heavily on single parents. Thus the ironies intensify: despite the fact that much academic scholarship in the humanities, especially in feminism and gay studies, critiques the nuclear family norm and reveals its nationalist, racist, homophobic, and sexist effects, academic work *practices* rely on the nuclear family as the most viable form of both raising children and achieving tenure and promotion. Opponents of proposals such as the AAUP recommendation are ignorant to the fact that by dismissing all child-care issues as complicit with a family values agenda, they make it difficult for alternative families to survive in the academy. Furthermore, the policy initiatives intended to benefit parents, such as spousal hires and job sharing, often assume a nuclear family model. Much discourse shaping perceptions of parenting in academia relies on this norm. For example, many of the *Chronicle*'s online career networks invoke heterosexual couples. In one column titled "How the Tenure Track Discriminates against Women," work/family scholar Joan Williams provides a list of suggestions for correcting the long-standing biases against mothers trying to achieve tenure. Her first suggestion is to "renegotiat(e) with your partner. Women typically fare worse than men in the conflict between work and family." Williams advises mothers to "make a list of everything you do, and everything your partner does. Then talk turkey about how to create a fairer household" (2000).[1]

For all women, married and single, having children decreases the likelihood of finding a tenure-track job and of securing tenure. In a report published in *Academe*, two scholars found that women who have babies within five years of earning a Ph.D. are 30 percent less likely than women without children of finding a tenure-track position. Of women who find such jobs and eventually receive tenure, 62 percent in the humanities and 50 percent in the sciences do not have children in the household. This contrasted with the situation of tenured men: 39 percent of tenured men in social sciences and humanities and 30 percent of those in the sciences do not have children (Masson and Goulden 7). Pursuit of tenure while raising children is daunting enough for some graduate students and assistant professors to leave academia. One *Chronicle* article told the stories of various assistant professors who quit before tenure because they couldn't balance work and family. Karen Gault, a single mother and assistant professor of anthropology at Hendrix College, decided after two years of combining mothering with teaching, committee work, and research to leave academe, "even though her provost assured she would receive tenure" (Fogg A10). This article is one of the few to mention the particular problems of single mothers. The Masson and Goulden report assumes marriage when there are children; says Masson, who is dean of graduate studies at the University of California at Berkeley, "Married women with children were far more likely than others to cite children as one of the reasons they changed their career goals away from academia" (5).

To the degree that the married couple remains the unexamined norm of recommendations for policy and other kinds of change, critics such as Cary Nelson are partially right: we *are* participating in a family values agenda. I do not want to dismiss the importance of policy and structural change for *all* parents, but rather to stress that in order to support different family structures—something which many academics would, in theory, advocate—it must be acknowledged that the needs of single parents differ from those of couples who can rely extensively on each other's labor and emotional support.

Community?

What is necessary to transform the university into a place that supports alternative families? Realistically, academia, at least the research university, will never be as communal as spaces where there is a common goal, such as the Puerto Rican Cultural Center, which I'll discuss in chapter 4. Our best hope, arguably, lies in going through policy, and for many of us, that means engaging with the corporate university. It could be argued that with the move toward more corporate-like structures and mentalities, universities finally have begun to consider child care a worthy issue that can enhance worker productivity, efficiency, and excellence. Policy does not represent the co-opted Other of some more radical politics. Rather, corporate policies can help produce more collaborative environments in which child care becomes a shared practice, even if the policies are not written with that goal in mind.

The question becomes this: How can academics produce communities that truly support all families, thus bridging the gap between what many of us argue in our scholarship and the way we lead our lives? How do we work, in the conditions that are given, to transform them? We can't be nostalgic for a community that never existed, nor for communities that exist outside capitalism. As Miranda Joseph puts it, the "romantic discourse of community" locates community

> in a long-lost past for which we yearn nostalgically from our current fallen state of alienation, bureaucratization, rationality. It distinguishes community from society spatially, as local, involving face-to-face relations, where capital is global and faceless; community is all about boundaries between us and them, boundaries that are naturalized through references to place or race or culture or identity, while capital would seem to denature, crossing all borders and making everything, everyone equivalent. . . . This discourse contrasts community to modern capitalist society structurally: the foundation of community is supposed to be values, while capitalist society is based only on value (economic value). (1)

As Joseph convincingly argues throughout *Against the Romance of Community*, the nostalgic desire for a community outside economics provides a rationale for moralizing, for false oppositions between us and them, because any kind of community formation that intersects with policy, for example, seems complicit with capitalism. Critics of the corporate university can maintain a position of superiority by disdaining engagement with policy, the realm of economic rather than ethical values. From that position, it is easy to judge others who have expectations of the corporate university and its members, who think that indeed the university could be a place where community could be formed, communities where everyone has equal opportunity to participate in job advancement, intellectual events, and social life.

Communities form because people recognize the different needs of bodies in particular spaces, at particular times; the usual denigration of dependency is replaced with a belief in support and reciprocity. This shift involves recognizing, as Eva Kittay argues, that "equality" as traditionally formulated is, like the public sphere, a liberal ruse:

> To the degree that equality is tied to a particular conception of society, one in which persons are bound together by voluntarily chosen obligations assumed for mutual benefit and self-interest, society cannot begin to comprehend the difficulties and dilemmas created by the facts of human

dependency. . . . The bonds of a human society tie not only those who can voluntarily obligate themselves and who are equally situated to benefit from mutual cooperation. Dependents are not in such a position, nor are those who must care for dependents. And as long as responsibilities for human dependency fall disproportionately on women, an equality so construed will disproportionately fail women in their aspirations. (27)

Kittay proposes an alternative conception of equality, asking not "what rights are due to me by virtue of my status as an individual equal to all others" but rather "what are my responsibilities to others with whom I stand in specific relations and what are the responsibilities of others to me, so that I can be well cared for and have my needs addressed even as I care for and respond to the needs of others who depend on me?" (27–28).

MARCH 10, 2003

The U.S. is about to declare war on Iraq, and I find myself often thinking about the last invasion, a little more than twelve years ago. January 1991. Alex is just a few weeks old. It's a Chicago winter, wind blowing off the lake right into our little apartment. There are blankets and diapers and towels everywhere. The futon is open in the living room and the bed in the bedroom is never made. It's pleasant and cozy and exhausting in its routines, the never-ending demand for nourishment from breast, followed by emissions of various sorts. The soiled diapers piling up, the stench of urine almost overpowering when I lift the lid on the pail as time inches nearer to the diaper service delivery of a fresh pile of cloth rectangles. But other people visit as well. Our friends from the various activist groups were so committed to us at a personal level—I looked at the photos the other day. Many visited our house in the weeks after Alex's birth; they hold him and smile, happy to be part of an extended family. They bring food: spinach lasagna, salad, garlic bread—the staples of activist gatherings. They wash the dishes, we talk politics. The U.S. has invaded Iraq, there's an antiwar demonstration at the federal building on Tuesday morning. Steve has taken a few weeks off work and we go, bundling up Alex until all you can see is his little red face and his dark curly hair falling over his forehead, his brown eyes trying to take in something of the chaos of the "el" train during morning commute. I hope that he doesn't need to nurse for the next two hours but strategizing just in case: Is there a coffee shop near the federal building where I might sit down and pull up my own bulky clothes, until his little mouth finds my nipple standing sore against an engorged breast?

I'm tired and cold, yet for a few minutes it all seems worth it. We're here, walking around in a large circle, chanting "No More War" as people rushing to work are forced to wonder who are these crazy people out in subzero temperatures. A few take our fliers, but mainly we just feel good to be together, expressing our dissent in the midst of madness.

And that's one reason I stayed hopeful for the first year of Alex's life, and why I struggle now, as the U.S. soldiers slaughter hundreds, including babies like my baby Alex and children like my boy Alex, to maintain some sense of connection. Twelve years in academia, especially the last ten, outside of Chicago, living in two university towns where my work has been defined by child care, teaching, and writing—mainly in isolation—has left me with little hope for the kind of community that seemed—indeed was— possible in Chicago. The commitment to politics was not just about U.S. imperialism but also about family, and our friends insisted I (they nearly made me) continue political work even when I felt a twinge of guilt about leaving Alex at home with them or with Steve, knowing Alex would want to nurse before I returned.

Things are never clear-cut. I was on the steering committee of CISPES, the Committee in Solidarity with the People of El Salvador, and I remember one meeting, at the office, which was at least twenty minutes from our apartment. The meeting ran late, some argument about recent guerrilla strategies: was it morally justifiable for FMLN guerrillas to kidnap mayors who were complicit with the right-wing government? I could feel my milk starting to leak, dampening my shirt. I rushed out, forced the key into the reluctant, frozen door lock, raced home down Western Avenue, scanning my rear-view mirror anxiously for cops. A right down Pratt Avenue, drawing close to the lake, parallel park with inexplicable skill, fumble in my bag for the key as I rush down the block to our building, run up the stairs to our apartment, imagine that I hear him crying, taking off my coat and unbuttoning my blouse before I'm even through the door. I grab him from his father's arms and thrust him to my breast. And now I can't remember: was he really crying? Call it the social construction of gender or a mother's instinct, it doesn't ultimately matter: a mother needs a strong support network in order to feel justified leaving babies even for short periods of time.

What enabled survival, more than survival, was the attention to bodies: my body, Alex's body, the bodies of people dying in Iraq and El Salvador. Bodies within spaces: our house, the activist offices, the streets of Chicago, the mountains of El Salvador, the deserts of Iraq. The attention to mobility: to what facilitated my movement between house and office, how that was connected to people trapped by war, people desperate to leave but denied asylum in the United States. I have felt none of that in academia, where the assumption is one of disembodiment. Mothers don't have needs because they don't have bodies; in fact, mothers with children are rarely seen at academic events: talks, conferences, meetings, social events mainly proceed as if children didn't exist. When fellow grad students and now professors occasionally comment "I haven't seen you in awhile" or "did you hear such and such a talk?" I wonder how they manage not to make the obvious connection. Some anecdotal memories:

Second year of the Ph.D. program at Illinois. Alex is 3 1/2; I've been separated from his father for six months and am desperate to go out. The annual departmental picnic is tomorrow night and I'd like to go, even if it's only for an hour, and I'd like to bring Alex, as long as I know there will be somebody there to play with him so I can eat and talk for a bit without distraction. I call my best friend, another graduate student, someone who has been recently elected to the graduate student organization with me. One of our key issues for the year, we've already decided, will be forming a child-care support group, to provide both emotional and physical support—trading off child care, for example, at departmental events. At the first meeting of the group, only a handful of people show—all graduate students with children, no professors, and no people without children. So much for community, I said to my friend. When she called several days later to see whether I was going to the picnic, I expected something more than this:

Friend: "Are you going to the picnic?"

Me: Probably not. It's too hard with Alex for me to really enjoy myself.

Friend: Oh. That's too bad.

Me: It's just that I'm always running after him, and it's hard to even find time to eat.

Friend: Yes, I can understand that. Why don't you get a babysitter?

Me: Guess I could. But part of me wants him to be there, to be part of the social life of the department. And he'll be with the sitter for part of the day while I work.

Friend: Yes, I can see that. Well, I'll talk to you soon.

Me: Yes, give me a call.

Click.

There's no malice here, just a deeply held and unarticulated belief that children are a private matter and that social events are for adults. If you want to bring your child, though, go ahead: no one will intervene. It's just not their responsibility. Another instance. Alex is eight, and we've just moved to State College. It's the first week of classes at Penn State, but since the local elementary schools don't start until two weeks after the university does, and I don't know any child-care people in town, I'm really scrambling to cover just the bare amount of time, when I have to teach, let alone do anything else a "regular" faculty member does during the first few weeks on campus, like go to one of the "happy hours for new faculty" or figure out the library or go to lunch with a new colleague. One day, I take a deep breath and ask a friend, perhaps the only person in the department I could ask because he's the only one who has more than said "hello" to Alex, if he would just watch Alex for the 1 1/2 hours it would take me to teach my class the next day. "Let me get back to you," he said. Later that day, he called to say he could watch Alex, as long as I left him in my office where he could play games on the computer and he would look in on him occasionally. Although I agreed with a false tone of gratefulness at that point, I realized it would be very hard for me to ask him again.

Relatively minor situations such as these accumulate into isolation and immobility. Limits on mobility keep the single mom from building important career contacts as well as just engaging in the conference camaraderie that stimulates intellectual work. For example, during my first two years at Penn State, I turned down four requests to speak at other universities, all of them requiring considerable travel, because I had no one in town that Alex and I had become close enough to, close enough so that I felt comfortable leaving him for the four or five days necessary. No doubt that is partially my fault, but it is also due to my friends' lack of any sense of responsibility for a single mother with a young child. Perhaps guilt about being a single mother kept me from hiring new people to take care of Alex, feeling like I should compensate for the long-distance dad by being at home as much as possible or at least by having friends care for him rather than strangers.

What I'm trying to describe, perhaps ineptly, is the feeling of isolation that derives as much from a general work climate as it does from specific policy initiatives, or lack of policies. As most of the reports on academia and parenting studies argue, what needs to change in order for mothers to feel supported is not just the policies but also the culture, one in which admitting one's need seems like an admission that work will not get done. I believe there's a connection: that working with the university to adopt more family-friendly policies not based on the nuclear family will lead to a more communal environment. Policy initiatives, however, may not change the fact that work is highly individuated rather than collaborative, which is perhaps the biggest element working against community formation in academia.

"The Ideal Worker"

In 2002, the Council on Anthropology and Reproduction issued a statement criticizing the gap between its own members' scholarship and its academic work practices, noting that scholars who study reproduction should be more attuned to the fact that academia is not a friendly place for parents: "The academic tenure system is structured around an image of the ideal worker, presumed to be a man without child care responsibilities, who is free to move around the country and to devote himself exclusively to his career." Asked the group rhetorically, "Should not we who devote our intellectual energies to understanding and critiquing how social systems operate also seek to understand and intervene in such processes as they play out in our own workplaces?" ("Reproduction in [and of] the Profession of Anthropology").

The ideal worker norm pervades academia. It is assumed that professors, especially pretenure, will basically devote their lives to their work, spending long hours researching and writing, traveling to conferences to build a disciplinary reputation, teaching seminars and attending meetings in late afternoon and evening hours. The AAUP Statement of Principles on Family notes: "The traditional tenure system was based on a model designed for men who were professors with wives at home caring for children."[2] Now, those wives are working as well, both at home and on their careers. Despite the move toward shared household labor, mothers are particularly vulnerable to the ideal worker norm because they have the babies and then continue to do most of the child care. Joan Williams notes that child-bearing and child-raising years—between twenty-five and forty-five—are the same years that careers must be built. Academic women have more flexible work schedules than many professionals, she says, but "often they find that the overall workload is so heavy that their flexibility seems less than one might think. From graduate students to full professors, academics not married to homemakers often feel caught between a work world that expects 12-hour days and the strong cultural expectation that raising children takes time" (October 27, 2000).

In this context, notes Williams, "caregiving activities signal that a faculty member is not an ideal worker and is therefore a substandard academic" (October 27, 2000). The statistics bear this out, as noted previously. Women who delay having children in order to meet the ideal worker criteria may find that the system discriminates against them in another way: since the average age of receiving a Ph.D. is thirty-four, and traveling along the tenure line usually takes six years, women who wait until their late thirties or early forties to begin a family may have trouble conceiving or having the number of babies they would like. Several studies have shown that academic women report some regrets at not having any children or as many as they would like because they didn't feel they could raise a family and secure tenure.

The ideal worker norm affects all parents, but it is particularly onerous for single parents, who again are more likely to be mothers and who are likely to be isolated from family such as their own parents and other relatives given the fact that both graduate school acceptance and securing faculty positions usually require one to move. In short, the ideal worker is abstracted from home and work conditions. This materiality needs to be restored before single mothers will feel supported in their child rearing and before academia will function as a true public sphere, one that acknowledges the connections between home and work.

Bodies

I started graduate school at the University of Illinois at Champaign-Urbana when Alex was seven months old. Because the university had no on-site child-care facility (and still doesn't, more than a decade later), I had him in a day-care center that was about 1 1/2 miles from campus for three days a week; on these days, Tuesday through Thursday, I would teach two sections of freshmen composition, meet with students during office hours, and attend two seminars, African American literature and postmodernism and anthropology. My Wednesday schedule was easy to manage because I had only one graduate class and used the rest of my "free time" while Alex was at the center to grade papers, prepare for teaching, and read for my seminars. Tuesdays and Thursdays were difficult, though, especially because Alex was still nursing. I dropped him off at 9 A.M., drove to campus hoping for a parking place close to the English building, dashed inside for my 9:30 class, taught until 10:45, held office hours until 11:45, and then drove to the center to nurse Alex, assuming he was relaxed enough after a morning in institutional day care to focus on nursing. Then back to campus for my other composition class from 12:30 to 1:45. After teaching my composition class on Thursdays, I went to my graduate seminar in African American literature, which met from 2 to 5 P.M. Engrossed in the discussion, I would often forget the time—except on those days when Alex had been too tense to nurse much at noon. Then, at around 4:30, my engorged breasts would start to tingle, and the harder I tried not to think about my baby, the more my breasts would ache. I remember one day hoping that class might end early, contemplating a quick departure but afraid to get up and reveal that the front of my shirt was soaked with milk. I waited until 5 P.M., held my books against my chest, raced to the center, and grabbed a hungry baby.

Universities have historically assumed a disembodied, transcendent worker, and this history is visible in the architecture. Try to imagine a university building with a lactation room, or even a bathroom with a diaper-changing table. Bodily fluids and excretions threaten to reveal the myth that the public sphere welcomes all subjects. Let loose, made visible, these emissions are proof of the materiality of the body, showing that not everyone travels freely through this space. Women must worry, for example, about containing their menstrual blood, and academia has accommodated for that need—generally—with "sanitary" napkin machines. In the older buildings on my campus, the machines are adorned with flowers and comforting words in cursive writing: "Feminine Napkins: Created Exclusively for Feminine Needs Away from Home." And such a deal: the oldest machines sell pads—those big bulky ones that feel like diapers—for only a nickel. But those dispensers are frequently empty, or the nickel or dime or quarter gets stuck in the slot, and many bathrooms do not have any dispensers at all, sometimes leading to frantic dashes up and down the stairs of buildings before class starts. It's as if the university is still not quite able to acknowledge that working women bleed—it's a bit of an embarrassment, a violation of public/private, one that would require the university also to acknowledge that women have babies—and what obligations would that entail? It's easier, and cheaper, to pretend that women and men have the same bodily needs, and some women would have it that way as well, as the pursuit of equality requires one to deny and contain the fluids of the female body, fluids that speak to bodily differences. As Julia Kristeva asks, "Where then lies the border, the initial phantasmatic limit that establishes the clean and proper self, the speaking and/or social being? Between man and woman? Or between mother and child? Perhaps between woman and mother" (Moi 85).

The spatial layout and architecture of university buildings require women—if they want to be seen as clean and proper, speaking selves—to adhere to a border between their womanly and their mothering selves. This is obvious in parental leave policy: a University of Virginia survey found that only 18 percent, or less than one-fifth of all institutions of higher education, offer paid parental leave beyond a six-week maternity leave. The schools that did offer paid leave were mainly private, elite institutions. Of those schools that do offer paid leave for a quarter or a semester, 25 percent do not provide full relief of academic duties ("Paid Parental Leave," University of Virginia News, January 29, 2004).

Even when policies are on the books, many women are afraid to use them. The director of the UVA survey said that although administrators insisted they do not stigmatize faculty who use the policies, "some academics told us they feared that using parental leave would mean increased scrutiny of their work and diminished career prospects." This phenomenon is what work/family scholars have termed "discrimination avoidance"—actions (or lack of actions) based on the fear that when people learn about your family commitments, you will not be taken seriously as a scholar. A survey at Penn State University conducted as part of an investigation into child-care needs found that out of five hundred new faculty who became parents between 1992 and 1999, only seven took advantage of the available parental leaves ("Final Report" 6).

This pressure to demonstrate lack of need is made obvious by the frequent firsthand accounts in the *Chronicle of Higher Education*'s career network from pregnant women fearing the reactions of prospective employers as they enter the job market or actual employers as they make their way along the tenure track. Jeanne S. Zaino, who had just secured a tenure-track job in political science after years of adjunct teaching, discovered she was pregnant and wrote about her fears in the *Chronicle*: "At first I was convinced that I couldn't possibly have a baby during my first year on the tenure track. The thought of telling the department chairman, dean, provost, and my colleagues that I was pregnant seemed unfathomable." Zaino had been following the discussion in the online *Chroni-*

cle forum on the AAUP proposal to allow professors with newborns more time on the tenure track, and the animosity voiced there made her even more nervous. She felt more hope when an ultrasound indicated her baby was due over winter break, and she thought perhaps she could avoid a maternity leave. She resolved to speak to her chairman. But then she read a special feature in the *New York Times* Sunday edition, "Education Life," that told the stories of professors who tried to make it and have kids: "By all accounts, the intense competition, the long hours, and the unspoken expectations of the academy's traditionally male culture conspire to make it really, really hard to have a baby and be a professor," said the article. A professor was quoted: "You simply can't give 100 percent to the academy when you have children" and "parenting is not a welcome event in the academy." The article, said Zaino, made her feel "queasy" (*Chronicle* career network). What's striking about Zaino's account is the lack of entitlement she feels to something guaranteed by law—maternity leave. She's already plotting ways to mask any appearance of bodily need or "weakness" produced by the baby.

Flexibility

In many ways, academia offers a flexible work schedule that other jobs don't. Teaching often can be scheduled so that one can be home by the end of the child's school day, for example, and there are days when one needn't go in to the office at all, accommodating school events or volunteer time. What this doesn't account for, however, is the heavy demands in terms of at-home work, whether it be grading papers and class preparation for those with a heavy teaching load, and/or research and writing time. As work/family specialist Lotte Bailyn says:

> The academic career . . . is paradoxical. Despite its advantages of independence and flexibility, it is psychologically difficult. The lack of ability to limit work, the tendency to compare oneself primarily to the exceptional giants in one's field, and the high incidence of overload make it particularly difficult for academics to find a satisfactory integration of work with private life. . . . It is the unbounded nature of the academic career that is the heart of the problem. Time is critical for professors, because there is not enough of it to do all the things their job requires: teaching, research, and institutional and professional service. It is there-

fore impossible for faculty to protect other aspects of their lives. (Qtd. in AAUP statement, 2)

The time crunch means mothers are often multitasking. Again, their stories fill the *Chronicle* career network and special publications on women academics and work. Here's one of my journal entries, from 2002:

All the crazy places I've graded papers. At stoplights. In a laser-tag maze, standing underneath a throbbing strobe light as eight eleven-year-old boys race around me. Time-outs of basketball games. Half-times of soccer matches. In the kitchen, waiting for the waffles to toast and the syrup to warm in the microwave. During commercials of *The Simpsons*. Walking the dog. The careful calculations: in order to return thirty-five papers of five pages each within seven days, I'll have to grade five per day. At thirty minutes per paper, that's 2 1/2 hours a day, which I can probably manage between teaching, housework, and child care. But I won't be able to grade any papers on Tuesday because I teach all day, then pick up Alex, then use whatever spare moments I have until his bedtime and later preparing for my graduate seminar on Wednesday. So add one paper to each of the five following days. That way I'll be without papers for three days before I collect the next batch of papers, thirty-eight five-page essays from the other class. In those three days, perhaps I'll have a little time to write.

Precisely because academics have the flexibility to work at home, most colleagues never see this balancing act. This lack of visibility intersects with what Bailyn calls the "unbounded nature of the academic career" to make it seem as if all professors have the flexibility to attend meetings and events when they're scheduled. Take, for example, the expectation that faculty will participate in the life of the department through attendance at afternoon meetings and talks, almost all of which occur at around 4 P.M. and last until 5:30 or 6, often after the time children must be picked up from after-school programs.

For most of their history in the United States, universities have relied on both the model of the ideal worker (as male) and the flexible work schedules to avoid addressing child-care issues in a way that many corporations have over the last twenty-five years. Only 5 percent of colleges and universities have policies allowing part-time work along the tenure track or within tenured ranks, compared to 57 percent of 1,057 corporations surveyed by the Families and Work Institute (R. Wilson 2002). Joan Williams and Bob Drago have been at the forefront of proposing part-time work on the tenure track. Explains Williams: "A part-timer would teach half of the normal teaching load, take on half as many committee assignments, and be expected to produce scholarship at half the rate. In return, he or she would be paid at half the salary, get a benefits package worth half as much, and proceed toward tenure at half the rate" (October 27, 2000). Their proposal has not been met with much enthusiasm to date.

Mobility

During my second year at Penn State, I was invited to speak at the University of Leeds as part of a seminar for feminists who had written about the "everyday" as a theoretical and practical concern. It was a wonderful opportunity, yet I couldn't figure out how to manage child care for five days, given the time it would take me to travel (a full day on either end) and attend the three-day series of seminars. Initially I said "yes," thinking I would just take Alex with me; then I said "no," realizing how impossible it would be to fully participate with a ten-year-old when no child-care facilities were available. Two months after rejecting the offer, I was stricken with a certainty that my career would never progress unless I went to these events, and also by a sense of utter entrapment as I watched friends come and go to conferences and other trips out of State College, returning invigorated by sharing their work, seeing old friends, meeting new people. So I called the conference organizer back: Was it too late? No, but now I would need to pay my own way. I managed to secure $500 from my department, arranged with Alex's father to take care of him for a few days in his hometown of Minneapolis if I flew him there, and bought two $400 plane tickets to Minneapolis for myself and Alex. I also bought a $600 ticket for me to fly from Minneapolis to Amsterdam to Leeds, stay for just twenty-four hours, then return, making the entire trip about three days. I found a dog-sitter (another $150). I contacted the organizer and said that I was coming after all, and she graciously worked me back into the program and arranged for housing. Then, the events of September 11, 2001, changed everyone's sense of the world.

As the media warned about travel abroad, I was besieged by a new set of anxieties. Should I travel with Alex? Should I cross the ocean alone? I convinced myself it would be OK and boarded the plane in State College with Alex, changed planes in Detroit, handed him off to his father in the

Minneapolis airport. Slightly confused but happy to see his dad, Alex gave me a hug and then put his hand in his father's. As they walked away, I watched them for as long as I could, panic rising inside me. I called a friend for reassurance. Go! he said. I bought a double espresso and went to the boarding area for the flight to Amsterdam, where I would change planes, arriving in Leeds early in the morning of the conference. Yet I couldn't erase from my mind the image of Alex, disappearing out the airport door. And I thought: What if something happens? Is it worth it? I knew I should go, but I couldn't move. I listened to the final boarding call. I sat and watched until the last person boarded and the door closed. Then I checked into an airport motel and graded papers for 2 1/2 days.

I have a feeling that my inability to make the trip will sound irrational to people. Indeed, it seems that way to me, looking back now and regretting the missed opportunity, along with a handful of other times I have turned down speaking engagements because it just seemed too complicated to arrange extended overnight and full-day child care. Yet I know why: uncertain about academia's acceptance of me, I chose mothering, full of the certainty of my importance to my child.

Universities could do more to help single parents attend conferences and give talks. They could, for example, consider child-care costs a valid research and travel expense. They could also subsidize child care at conferences and events so that parents, especially those of babies still nursing, could feel comfortable about bringing their children along.

The need to negotiate the space between home and work becomes even more complicated in relation to fellowship and postdoctoral positions that require one to move for a semester or year. I frankly have never even considered these options, despite increasing pressure in the humanities to prove your reputation by securing outside grants. It would be hard on Alex to move to a new school for a year, as it would be for any child, from whatever household. Yet at least a two-parent household can support each other in the move. If the child of a single parent is troubled or having difficulty adjusting, that makes her life hard to manage, leaving even less time to focus on teaching and scholarship. Thus, the decision not to relocate for other opportunities is as much about my needs as Alex's, or perhaps, better stated, it's about the inability to separate those two.

A final category of mobility also discriminates against mothers, writes Joan Williams (April 18, 2003): the fact that merit raises are often linked to outside offers. Everyone knows, and even the AAUP acknowledges, that the main way to get a significant raise in this profession is to receive

an offer from another institution. Williams notes that women will sometimes consider moving if their husband gets a good offer (again, she assumes a married couple in relation to children), yet many women will not
even seek these offers because they don't want to uproot their families.
This practice helps explain the pay gap between men and women in academia: "A salary advantage held by male faculty members over female faculty members exists at all ranks and institutional types. The salary gap is
largest at the rank of full professor where, for all institutional types combined, women are paid, on average only 88 percent of what their male
colleagues are paid" (AAUP, Statement, 1). The entire practice may in fact
constitute a form of gender discrimination, says Williams; to remedy this,
she urges departments to link raises to excellence in scholarship, teaching,
and research rather than to outside offers.

Corporate Bodies

I want to make clear from the start of this section that I am not idealiz-
ing corporations. The fact that I am even writing about their child-care
policies indicates the paucity of options in the United States, which, unlike most European countries, has virtually no publicly subsidized child-
care program. In France and Belgium, for example, about 95 percent of
preelementary-school-age children are in publicly funded child care
(Williams, *Unbending Gender,* 2000, 49). In the United States, by contrast, women who have wanted to pursue careers and also raise children
are usually forced to look for private child care.

Taking seriously the theory of domestic intellectuals, that we work
from where we're at, shouldn't we consider what corporations have done
to recognize and value maternal labor? In the early 1990s, corporations
started to recognize that women professionals were leaving because of
child-care concerns. Ann Crittenden details numerous cases of women
failing to make advances in the 1990s: the accounting firm Deloitte and
Touche found that between 1982 and 1992, the percentage of female
partners had barely risen, from 1 to 5 percent—mainly because the
women felt that there was no way to have children and be promoted. In
the legal arena, the American Bar Association announced that the "partnership rate for women fell even further behind the rate for men during
the 1990s" (Crittenden 39). A survey of male and female MBAs showed
that "among those who have risen to within three levels of the CEO po-

sition, fewer than half (49 percent) of the women have children, compared with 85 percent of the men" (35). Policies such as part-time tracks intended to accommodate mothers had actually penalized them by creating "mommy tracks" as corporations continued to rely on the ideal worker norm. Many women were understandably reluctant to follow these mommy tracks; a 1990 study of Fortune 500 manufacturing firms "found that while 88 percent offered part-time work (either informally or as part of a formal program), only three to five percent of their employees took advantage of it. Another survey showed that less than three percent of lawyers used part-time policies despite the fact that 90 percent of firms surveyed offered it" (Williams, *Unbending Gender,* 2000, 94).

In response to the failure of the mommy track, some corporations started building on-site child-care facilities, on the theory that by providing more services at work and saving mothers the time of travel to and from child-care centers, they could create more time for mothers and thus provide an alternative to flextime. When corporations have decided to devote more resources to child care and parenting—and certainly there are still many corporations, especially smaller companies, who do little to address these needs—we can identify two tendencies, both of which recognize the home as a site of labor because of its articulation to market production. In contrast to previous characterizations of the home as a nonproductive site, then, corporate child-care policies see the home as productive because, in doing so, they can make the workplace more efficient. One strategy makes the workplace friendlier to mothers and children through on-site child care, flexible work time, lactation rooms, and maternal leave time. Another strategy makes the home friendlier to work by allowing mothers to work from home, a practice becoming more common due to new information technologies. Not only do these policies recognize the home as a productive site, they also recognize that women's upward mobility is connected to their outward mobility—the paths one must travel between sites (home, work, grocery story, children's schools, doctor's office, orthodontist, etc.). Furthermore, bodies matter—the pregnant body, the nursing body, the sick child's body. The recognition of specific mothering bodies is part of the corporate embrace of diversity; difference is now seen as a means of legitimating corporate authority.

Of course, this attention to the specific, corporeal needs of employees is all in the interest of greater profits and efficiency, and thus one might say that the domestic sphere has merely been co-opted in the interest of a better bottom line. To argue in this manner, however, would take far too lightly (from a moralistic position) the everyday complexities of balancing work and child care—realities that are more likely to change when women have the energy to address them and form networks of support than if women are so exhausted they can barely crawl into bed at the end of an eighteen-hour day.

It's also important to recognize that while the policy of "flexible working schedules" may lend itself to corporate downsizing strategies, it is not always in the interest of potential downsizing but rather due to the corporate desire to retain women employees with children. When Deloitte instituted flexible schedules, it started retaining more women; by 1997, 10 percent of its partners were women, the highest percentage among the big accounting firms (Crittenden 36). Yet these corporate strategies do coincide with the fact that the New Economy relies on a highly mobile and flexible workforce, a workforce always ready to labor, whether at work or home. Interestingly, work/life labor consultants see in this growth of flexibility an opportunity to recognize that women have always had to work at both home and job. In fact, they suggest that corporations make the links between home and work an explicit part of their policy agendas, or risk gender and family discrimination: "In the future, it will no longer be possible to fall back on the assumption that family issues are individuals' private concerns, since the costs of this assumption are becoming increasingly evident"—in the form of employee stress, attrition, and low productivity (Bailyn 76). The idea is to go against "deeply held beliefs about the separation of work and family spheres," to produce a "dual agenda," the "bringing together of work practices with the needs of employees to integrate their work with their personal lives" (Final Report, Penn State study 25). Toward this goal, there are signs of a move to redefine the ideal worker as someone who actually needs to spend less time in the office.

Two major concerns arise. First, flextime and telecommuting may replace on-site child-care commitments because they're cheaper and easier. It may turn out, in this scenario, that flexible work time for women who want to spend more time at home with their children coincides with company motives to cut on-site expenditures. There's already evidence of a shift from on-site child-care structures to flexible working arrangements. A 2001 survey by the Society of Human Resource Management found that the number of U.S. companies with on-site child-care centers had dropped to 5 percent in 2001 from 6 percent in 1997; during the same time, the percentage of employers offering child-care referral services rose to 20 percent from 15 percent, and 69 percent offered dependent-care flexible spending accounts, up from 58 percent (Rosenberg 2). Second, what if these corporate strategies toward the dissolution of home and work make the home so much like work that there is no retreat, no escape from the corporation?

In response to these concerns, it is important to insist that a material, visible commitment to child care and parenting is retained at work in order to help mothers *and* to demonstrate to all employees that mothering is a valued activity. Home and work must be thought of as distinct yet related sites, with the corporate commitment to on-site facilities and policies maintaining equal importance to policies that play out at home. The distinction between work and home is as much a matter of everyday life as it is of policy, however. A harried mother might well say that there's no point in trying to maintain a distinction since that distinction dissolves in the constant attempt to get things done, to multitask. By recognizing the hybrid identities of mothers as these identities take shape at particular yet overlapping sites and by acknowledging that the demands of work and life take a toll on the mother's body, corporations help create a situation in which the details of everyday life are spoken, made visible, for all to see. If the institution treats child care as work (even if in the interests of better productivity on the job), then women aren't expected to be self-sufficient, and child care moves from a private, individual concern to a validated, public matter. Mothers feel more valued and are less likely to burn out either at home or at work.

The atmosphere of inclusion depends on both policies and the perception that work at home is valued, which in turn makes women feel more motivated to work for the corporate team. It's a philosophy that most corporations now accept, says Williams, who cites a "highly respected survey" in which "80 percent of corporations agreed that they could not remain competitive in the 1990s without addressing work/family and diversity issues." Another survey, by the Conference Board business group, found that "two-thirds (of human resource managers) named family-supportive policies as the single most important factor in attracting and retaining employees" (85). In part, this support is due to studies showing that companies save money on rehiring and retraining workers when they can retain women employees—and one of the best ways to retain them is to make it easier to balance family and work.[3]

If corporations have come to the point of valuing household labor as much as they value market labor, we might invoke Engels's theory of how capitalism profits when women reproduce workers for the system at no cost to the system. Now, it would seem, capitalism is functioning even more smoothly when women's household labor is valued in market terms and perceived as worth a cost to the system. Hence the question becomes: Child care in the service of what? What if we thought of child care not only as valuable in the sense of producing better products (children and information, for example) *but also* as part of a collaborative attempt at the redistribution of wealth and the creation of social justice? As Miranda Joseph suggests above, what if economic value and values coincide? And perhaps this critique could happen at the university, where critical knowledge is produced. If so, then we should do at least as good a job as corporations do in treating the home as a site of productive labor.

Talking to the ISAs

Tony Bennett and others in cultural policy have argued that cultural studies would have greater societal effects if we abandoned moralistic positions of critiquing governmental bodies—what Althusser called "ideological state apparatuses." Bennett says scholars should be "talking to and working with what used to be called the ISAs rather than writing them off from the outset and then, in a self-fulfilling prophecy, criticizing them again when they seem to affirm one's direst functionalist predictions" (1992, 32).

Not everyone would agree. Many cultural critics who have recently written about the corporate university are taking refuge in the notion that culture can be most politically effective when it is least contaminated by the market. Henry Giroux, for example, defines "corporate culture" as the "ensemble of ideological and institutional forces," including the corporate university, that works to "produce compliant workers, spectorial consumers, and passive citizens" (1999, 9). This kind of skepticism about the corporate university inhibits academics from engaging with child-care policies that are premised on the corporate goals of productivity, efficiency, and excellence, because to engage with these policies must mean that one is co-opted. Yet if we are to think of the university as an alternative site, we need to acknowledge the conditions that make it more/less likely for certain groups to "go out" in public; we need to re-socialize academic space. This means acknowledging parenting, especially single parenting, as a condition that inhibits attendance at public events such as talks, conferences, parties, and so on. In fact, in some situations, the discourse of excellence and efficiency may lead to a more "progressive" commitment to solidarity and reciprocity in which child care is seen as a political act. Policies encouraging administrators to take responsibility for child-care relief and material commitments to spaces for children on campus are examples of the intersections of excellence and community.

Interventions into university policy are especially necessary if the policy is to include all families because as they are now written, much policy and discourse shaping it assumes that families are composed of heterosexual couples. Nearly all of the stories above drawn from *Chronicle* articles describe the lives of married couples. Some university policies will benefit all parents; many of the proposals made by the AAUP would do so, including extended pregnancy and parental leave times, stopping the tenure clock for newborns, on-site and affordable child-care centers. Other policies, however, will create the impression of family values but only help certain families.

For example, spousal hiring policies are considered one of the primary ways a university can demonstrate its commitment to families, in part because of the recognition that providing jobs for two spouses will increase the productivity of both, especially if they have children. Penn State prides itself on its Dual Career Program for new faculty, and the university "makes a serious effort to hire academic couples" (Final Report 9). Departments believe they are fulfilling their obligations to families by providing support for spouses when, of course, spousal hires are of no advantage to single parents. Two-parent households must juggle child care and work schedules, but at least they have the option of juggling. Travel for conferences and research, for example, is possible because one parent stays home with the kids.

Job sharing and half-time tenure track positions have been proposed to help parents, especially mothers, cope with the pressures of tenure and child rearing. However, universities that offer job sharing—and these are not many—often assume that the job will be shared by spouses. In urging more universities to offer job sharing, Joan Williams says that "academics are in a particularly good position to set up job shares because they know fellow graduate students in their fields—they may even be married to one" (October 27, 2000). If job sharing is going to benefit single parents, universities will need to arrange shares between colleagues who don't share a household.

How can policy initiatives help produce a shift in the academic culture of self-sufficiency that keeps so many parents, both single and married, from using the policies once they're on the books? It is clear from the research that the culture of self-sufficiency won't change until the work of mothering is made visible in a manner that shows how it shapes work generally perceived as productive. Until then, even if family-friendly policies are in place, there will be little support to change the burden of care simply because domestic work is still not assumed to be "real" productive work. Policy may be able to encourage this shift in small but significant ways. For example, the Penn State study on work/family issues makes the following suggestions, all of which would make the work of parenting more visible on campus: parents and staff should be permitted to bring children to the workplace when local schools close for an in-service day, women should be allowed to care for young children at work in order to promote breastfeeding, and buildings should be redesigned and refitted to make them friendly to young children and parents (Final Report 8). Short of these material changes, I would argue, faculty without children may not even recognize the pressures on parents, especially single parents, who really have to scramble to find child care in situations such as school vacation, child illness, and regular meetings and events after school or day care closes. Ideally, bringing the domestic into the workplace will illuminate the heterogeneity of the domestic sphere, forcing into recognition what most academics purport to already know: there are many different kinds of families.

In another permutation of self-sufficiency, current policies often require an individual faculty member to negotiate with her departmental head for extended time on the tenure clock or maternal leave, explaining why she isn't getting work done on schedule—and no one, especially nontenured faculty, relishes making that admission. The Penn State study recommends a number of things that would lessen this sense of individual responsibility: introduce an ombudsman into negotiations for parental leave and reduced workload, include recognition in annual statements for administrators of units where new parents use existing policies, and shift the burden of requests for parental leave from faculty members to the university (Final Report 7–8). The language of excellence and accounting dominates the report at this point, as in this suggestion: "Reward and recognize administrators who successfully promote policy utilization." However, the effects of this accounting may exceed measurement. Even if the point needs first to be made on the grounds of excellence, this very valuing may lead to a greater sense of support for parents with unequal access to the events that most academics take for granted. This support may lead to community formations, such as shared child care at events, in which dependency is not something to be overcome but something to be shared.

Of course, the commitment to communal work will always be mitigated by the overwhelming valorization of individual publications in the humanities. To the degree, then, that we can begin to recognize child care as worthy work, we may also begin to valorize other kinds of work unrecognized in the emphasis on individual publications. Mothering, as argued in the introduction, is a lot like organizing: the everyday work that undergirds the more visible work yet rarely gets recognized as such. This would require us to pressure departments and universities to significantly alter the conception of worthy work, to broaden the basis for what counts as tenure rather than simply extending the number of years before one goes up for tenure. In this conception, organizing events (which commonly falls under the demeaned category of "service") and collaborative projects would count as much as single-authored books; indeed, one would see that organizing and collaborating enhance writing. A collaborative model does not preclude writing and intellectual work, as the members of the Centre for Contemporary Cultural Studies in Birmingham demonstrated with their jointly authored working papers and books in the 1970s. As the value of work shifts away from the single-authored book or article, so too does the notion of what counts as work. If scholars work together rather than competing, they will see the benefits of sharing child care so parents can contribute as much to the project as nonparents. Mothers (and it's possible for fathers to become mothers) may be the paradigmatic organic intellectuals: the ones who organize, in Gramsci's terms, from the bottom up.

3

The U.S.-Mexican Border

Border woman/writer Gloria Anzaldúa describes the U.S.-Mexico border as "una herida abierta," an open wound, "where the Third World grates against the first and bleeds." Yet it seems this bleeding is productive: "Before a scab forms it hemorrhages again, the lifeblood of two worlds merging to form a third country—a border culture" (3). The border is both a line that divides "us" from "them" and a fluid space, the borderlands, whose inhabitants include the "perverse, the queer, the troublesome." They are "los atrevasados," those who "cross over, pass over, or go through the confines of the 'normal'" (3). The borderlands defy clear categories of identity and perhaps produce a "tolerance for ambiguity." That very ambiguity produces fear, however, and that fear leads to increased surveillance of the border between "us" and "them." Those green border patrol vans have no respect for ambiguity.

This struggle is all very evident where Anzaldúa grew up, in the Rio Grande Valley, the southernmost tip of Texas, land that used to be and in some ways still is Mexico. I worked as a freelance journalist and activist here in the late 1980s, and I've decided to return in the summer of 2003 to interview undocumented single mothers from Mexico and Central America now living with their children in the valley. How does a single mother survive, build a life for herself and her children when she does not have legal status, when she is not recognized by the state, at least officially? She is recognized in unofficial economic terms—as a worker in middle-class homes, in factories, restaurants, strip clubs, and fields. She is also recognized in national debates as a "breeder" who threatens the purity of the nation. To wit, the latest diatribe by Harvard professor Samuel Huntington, whose article "The Hispanic Challenge" warns that "the most immediate and most serious challenge to America's traditional identity comes from the immense and continuing immigration from Latin

America, especially from Mexico, and the fertility rates of these immigrants compared to black and white American natives" (2).

As with many single mothers, then, these women occupy an important position in national debates about immigration, citizenship, work, and the family, yet their voices are rarely heard. In returning to the valley to gather the stories, I also wanted to pursue how, in this particular space, undocumented single mothers might emerge as domestic intellectuals. Undocumented single moms face a particular set of issues connected to legal status, which in turn intensifies the problems many single moms face. Unlike most of us, they live in fear of deportation and separation from their children. The simplest acts, such as driving a car, become dangerous practices. "I'm very afraid every time I leave the house," says Esperanza, a thirty-six-year-old single mother of nine-year-old Dolores who moved to the small south Texas town of San Benito from Zacatecas, Mexico, in 1990. "I ask God to help me, that *la migra* don't arrest me, mainly because of my daughter, because I don't want to be separated from my daughter. This is the biggest fear I have." The freedom to work for a sustainable wage, to take English classes, to obtain a driver's license—these are all rendered difficult or impossible when one doesn't have papers. Hence, the intensification of the situations of most single mothers: the struggle to make ends meet, the feeling of isolation and the difficulty of building community, anxiety about being a good mother and ensuring the well-being of your children. Positioned by these political, economic, and social conditions, these mothers are poised to rearticulate them as well.

Rearticulating these conditions sometimes requires one to work through the very policy realms that have made life difficult. In this case, "passing through the confines of the normal" means conceding that the route to freedom lies in going through immigration and welfare policy, with the goal of coming out the other side with greater mobility. Perhaps one must play the game of normalcy before becoming "abnormal," or, in Anzaldúa's terms, queer—if single mothers can be said to be "queer" when we live on the border of what's still perceived to be the normal family.

In many ways, these policies seem purely punitive. In addition to the imperative to deport undocumented people, welfare and immigration policy often work in tandem to make it difficult for immigrant women to qualify for welfare. For example, almost half of the projected $54 billion in savings from the 1996 Personal Responsibility Act (PRA) was achieved by restrictions on immigrants—even those who are legal but are not citizens.[1] Immigration reform intended in the past two decades to provide amnesty to some undocumented immigrants excludes applicants if they are likely to become a "public charge," a policy that discriminates against mothers who fear that seeking even temporary benefits for their children will prevent them from acquiring legal status.[2]

Another route to legal status—political asylum—is extremely difficult to win, especially here in the valley, where immigration judges have been skeptical of claims made by Central Americans. The main political asylum legal project in the valley—Proyecto Libertad—has won only a handful of asylum cases for Central Americans in its two decades' of existence. In this chapter, I tell the story of one Guatemalan woman, Juana, whose successful bid for asylum helped her maintain independence from an abusive husband and support herself and her son.

There is one other way that immigration policy provides the opportunity for legal status: marriage to a citizen or legal permanent resident. Marriage, as we have seen in relation to welfare policy, thus serves as the conservative solution to dependency. It is a deeply problematic solution. First, the right to gain citizenship through marriage has been guided by congressional mood swings regarding immigrants and nationhood. Granting immigrants the "freedom" to marry has been seen as another way to extend democracy; it's a step one takes toward becoming a fully enfranchised citizen. Congressional debates since the 1875 Page Act—the first to restrict immigration to the United States and aimed at excluding Chinese women typecast as prostitutes—have often linked marriage to whiteness and "moral purity." Suspicious of immigrants who have figured out how to use the system, Congress has made it increasingly difficult to secure legal status through marriage, particularly since the Immigration Marriage Fraud amendments passed in 1986.[3]

Furthermore, Nancy Cott has shown in her history of marriage in the United States how the legality/marriage link perpetuates gender inequality, subordinating wives to husbands. Even when policy has encouraged women to join husbands, it has positioned her as dependent rather than as a full citizen (Cott 143). These patriarchal assumptions shape the relationship after marriage. In the valley, the imperative to marry for legality has produced many problems in the lives of undocumented women, as spouses and boyfriends have used their power to physically and emotionally abuse their partners, seeing in their vulnerability an opportunity to keep them trapped within the home, unable to report abuses.[4]

Ironically, the route to freedom is sometimes found by passing through the confines of marriage. The Violence Against Women Act (VAWA), passed in 1994, allows undocumented women who have been abused by their spouses or parents to apply on their own for permanent residence status rather than having to depend on their abuser to make the claim on their behalf. Proyecto Libertad carries more than three hundred VAWA cases, a remarkable number given the fact that it's often hard to get the women even to talk about domestic abuse. About one hundred of those women have been granted a temporary work permit; some of those cases have proceeded to the next stage, applying for permanent legal residency. Chances of winning are very good; Proyecto has not yet lost a case, and nationwide about 98 percent of all applications submitted have been approved.[5]

Los atrevasados—those who cross over, pass over, or go through the confines of the normal. Yet what these mothers want is a stable life for their children. They work for paltry wages in Tex-Mex restaurants and nightclubs, they care for the babies and clean the houses of the middle class, they sell Mary Kay cosmetics and plastic flower arrangements for the coffee tables of Mexican Americans who sometimes despise them precisely because of the connection that exists despite the border of legality. In this chapter, I reconstruct these lives in some detail, presenting "everyday life" on the border. The desires voiced most frequently in my interviews were quite simple and material: a job, a home, education for the children. To be a domestic intellectual along the border means creating a life for your children that may look to some like the stereotypical American dream.

Mobility: Harlingen, Texas, Summer 2003

Mobility can only fully be understood in relational terms, which is one reason I'm returning to the Rio Grande Valley of Texas after fifteen years. I worked here as a journalist and activist before I was a mother, when my mobility was pretty much unencumbered. Twenty-four years old, single, no kids, I sold everything I owned, left a good job as a reporter for a major city newspaper, and followed my heart to the border, to work alongside my partner, Steve, and other lawyer/activists at the nonprofit legal and immigrant rights' group, Proyecto Libertad. My questions about mobility then had to do with the mobility of white privilege—Anglos helping brown people, possibly building an identity based on "doing good" or "opposition to injustices," or some combination of the two. Yet we took refuge in the politics of the work: we weren't missionaries of any sort, we didn't believe ourselves to be bringing salvation of any kind. We were there to work against the effects of the U.S. government's destructive policies in Central America, to disclaim the privileges of white middle classness and U.S. citizenship. It was the late 1980s, and thousands of Salvadorans and Guatemalans were fleeing right-wing governments and death squads backed by the Central Intelligence Agency (CIA). Proyecto Libertad is in Harlingen, a town thirty miles north of the border that was made famous by Ronald Reagan, who warned in 1986 that the town was just "two days' driving time" from the "communist" Sandinistas in Nicaragua. Steve made $18,000 a year for twelve-hour days filled with frustrating encounters with representatives of a system who could care less about the legal rights of "aliens"—Border Patrol agents, prison guards, and judges who refused to grant political asylum to people who had been tortured in countries that the United States insisted were democracies. When lucky, I made $10,000 a year as a freelance journalist, traveling up and down the border, from Brownsville to Tijuana, recording the stories of undocumented women raped by smugglers and law enforcement officials, of Mexicans who lived in poor barrios contaminated by the wastes of U.S.-owned factories, and of farm workers barely surviving on land their ancestors once owned.

The valley, now and then, functions as a huge detention center, some call it a war zone, a four-county area bordered on one side by the Gulf of Mexico and on the north by the desolate King Ranch. It's very difficult for an undocumented person to get out of the valley by land. There are only two highways north, and both contain immigration checkpoints within sixty miles. People have tried to walk, but they must pass through hundreds of acres of desert. It's here that refugees sometimes die, in the heat of the unpopulated ranchland or, if they've paid a smuggler, locked in the back of air-tight trucks. They're dying on land that used to be Mexico, and Mexicans and Mexican Americans are still the majority population. On this return trip, I stop for breakfast in Robstown, at the northern edge of the King Ranch, at the Taqueria de los Altos de Jalisco. It's bustling on a Sunday morning—mainly Latino families in their church clothes enjoying *huevos rancheros* and *licuados*. A few older Anglos come in as well, dressed in Bermuda shorts and looking as if they're heading for some golf course. In the 1800s, Anglos simply moved in and took this land, buying entire towns of Mexicanos who then went to work for the King family. In 1845, for example, according to Texas historian David

Montejano, Richard King bought the herds of a drought-stricken Mexican village, then "extended an offer to the village: he would resettle the entire community on his ranch where they could have homes and work." The village accepted, and thereafter became a loyal band of employees, "providing the critical armed guard during the 'troubled times' of the region" (80–81).

The signs along Highway 77 further testify to the complex hybridity of this place—"Best Beef Jerky in Texas," "Come to Alice, birthplace of the cowboy," "Next right: Cactus Nursery." On this return, I'm still trying to figure out where I belong. Certainly not with the Anglo golfers. Yet neither with the Latinas I'm about to interview. Now the return has become a way to put my own middle-class experiences of single mothering into a bigger picture, to understand what I have that other women don't, and as well what they have that I don't. Trying to find the intersections that make hybridity a politically useful category. I'm aware of the complexities of "giving voice" to these mothers. I'm struck by how these questions of privilege become particularly intense once one actually leaves the academy to go to those places and talk to those people we often write about with little direct contact.

Coming from the other direction, from south to north, women, many of them mothers, cross the border from Central America and Mexico into the United States, seeking a better life for themselves and their children. More Mexican and Central American women are migrating to the United States than ever before, and many of them come alone, sometimes with their children, a marked departure from the years, pre-1985, of mainly male and family-based migration. Single women are now part of the culture of migration that shapes Mexico, and they look for greater mobility in the United States than they have experienced in Mexico—in terms of family, for one. Many single mothers told me they felt somewhat optimistic that in the United States there would be less shame and stigma attached to being a single mother than there would be in Mexico, especially if they had come from small villages. On the other hand, they had given up the support of extended families and friends.

They often cross alone, and if not, they often end up alone in the valley, vulnerable to a host of abuses that are sometimes particular to and always exacerbated by their undocumented status. Their mobility across the border—no small feat—has rendered them relatively immobile, often isolated and trapped. It's hard to travel north without some kind of legal permission, and such status is hard to secure. "Being denied the right of mobility has all these other repercussions, to every situation you can imagine: work, housing, education. You name it," says Nathan Selzer, a community organizer for Proyecto. Even a trip to the grocery store could result in deportation, if it's a grocery store where *la migra* happens to be on the lookout, cruising the streets in their army-green vehicles. There has been a steady increase in Border Patrol agents over the last decade, especially since September 11, along with new kinds of technologies for monitoring the line between "us" and "them." Compared to these restrictions, my own problems traveling due to child-care concerns seem insignificant.

Yet I know that privilege is not always the most constructive approach from which to view every situation. Privilege produces guilt. How can we produce alliances, new possibilities for living, if we're divided based on who has the hardest life? Is there another way to think about it, other than privilege? Is identity always about difference and marginality? How does one keep track and understand the relationship between all the identity categories that comprise us, that overlap in complicated and inextricable fashion: gender, sexuality, race, class, age, religion, legal status. Perhaps there is something useful in the critique of identity politics made by Lawrence Grossberg. He argues that rather than locating choice—or lack of choice—in individual subjects and the realm of consciousness, it would be more productive to think spatially, in terms of the structuring of mobility. He defines agency as

> a matter of the structured mobility by which people are given access to particular kinds of places, and to the paths that allow one to move to and from such places. . . . If subjectivity constitutes "homes" as places of attachment, temporary addresses for people, agency constitutes strategic installations; these are the specific places and spaces that define particular forms of agency and empower particular populations. In this sense, we can inquire into the particular conditions of possibility of agency, for agency—the ability to make history, as it were—is not intrinsic either to subjects or to selves. (101–102)

How can an undocumented single mother define the United States as a place of belonging when her address is almost always temporary? This is surely a question of what structures mobility, for if movement between sites of work, school, and home can be facilitated by even temporary forms of legality such as a work permit, then agency has increased, and home becomes more permanent, more stable. The problem is the gap between the individual subject and these structures. Aside from Proyecto Libertad and a few other social service and immigrant rights groups in the valley, there is little in place to help women negotiate the system and survive in this economically depressed area. Over 35 percent of the border population of Texas lives in poverty, and the situation is especially dire for mothers and children, who have very limited access to health services, especially since the PRA basically denied coverage for all medical care except for emergency services.[6]

As I wander Harlingen in the summer of 2003, looking for old haunts, I drive up and down pot-holed streets lined by tiny little houses, run-down apartment buildings, and mobile home parks. The poorer Mexican Americans and undocumented folks live here on the west side; when you cross the railroad tracks, income levels rise and the number of Anglos increases. I remember the fair held every year, still going on: the Algodon Festival, whose organizers appear unaware of the history of cotton and slavery in the state—or perhaps they are all too aware, as the queen and king are nearly always Anglo. Clearly, the towns that dot the valley bear the traces of the segregation that began in the early 1900s, when Anglo farmers moved south and began irrigating the land, transforming the region from cattle ranching to commercial farming. Jim Crow segregation defined the valley as it did the rest of the South—separate schools, neighborhoods, shopping areas. Mexicans and Mexican Americans went to work as migrant farm laborers, a practice that continues today. One single mother I interviewed, Rosa, recounted for me how in her first months in the valley she worked in the fields, pushing her baby in a stroller for six miles to arrive at her workplace, then parking him in the shade, returning as frequently as she could to nurse and care for him.

Rosa says she chose to come to the United States, but choice is a complicated category, and upward mobility is determined by what one leaves behind as much as what one moves toward. I'm looking on this trip for a friend, Olga, a single mother, knowing it will be hard to find her after fifteen years. I learn that the strip club where she worked as a waitress, the Foxy Lady, has recently shut down, although it's unlikely that she would still be working there, anyway. The phone book has no entry under her name. Perhaps she did marry an Anglo; she received frequent proposals but always resisted, suspicious of the men's motives even while she was tempted by the chance for legalization. I drive one day to the Mexican border town of Rio Bravo where her mother Marcelina lived, and I search for her *colonia,* but the neighborhood seems to have disappeared, replaced by a huge junk yard. I've kept the notes I took then on the lives of Olga, Marcelina, and Olga's sister, Panchita, who worked in one of the one thousand–plus U.S.-owned factories called *maquiladoras* that line the Mexican side of the border. There are now almost one million Mexicans, mainly women between the ages of fifteen and thirty, working in the four thousand–plus maquiladoras for an average of between $25 and $35 a week.

To me, Olga is the paradigmatic domestic intellectual: she resisted marriage in both Mexico and the United States and carved out a life for herself and her daughter in a space where there are few options for undocumented single moms. She maintained this space even after her legal status made her vulnerable to the predatory advances of a local constable, and she bravely told her story of abuse even when it meant further scrutiny by the state. Olga's story illustrates many conditions of border life, not the least of which is how vulnerable one's body is without the legal status to prove you "belong." I begin here with Olga and proceed through the stories of four other undocumented single mothers living in the valley, using their narratives to illustrate the key words central to understanding the conditions shaping their lives: bodies, mobility, community, everyday life, and policy. Cumulatively, what these portraits indicate is that women's bodies on the border are subject to violations of power that make it difficult for them to feel much freedom or mobility in their everyday lives. Activists at Proyecto Libertad have been able to work through the realm of immigration policy to make some improvements, however, indicating that domestic intellectuals must consider appeals to the state as one strategy among others for social change. In arguing for policy work, I am not forgetting the cautionary words of Wendy Brown and other feminists who have shown the dangers of appealing to the very governing entity that has denied women's agencies. This caution is particularly relevant for undocumented women, subject as they are to state authority. However, that caution should not preclude us from using policies to address the immediate needs of single mothers and their children even as we work for the conditions in which marriage is *not* one of the most viable routes to legality and freedom.

Bodies

When Olga was sixteen, she decided the meager existence of her family in Rio Bravo wasn't enough for her and her newborn daughter. She contemplated her options. Marriage to the father of her child, which her parents urged. But she resisted: "He was lazy. He begged his mother for money to take me to the movies." She could work in one of the maquiladoras, like her sister. Or she could cross the Rio Grande River into south Texas. She had no land-of-opportunity illusions, but she knew she could make a better life for herself and Brenda there, even if it meant living with the constant threat of deportation.

Olga had never before been to the United States, but one early morning she paid a young man from her neighborhood $20 to push her across the Rio Grande River in an inner tube. With a satchel full of short skirts and tube tops, Olga began her career as a *cantinera*, a sort of cocktail waitress/dancer/companion in the bars that dot the towns of the Rio Grande Valley. It wasn't hard to find work—the cantinas thrive on the labor of undocumented women. The bar owners hire fifteen to twenty women, paying them only a dollar or two an hour, expecting them to live on the tips they earn by keeping the largely male clientele entertained for the evening. Initially, she left Brenda at home, stayed with friends in Harlingen, and returned to Rio Bravo often to see her daughter, whom her mother grudgingly cared for, her reluctance mitigated by Olga's generous contributions to the household economy. Gradually, Olga stayed longer and longer on the U.S. side, securing more and better-paying work and putting some money aside for her own place. When Brenda was three, she took her across the river to live in a two-room dilapidated house with two friends, also *cantineras,* in Harlingen.

Olga quickly caught on to the art of the *cantinera*. She explained it to me one day as she and her three housemates prepared for work. Holding an eyelash curler to her large brown eyes, Olga explained, "We have to look good, a little sexy, but not too much. We're not *putas* (prostitutes), and we don't want anyone to think we are."

The incongruities of the lives of these young, Catholic Mexican women from traditional households is evident in their belongings: on one poster, the Spuds McKenzie Budweiser dog proclaims, "The greatest party animals in the world come from Texas." Next to the poster is a small plaque that reads, "*Dios es mi fortaleza*" (God is my strength). Several votive candles with pictures of saints sit on the shelves. On the dresser is a program from mass at Our Lady of Guadalupe Church of Harlingen, sharing space with lipsticks, blushes, mascara, hair rollers, hair spray, brushes, and a naked Barbie doll, blonde hair tangled. Black pantyhose hang over a closet door. Spike-heeled shoes peek out from under the two beds.

There are bags of groceries on the small table; it has been a good week for the women in terms of tips. Brenda is munching on a cracker. They share the costs of rent, utilities, and groceries, and Olga's friends help care for Brenda. At nineteen, Olga enjoy a freedom she wouldn't experience in Mexico—living as a single mom, with her friends, meeting lots of men, staying out late in clubs. Yet because she's undocumented, Olga's mobility is always at risk, and this risk is due in part to her job.

She held her steadiest job at the El Tenampa cantina in nearby Santa Rosa, where she made $125 a week plus tips. The bar closed, however, after a much publicized incident in which Olga and two other cantineras were kidnapped by an off-duty constable named Albert Tovar. Olga tells the following story.

At about 5:30 P.M., a medium-built Latino man in his early thirties came to the bar and checked his gun with the bartender. Olga served Lite beers to him and his friend. The man started talking to Olga, asked her to sit down, and called her friend Rosa over to the table. He danced with Rosa. He eventually offered them $200 to "go and party" with him for the evening. They refused, explaining that the owner didn't permit them to leave.

"You don't realize who I am, do you?" Tovar asked the women. "You don't know I have more power than any policeman or sheriff."

He told them to ask the bar owner to allow them to leave, and when Olga did and returned with the same answer, Tovar exploded. "I'm going to close this fucking whorehouse down! You won't be serving any more beer here."

He began checking identification papers and found that all nineteen of the *cantineras* were undocumented. He called the Santa Rosa police, who arrived to help him arrest the women. The police took sixteen women in three cars. Tovar took Olga and Rosa in his car. Just as their other friend, Luisa, was getting into a police car, he told her to get in his car. He then drove off, telling the women he was taking them to Immigration. But it soon became clear that Tovar had no intention of turning the women in. He dropped the three women off at a bar in La Feria, left, and soon returned with another friend. They bought some beer and drove to the Rodeway Inn in Mercedes. At this point, Olga began protesting strongly.

"In the car he told us he wanted to help us, that he could get us work permits that would prove how powerful he was," she remembers. "I told him I didn't want his help. He got mad and told me I should be afraid of him and his gun, that he could deport me. He thought because we didn't have papers he could do anything he wanted with us. I told him I'd rather be deported a thousand times than do anything with him."

Tovar borrowed money from his friend Manuel Perez to pay for a two-bedroom suite and took Rosa in the back bedroom. Olga and Luisa managed to escape after a scuffle in which Perez hit them and threatened to kill them. Rosa did not escape. She pleaded with Tovar not to rape her; she had just had a baby a month earlier and was still recovering. But he ignored her.

After the rape, Tovar dropped Rosa off in Harlingen. She made her way back to El Tenampa bar, as did Olga and Luisa, and they told the owner, Nick Canales, what had happened. He called the Cameron County sheriff's department, and Tovar was arrested the next day. Several months later, he was convicted of abuse of power in illegally detaining the women. It is rare that the rapists of undocumented women are brought to trial because the women are reluctant to report the incidents, realizing they risk deportation when they walk into any law enforcement office.

All along the 2,000-mile border, from Brownsville to Tijuana, undocumented women tell stories of abuse. I interviewed nearly one hundred women who had been abused when I worked as a journalist there, traveling from Harlingen all along the border to Tijuana. Nearly all lose their money and other meager possessions in bribes to Mexican officials to allow them to survive in the corrupt machination of state power. "Coyotes," or human smugglers, charge exorbitant rates and many times do not deliver on their promises of reaching the United States. Crossing the border, women fall prey to river bandits who rape and rob. The next hurdle is the U.S. Border Patrol, more men who have the power to detain and deport. If they manage to make it into the United States, women then face exploitation in the workplace from employers who know they are powerless to report abuses.

For Olga, life became much harder after the incident with Tovar. In part due to that situation, El Tenampa closed. The passage of the Immigration Reform and Control Act (IRCA) of 1986, which mandated fines for employers who "knowingly" hired undocumented employees, made other bar owners nervous about hiring the cantineras. Olga found work at a topless bar in Harlingen called the Foxy Lady. She worked, fully clothed, waiting tables, and could make about $50 a night in tips. "It makes me ashamed to work at a place with these women, undressing in front of men," she said. "But the law doesn't give me much of a choice." Each week, it became harder to make ends meet. When the owner of the Foxy Lady got cold feet about giving her work, Olga went to another topless club and worked for a few days. Together with her friends, they put together just enough money each week to survive.

The second part of IRCA was an amnesty program for undocumented immigrants who could prove they had been in the country continuously since at least 1982. Many *cantineras* and other women immigrants found it very hard to meet the burden of proof, however, because that meant submitting things like rent receipts and pay stubs, and many women are paid in cash, move frequently, and become accustomed to destroying rather than retaining evidence of their presence in the United States. Still, the amnesty offer was tantalizing to Olga, and she heard that you could buy some time between the application and the decision, time during which you were granted a temporary work permit. So she scraped together the $75 for the notary public seal she needed on the application. She made it before the deadline, but then she needed another $185 to continue, and at that point she gave up.

Olga's friend Silvia, another *cantinera*, had been in the United States since 1981 and thus had a better shot at the amnesty program, even though it would be hard for her to gather the necessary proof. However, Silvia heard that she shouldn't even bother applying because she had received Aid to Families with Dependent Children (AFDC) for her daughter for several years. In a particularly cruel twist—and one that shows immigration policy's bias against mothers and especially single mothers— IRCA included a provision that denied amnesty to anyone "likely to become a public charge" and imposed a five-year ban on AFDC and food stamps for anyone who did qualify for amnesty. Thus, if a mother had ever received AFDC for her children, she couldn't qualify for amnesty, and if she wanted to apply for amnesty, she was then disqualified from applying for AFDC for the next five years. As Grace Chang argues in her book *Disposable Domestics,* the policy consolidated a pool of cheap female labor, women who are forced to remain in exploitative conditions, without state aid, if they want any hope of becoming legal. They can't seek legal status if they aren't already "self-sufficient," and they can't use food stamps, even temporarily, in order to help them achieve self-sufficiency. The bias against dependency is linked to the popular myth that immigrant women, especially Latinas, come to the United States in droves to have their children here and soak up social service resources. Actually, immigrant women use social services at very low rates, says Chang.

Despite these obstacles, Olga was determined not to return to Mexico and the factories, where she had worked for a year when she was fifteen. She's scornful of her family even as she fears their condemnation of her work as a cantinera. Her parents pretend not to know what she's doing. "But," Olga says, "if my neighbors and relatives knew, they would treat me like garbage. In Mexico, women don't go to bars—only the prostitutes." Yet she believes her parents are proud of her independence. Gesturing at her little house and her meager possessions, she notes that it's a "palace compared to where my family lives."

Olga's home was a step up from her parents'. After winding through the unpaved streets filled with potholes nearly large enough to swallow my car, I find Olga's mother Marcelina sitting in some shade in the late morning heat of the Colonia Benito Juarez. At first distrustful, she warms up on sight of the photos I give her of Olga and Brenda. She invites me inside. The house is bigger than Olga's but has dirt instead of wooden floors and no refrigerator. Three beds suffice for Olga's parents and four younger brothers and sisters.

The conversation continually drifts back to the subject of money. Marcelina's husband is barely making any money now as an occasional agricultural worker. Marcelina wants to know how much money Olga makes a week, and I reply, lying but with good reason, that I really don't know. When I'm there, Olga's aunt and cousin drop by. They ask how Olga is doing, and I say fine. They remember how Olga as a child was more outgoing and independent than her sisters. "*Puro fuego,*" says Marcelina. Pure fire.

But when the relatives leave, Marcelina turns slightly bitter. "I miss her, but she never tells me what she's doing, and she never brings me money. I scold her sometimes, I ask her why doesn't she share what she earns. She used to come and see me more—when the child was here. But now she doesn't come hardly at all. When you see her, tell her to send us a little money."

Olga's younger sister Panchita is without a doubt the pride of the household. Marcelina goes into the communal bedroom and returns with a certificate that says *"Empleado del Mes,"* employee of the month, awarded to Panchita in January. The sixteen-year-old makes about $27 a week in the Delnosa maquiladoras. The maquiladora industry has grown dramatically since they began in the 1970s as a twin-plant concept. U.S. corporations such as Zenith and General Motors set up plants in Mexico and pay workers wages that are below subsistence level. The near-finished goods are then transported without import tax to the U.S. border town, where they are packaged and sold in the United States at huge profits. Delnosa makes parts for General Motors cars.

Every morning, Panchita rises at 5 A.M. She prepares carefully for work: purple eye shadow and matching mascara, pink blush and lipstick. Pink nails. White hose and a freshly ironed blouse and skirt. Earrings and a necklace with a cross. This is the fashion of the thousands who provide the bulk of the labor force to the maquiladoras, teenage girls for whom factory work replaces high school.

At 6 A.M., Panchita walks to the edge of the colonia, where she boards a public minibus that will take her about fifteen miles to one of the U.S.-style industrial parks that stretch along the road between the border towns of Rio Bravo and Reynosa. From 6:42 to 4:48, Panchita's job is to make sure that the buttons of auto air conditioner panels are the right size and shape. If the edges are rough, she files them down until they fit smoothly. She gets a ten-minute break in the morning, five minutes in the afternoon, and thirty minutes for lunch. If she is late at any time, even by a few minutes, her pay is docked accordingly.

Panchita speaks with subdued awe about Olga. Occasionally, she gets to see her sister, usually in the middle of the night, those times when Olga is deported by the Border Patrol and makes her way home. The Immigration and Naturalization Service (INS) recently raided the Foxy Lady and found Olga working without papers. They took her to the international bridge at Progreso, about thirty miles from Harlingen. From there, Olga took the last bus, leaving at 1 A.M., for Rio Bravo, about twenty miles away. She arrived around 2 and crawled into bed with her sister. She woke early, took another bus to Matamoros, about fifty miles, waded across the river, walked to the bus station, and took a bus from Brownsville to her Harlingen house, where Brenda was playing with Silvia.

Many *cantineras* find that their best hope for mobility is marriage. Olga was tempted by a proposal from a middle-aged Anglo, the owner of a mobile home park, who gave her money for clothes. She considered it for several weeks; her roommates were in a tizzy about what she should do. She finally decided no. I asked her several weeks later what had happened to him; she smiled ruefully and said, "He just wanted to fuck me. And I won't be fucked."

I realize now, looking back and writing this story as a single mother, how strong Olga was to resist marriage. Marriage is a patriarchal institution, but it can create some paths of mobility even as it shuts down others, and sometimes the longing for the former can preclude one from thinking of the latter.

Policy and Everyday Life

Marta convinced herself that marriage would be a good thing. Now twenty-six years old, she came here from Monterrey, Mexico, for the first time in the early 1990s, crossing the river with her two children. Her son Diego was born in the United States in 1993. Marta returned to Mexico not long thereafter, and her daughter Alma was born there in 1995. That same year, she returned to the valley with both children (who have the same father). There she met Joe, a Mexican American man from the valley, and agreed to move in with him. In 1998, they decided to get married. At first, things with Joe were good. But he started drinking heavily, cheating on her with another woman, then hitting her. He kept saying he would change, but he only got worse and started hitting the children as well. Marta occasionally left him, moving in with her sister who also lives in the valley, and returning to Mexico for a year at one point, but then letting Joe talk her into giving him another chance. Finally in 2001, she had enough. She left him, and now she's receiving assistance from the local women's shelter and Proyecto Libertad, which is helping her apply for legalization under VAWA.

Marta now lives in a small apartment in Los Vecinos housing project in Harlingen. She pays $168 a month for the four rooms. On a typically hot day in June, late in the afternoon, she has her hands full, but things are under control. Her two teenage nieces are visiting, helping out by preparing food at the kitchen table. In the small living room, Cartoon Network is blaring on the television. Diego and Alma are lying on the linoleum floor, just a foot or two in front of the TV, mesmerized. Alfonsito, Marta's ten-month-old baby (Joe is not the father), crawls around on the floor. I've brought fresh-squeezed lemonades from a stand down the street, and he goes from one Styrofoam container to the other, trying to suck on the straws. Marta keeps asking Alma to care for her brother, which she does for a minute, then, quickly bored, returns to the TV. The room is hot but not unbearable, though Marta speaks longingly about owning an air conditioner. She's going to ask the people at the church who help her out with food and Pampers occasionally if they might get one for her. She wipes the damp hair from Alfonsito's forehead when he gets fussy and excuses herself to nurse him. When she returns, she describes all the ways Joe has abused and mistreated her and the children, including threatening to report her to Immigration, hitting them, and selling drugs from their apartment.

First, Joe refused to apply for legal status for Marta, which she could get based on the fact that he is a U.S. citizen. He told her they didn't have enough money and rejected her offers to take care of children in their house in order to earn the necessary money. He used her undocumented status to control, isolate, and threaten her. When Marta left him once to stay with her sister, she remembers how

> Joe used to call on the telephone and say: prepare yourselves! The *migra* is coming (to get you). We were so scared, we wouldn't leave the house all day long. This lasted for one month. And my family started to blame me: they said it's your fault, Marta. I thought to myself: I have to do something. So I told Joe: if you report us to Immigration, I'm going to call the police and tell them that you sell drugs. I was so scared to be separated from my children that I would listen to his threats. When we lived together, he would say the same things—that we shouldn't leave the house. He would have people over to the house, men to drink, and I would go in a room with the children and shut the door and stay there for hours.

In 1994, President Clinton signed VAWA into law, including a provision that allows immigrant women to apply on their own for legal residence status. Previously, immigrants could apply for a family-based visa only through the sponsorship of a spouse or parent. Under VAWA, children of the battered spouse can also be granted legal status as derivative beneficiaries. The law has been an extremely important way to address the abuses of power wielded by husbands against their undocumented wives, who previously risked their own deportation and separation from children by reporting abuse. As Nilda Prado, the paralegal in charge of the program at Proyecto Libertad, tells me, "In most cases, that's what the husbands use as a threat—they say, 'I'm not going to apply for you, because as soon as you get your papers, you're going to leave me.' A lot of times, they go through the whole [application] process, and they [the couple] get ready to go for the interview [to the INS]—and the spouse says, I'm not going to go. If he doesn't go, then the INS is not going to grant the request."

While the approval rate for VAWA cases has been high, it's not easy to gather all the necessary documentation. Nilda tells me that Marta is having a hard time getting things together. Nilda has to provide proof that Marta is of "good moral character," that she entered into a "good faith marriage" and lived with her spouse, that the abuser is a U.S. citizen or legal permanent resident, and that he subjected her to extreme mental or physical cruelty. The information is often hard for abused women to gather, says Nilda, as "a lot of times they just pick up with their kids and leave, and don't bring anything with them, and they don't want to go back." Sometimes what would seem like easy proof to gather—like showing a report card signed by both parents, indicating they lived together—is difficult when the abuser, like Joe, is rarely around and ignores the kids. For "good moral character," Nilda gathers affidavits from friends and family, which usually suffices, although the applicant must also get a police report showing they have no record for the previous three years. To lessen the possibility that the police will turn the applicant in to Immigration when she goes to get this clearance report, Proyecto sends along a letter, explaining to the police that the woman is going through the VAWA application process. Nilda says the police have been quite cooperative, and the Brownsville station is even waiving the $7 fee, but that, understandably, many women are still afraid to go to the police station.[7]

Marta is overwhelmed by this whole process, but she's determined to prove the many ways in which Joe abused her. He rarely held a job, she says, preferring instead to spend his time drinking. He sold drugs from their apartment. And he hit her and the children. At this point in Marta's story, Alma leaves her post by the TV and comes over. "He used to hit us with a board," she says in English, then returns to Cartoon Network.

Joe was also seeing another woman. "It made me feel so ugly, so sad—after all that time together. He tried to deny it, but the other woman had already told me all the details. So I got angry and packed all our stuff, eight suitcases. He pulled my hair and pushed me, made me cry, and the children cry. I got my children together and we went back to Monterrey." They stayed for almost a year, but it was difficult because Diego and Alma had trouble in school as they didn't speak, read, or write Spanish well. "My mother told me to go back—to stay with my family here (not with Joe). And she gave me some advice: if you're going to look for a man, look for a man who cares for your children. First your children, then you."

In 1999, Marta returned pregnant with the child of a man she had met in Monterrey, a man she says she slept with once, mainly out of a sense of rebellion against Joe's infidelities. When she returned to Harlingen, she stayed with her sister. Joe was living just a few houses down with another woman. Marta remembers, "At first I said, that's life. To each his own. But then he came to me, crying, begging my pardon. He came around, promised to change—he said, 'I won't drink, I won't sell drugs.' He told the woman to leave, and he said we could get back together. I didn't answer, until the next day. The woman told me many ugly things—what they had done together. I didn't know who to believe—her or him. I was very confused."

The two agreed to try again, and Joe said he would forgive her for getting pregnant. Marta told him she forgave him for his abuses. He said he would give the baby his last name, she agreed, and they moved back in together. Yet soon he started to hit Marta again. One time, he and his cousin Rick left the house with Diego, then six years old, and didn't come back for five hours. When they returned, Marta could tell they had been at a bar—Diego smelled like smoke and the two men had obviously been drinking. When Marta confronted Joe, he became angry. Rick recounted the incident in a four-page letter he submitted as part of the evidence for Marta's VAWA case. Marta and Joe started arguing, he wrote, and

> then he slapped her hard then she fell to the floor. I told him not to hit her but Joe just told me to leave the hous [*sic*] so I left the next day. Marta told me that he hit her a lot she showed me some bruises where he hit her and her busted mouth. I am Joe's cousin so I saw lots of time he would hit her kids and pinish [*sic*] them a lot.

In 2001, Marta left her husband for good, getting the apartment in Los Vecinos. Yet Joe still haunts her. One day, he came to visit Antonio, the child to whom he gave his last name. Marta was just returning to the apartment when she saw him getting in the car with the child. He said he would just keep him for a few hours, but he never returned him, claiming that he was really his son. Because the boy does have his last name, Joe's claim has been recognized by the court system, and the two are now embroiled in a custody battle. During the first hearing, the judge told Marta he wouldn't return the child because she was from Mexico, and she would only take him there. She swore she wouldn't leave—that the only reason she had left Joe before was because he beat her. The judge responded that the hearing was not about domestic abuse. Joe charged that Marta was not a good mother, that she left the kids alone to go dancing and work in strip clubs.

As she recounts these charges now, Marta expresses her bewilderment but also her outrage, and delineates for me all the ways in which she is a good mother: either she's home, or she arranges for her sisters or nieces to be there. "My children always have food, clean clothes, everything neatly laid out for school each day. I iron their clothes. They like it very much when I iron their clothes." Both Diego and Alma are doing well at school, especially Diego, who received good report cards and only missed one day of school, when he had to go to the dentist. "He says to me, do you know what, Mami? When I get older, I'm going to work so that you don't have to. I'm going to be a doctor."

At the end of telling her story, Marta is clearly exhausted. She admits that she has been feeling very upset and agitated lately, prone to crying and impatience. She has received some counseling from a local women's shelter, but she realizes she needs more help—maybe some antidepressants. She is determined to become self-sufficient now. "My goal is to go forward, by myself, with my children, without needing any man. I want my children to study, and to get my papers in order." She rephrases and repeats her mother's advice: "If I do have another boyfriend, he will have to care first for my children, and then for me. He will have to demonstrate that he loves my children, that he won't mistreat them. Maybe in the future, God will send me such a man. But for now, I just want to work, taking care of old people, or perhaps in a restaurant."

The VAWA allows Marta and other abused women the possibility of independence and mobility based on legal status outside of marriage, yet it also premises this mobility on marriage itself. Important as the law is, it perpetuates the heterosexual, familial basis of immigration policy, because the requirements for proving one's VAWA case include the following: "must have entered into the marriage in good faith, not solely for the purpose of obtaining immigration benefits." As Anannya Bhattacharjee notes in her discussion of South Asian immigrant women, the law's insistence on the "good faith" of the applicant mandates that a woman's primary motivation, presumably, should be family commitment to the man she marries, not legal status for herself. She must demonstrate "good faith" with wedding photographs and invitations, official documents, and oral narratives proving that they have lived together as a "proper" couple, and that they did not marry for immigration benefits. In other words, she has to prove the nonexistence of immigration reasons. (315)

This interrogation suggests women's untrustworthiness and leaves the motives of the petitioning husband unquestioned, notes Bhattacharjee—he may want a domestic servant or free sex, but it doesn't matter to the INS. And immigration law is clearly biased against lesbian couples and against single mothers, none of whom can petition for residence based on any kind of marriage. Single mothers who are abused by men with whom they live obviously cannot use the VAWA.

Still, it's hard to dismiss the effects that legal status would have on Marta's everyday life. These are the moments when I have to question the abstractness of the critiques of the "heteronormativity of marriage" that come from queer theorists like Michael Warner, Lauren Berlant, and Judith Butler. In a way, they're right; yes, of course, marriage is an oppressive, heterosexist, patriarchal institution. Yet it can also—no, it must also—be manipulated from within, because those are quite often the terms that are provided, the terms through which everyday life is negotiated. The difference legal status makes is apparent in the life of another single mom, Maria, who with her work permit secured a job, bought a car, and rented a house for herself and her daughter. From afar, Maria appears as a statistic, another minimum-wage laborer willing to work within the capitalist grind, the Mexican immigrant who both Presidents Bush and Fox acknowledge keeps their economies running. Yet from the living room of her home in San Benito, Maria appears as a proud and self-sufficient single mom, using her new work permit to resist remarriage.

Working at What-a-Burger

Maria greets me on the steps of her front porch. She recently got home from her $6.70-an hour job at the nearby What-a-Burger. Her long hair is damp and she explains that she just showered to get rid of the hamburger smell. She's wearing a yellow shirt with spaghetti straps, white shorts, and sandals that reveal neatly manicured, pink-painted toenails. She's clearly very proud of her seven-year-old daughter Ana, who has just returned from her karate lesson. She wears a white jacket and a yellow belt and flips her long black hair over her shoulder before she demonstrates a kick.

This is a girls' place, I think, as Maria shows me around the immaculate house. There's a long, narrow living room stretching across the front of the house. At one end is a set of shelves surrounding the centerpiece— a television tuned to a Mexican *telenovela*. The shelves around the television are filled with various decorations, many ceramic angels and cupids, and two photos of other women with their children. Two doors lead off either end of the living room, one into the kitchen and one into the bedroom. In the bedroom, one large bed has a pink spread, and there's a white dresser at the end of it, against the wall. The bathroom is carpeted and smells like perfume, and there's a lacy bra drying on the shower rack. The kitchen is a little more cluttered, as if Maria hasn't yet had time to wash the dinner dishes, but it has a nice, homey feel. Ana's toys, books, and colors are all in their place, and she sets herself up in the bedroom with some paper and colors.

Maria came to the United States in January 1994 at the age of twenty-five from Vera Cruz to visit cousins who were living in the valley and decided to stay because work was so limited in her hometown. At first, she worked in Brownsville, taking care of children. In 1995, she met her husband, Jorge, also from Mexico but at that point a legal permanent resident of the United States, and got pregnant shortly thereafter. "I asked him: Are you going to help us? Because I want this baby. I'm already twenty-six. And he said, 'It's your decision: if you want to keep the baby, I'm going to help you.' So we continued together and got married six months after she was born."

It was OK for awhile, but then Jorge began to change. He started to lie and hit her (she lowers her voice and searches for euphemisms that Ana won't understand). "Actually, the first time he hit me was when I was eight months pregnant. But he knew exactly what he was doing—he didn't hit me anywhere except in the face."

Maria put up with the physical and emotional abuse for a while, but she decided to leave when she found out he was seeing another woman. "I thought I can put up with a lot of things—but not this." She left in 1999 and went to the Mujeres Unidas (United Women) women's shelter in nearby McAllen. "I had nothing, not even a place to live," she recalls.

But the shelter helped her out, and the legal staff at Proyecto Libertad filed her VAWA case. She was approved for deferral of deportation and then for work authorization, which has been reapproved every year since then. She's awaiting the decision on permanent residency, which Nilda believes she will eventually win.

With the work authorization, Maria was able to secure a good job just a few blocks from her house at the What-a-Burger fast-food chain, on Business 77, a strip of McDonalds, Exxons, and convenience stores. Two days a week, she works ten hours a day. The other days, she works fewer hours, perhaps seven or eight, for a total of between thirty-eight and forty hours a week, at $6.70 an hour. She cooks, takes orders, cleans, and prepares food. With her salary, she can pretty much support herself. She gets occasional help from Ana's father, with whom she now has a fairly decent relationship. He works in Corpus Christi but comes to see his daughter every two weeks. And when Ana isn't in school and Maria is working, Ana's father's mother, who lives just fifteen minutes away, cares for her, a situation Ana likes very much.

Clearly, the work authorization has given Maria, now thirty-four, a certain security and confidence. She doesn't live in fear of deportation. She is not dependent on any man or relative. She has a small group of friends, all single mothers, and she's in no hurry to remarry. Her dream? To obtain permanent residency and to buy her own house. This wasn't the life she imagined she would lead, but now that she is, she's at peace with her situation:

> [A single mother] has to work on her own. No one is going to come to your rescue. The family, yes, but if you don't have family nearby, you have to do it alone. I think that as mothers, alone, we have to try to do what's best for our children. We have to teach them good values, because the values that we give them now are the values that they'll have as they grow up. Thanks to God, I come from a good family—my parents were together, they're still together. I never thought my child would grow up without a father, and I struggled many years to make it work with him. But there are things that, as a woman, you shouldn't have to put up with. It's better like this.

As I get ready to leave, I notice that Ana is furiously coloring away, and I walk over to comment on her art. It's a flower with a heart at its center, surrounded by a butterfly and what appears to be a whimsical bird. She has written "Jane" above the flower and on the reverse, "Ana." She asks me to wait a few minutes while she finishes coloring it, then hands me the sheet with a big grin. As Maria shows me out of the house, I comment on the car in the driveway—an addition from my previous visit. She smiles broadly: "My birthday present to myself," she says. With her new legal status, she can get a driver's license, introducing into her and Ana's lives a whole new level of mobility.

Community

What emerges from the stories of all these mothers is the rather intense isolation produced by the combination of being undocumented and a single mother. While some women join family members already in the United States, many more have left their extended family in Mexico or Central America. It's difficult to build a support network when going out in public could lead to deportation. Even when they acquire legal papers, like Maria, the old patterns of "going quietly about one's business" remain, exacerbated by the fact that she simply doesn't have time to devote to building community. Perhaps the most common sentiment expressed was a variation on Maria's comment: "A single mother has to do it on her own."

Organizers at Proyecto Libertad are trying to counter that sense of isolation through the development of grassroots, community-based networks. Over the last decade, Proyecto has moved increasingly from arguing political asylum cases for Central American clients to community organizing for local immigrants. This shift is due in part to the changing political conditions in Central America, as fewer refugees arrive now than in the 1980s and '90s. In those years, when Steve and I worked here, Proyecto had very little relationship with the town; in fact, there was at times a palpable hostility toward these "outsiders" who were seemingly encouraging "illegal immigration" into the valley.

The shift is also due to a recognition that immigrants must move beyond victim status to thinking of themselves as community members able to reshape the structures of their neighborhoods even if they don't have papers. Selzer, the community organizer for Proyecto, has been working for the last three years to assist different neighborhoods, composed mainly of undocumented people, in organizing *comités*—coordinating committees—to address four areas: drivers' licenses, workers' rights, elimination of abuse of authority, and legalization. The first step is simply to establish a space where people come for regular meetings to speak their concerns. The next step is to recruit rights organizers, who then go through a six-week training period. Selzer calls this a "process of consciousness raising—of understanding reality and then saying well screw this—to say this is my need, so this is my right, which is a tough leap. It's not something people just naturally do. They're more likely to think 'we have lots of needs and lots of problems, but *no tenemos papeles* (we don't have papers).'"

Esperanza, the thirty-six-year-old single mother I mentioned at the beginning of this chapter, doesn't have papers, and despite the fact that she has worked in the United States since 1990, she can't qualify for legal status. She has resisted getting married because she has seen too much abuse. Despite her fear of deportation, or perhaps because of it, she has decided to join the organizing committee in her neighborhood in San Benito. She brings to it the skills she practices within her everyday life.

Because she can't afford her own place, she lives with her daughter Dolores in a trailer with her sister, her sister's U.S.-citizen husband, and her sister's two children—a baby from this marriage, and a seven-year-old from a previous relationship. The situation is tense; they were supposed to pay her for housework and cooking, but they haven't yet. And "her husband is very strict, a harsh disciplinarian. He wants the house completely clean at all times, yells at the children. He wants everything to be quiet all the time. He orders them to pick up their toys. Everything is cramped, and the children don't have room to play. Dolores doesn't feel at peace there and wants to leave. But I can't afford it."

Esperanza's options are limited because without work authorization, she must rely on the meager wages she earns by selling Mary Kay cosmetics and Home Interior flower arrangements in the neighborhood. During the day, she gets up at 6 A.M. to get the older children ready for school, then she takes care of her sister's baby, cleans the house, and prepares dinner. When her sister returns from work at the meat-packing plant at 5 P.M., Esperanza leaves to do her work, going door to door to collect payments or try to sell more products. Dolores tags along because she doesn't want to stay in the trailer. Because people are quite poor, Esperanza accepts payments over many weeks, and while they do eventually pay, she must make several return trips to collect the money. She usually works until 10 P.M. She's proud of her hard work, but, she says, "I'd like to improve my life, so I came here to Proyecto seeing what I could do to become legal, but they said, there's nothing I can do. It's difficult to improve your situation, when you aren't legal. You can't get a secure job."

Through her work, Esperanza has met most of the people in the neighborhood and gathered all the gossip, good and bad. She frequently is called upon to organize baby showers and birthday parties. She recently found out that a woman who needed surgery didn't have health insurance and couldn't afford the operation, so she organized a large sale of food and raised enough over several weeks to pay for a large chunk of the medical bill. Surrounded by these friends, she no longer feels so scared when she leaves the house. "I'm not peering over my shoulder at every turn," she says. And despite her dependence on her brother-in-law, Esperanza expresses little desire to get married to someone as a strategy of legalization or escape: "Right now, I'm thinking I don't want to get married to anyone else. If not the father of my child, I'd rather be alone. I've seen too many husbands mistreat the children of other men. I'm especially not going to marry someone who doesn't treat my child well. Until this moment, I haven't met this person. It's better that I be alone with my daughter than to be with a man who doesn't respect me and my child."

Esperanza looks at her daughter and describes how she is trying to instill a spirit of self-sufficiency in her: "I tell her—I'll do whatever I can for you, but in reality, the responsibility is yours. Sometimes, when we see a house, she says to me, 'Mama, wouldn't you like to have a house like that,' and I say, 'Yes, m'ijita, when you have a job as a teacher, you can buy me one.'"

Going Home?

The desire for a secure home for one's children includes not just the material structure but also a sense of belonging. Yet belongingness stretches between this new, rather provisional home, and the home left behind in Mexico or Central America. How to re-create home here, in this in-between space? This endeavor can be especially painful when a mother leaves children behind in her home country, as some, like Juana, are forced to do. Children growing up here are also caught between what used to be their mother's home and this hybrid space.

To get to Juana's house in Harlingen, I must pass through a gauntlet of barking dogs, their teeth just inches from my leg as I wend my way through the front yard and driveway of the owner's house, into the backyard, where, next to the alley, sits Juana's tiny house, barely bigger than a child's playhouse. The flesh-colored paint is wearing thin, and a small window air conditioning unit isn't working. Juana has told me this on the phone and asks if it will be all right if we sit outside. I say of course, wondering how we'll endure the 95 degrees and 95 percent humidity, but the backyard turns out to be pleasantly breezy and shaded. When I arrive, midafternoon, Juana is waiting for me, seated in a wheelchair because she recently broke her ankle. Juana is dressed in blue stretch pants and a white T-shirt etched with the skyline of New York City. She's wearing pale-blue eye shadow that matches her pants, a gold filigree ring on her middle finger, and a sterling silver ring on her other hand.

The wheelchair is pulled up to a picnic table that is shaded by a wonderful, twisting mesquite tree. This little stretch of land has become an extension of Juana's house. On the tree is nailed a picture of Jesus on the cross, and a boombox resting in the branches of a mulberry tree is tuned to a Spanish radio station. The backyard is also a garage of sorts for Juana's friend, a man named Joe who uses this space to fix small machines. Broken weed wackers, lawn mowers, a washing machine, and a shopping cart, sans wheels, are scattered about. Juana has arranged chairs for us—old office chairs with the small bottom wheels removed. I wonder what uses Joe has found for wheels of various sizes. As we talk, Joe roams about—he brings Coke in cans with glasses of ice. He hoses down a rust-colored mutt in an old bathtub. A 1970 Chrysler Le Baron is parked between the picnic table and the alley—$600 is the price on the windshield. Juana pays $250 a month in rent.

As we sit down, Juana's sixteen-year-old son Otto wanders out of the house, and Juana calls him over, saying proudly, in Spanish, "He speaks English very well." He's wearing baggy pants and a bright yellow T-shirt emblazoned with "Tommy Jeans." Expressionless, he sits down next to his mother, barely responding to our greetings. To the questions I direct at him, he mumbles yes or no, with the suspicion of a teenager. But gradually, he relaxes and his responses become longer—full sentences even. He leans against his mother's arm and later asks if I want some more Coke. He says he traveled through Pennsylvania with his brother-in-law, a truck driver.

Otto's father left them for good seven years ago, but he hadn't been around much even before that, from the time they arrived in the valley in 1992, fleeing political violence in Guatemala. It has been a tragic decade for the family: two of Juana's children, older than Otto, were murdered in Guatemala. One of them, Yoni, was killed after he was deported from the United States in 1998; the other, Blanca, had never left her country and was murdered by the same men who killed her brother. After their deaths, Juana was finally able to win political asylum here, a bittersweet victory illustrating just how unfair the asylum process is for Central Americans fleeing countries that the United States has deemed "democracies."

The family came here in 1992 after Juana and her husband, Frederico, received death threats from a political party that didn't like their party. Otto was only four years old at the time. One day, men arrived at their house in Guatemala City and threatened them—hitting her older son Yoni, then fifteen years old, in the head with a gun and then holding his head in a barrel of water. They tied her husband to a tree so he couldn't help his son, and they kicked Otto. "Tell her how you remember this," Juana urges her son now. In a flat tone, with as few words as possible, Otto concurs with his mother's story.

Juana's husband left the country first, then sent for her and the two boys. Two of Juana's older children, Frederico and Blanca, already married with families, decided to stay in Guatemala. Juana, Otto, and Yoni made their way on buses through Mexico and then paid a man to help them cross the Rio Grande River. When they reached a little store on the U.S. side, she phoned her husband, who had already joined their older daughter, Emma, already living in Harlingen.

Shortly after their arrival, Juana received word that the husband of her daughter Blanca, then twenty years old, had disappeared and was presumed dead, again due to political violence. She filed a claim for political asylum in 1994 and was promptly denied, as was her appeal to the Board of Immigration Appeals later that year. Because her asylum case was denied, Juana was living as an undocumented mother of undocumented children, without work authorization. To make matters worse, her husband was not much help, either financially or emotionally. He was often gone, and she began to suspect he was having an affair. Although he initially denied any infidelities, Juana kept hearing rumors. One night she went to look for him:

> I found him at the Cantina Mango, with that woman, and I was so mad that I slapped her. He got mad, and when he got home, he threw me on the floor and banged my head against the floor, pulling me up by my hair and then pushing me back down. Then he kicked me. Another time, I

was working in the Restaurant Serape, cooking, and I received an order for huevos rancheros and chicken mole. I brought the plates out and there he was with that other woman. We had another fight after this—he punched me in the face. I started to cry—to ask him why, after all these years together? Why abandon me for another woman? And he told me—if it's going to happen, it's going to happen, that he was going to leave me to marry this woman so that he could fix his legal situation. He said after he fixed his papers, he would return to me and our children. But this was a lie.

At this point in her story, Juana again turns to Otto and urges him, "Tell her how you saw your father hit me, tell her what you said." And Otto, again in his monotone, says, "I said: Stop hitting my mom." Frederico did marry the woman, but the marriage wasn't recognized by the INS and he was eventually deported to Guatemala.

Undaunted, Juana worked a variety of restaurant jobs, sometimes for just a few dollars an hour, often having to relocate when her various employers became nervous because of her lack of work authorization. Together, she and Otto reconstruct her work history, going back and forth trying to remember the names of all the different restaurants. "She's just working all the time," says Otto.

In June 1997, the Border Patrol picked up Yoni and began deportation proceedings. Juana was unable to get the paper work together to forestall the deportation, and Yoni was deported in January 1998. He was afraid to return to Guatemala, says Juana, afraid he would be killed. He moved in with his brother and resumed political work, thinking his colleagues would be able to protect him. He worked in the party office, put up posters, demonstrated at local rallies. Eight months after he was deported, he was murdered by six men—shot twenty times on October 27, 1998, when he was twenty-two years old. When Juana went to the INS office to see if she could go to Guatemala to attend her son's funeral, they responded by detaining her for forty-three days in the Port Isabel Service Processing Center.

In Guatemala, Yoni's sister Blanca confronted one of the men who she knew had killed Yoni. He warned her not to keep asking questions or the same thing would happen to her, and he told his friends about her questions. Blanca called her mother at this point, and Juana asked why she didn't come here. She couldn't figure out how to travel with her three children, and she refused to leave them. Juana remembers, "I told her—at least, run from danger! Don't go out in the street or talk with just anyone on the telephone. I talked to her on April 20, and her birthday was coming, on April 25, and I said, 'What are you going to do for your birthday,' and she said, 'I'll have to see, Mami.'"

On April 26, 1999, Blanca was murdered. Her neighbors in the apartment complex witnessed the event. A young man came to her door and told her that some men were looking for her. She followed him outside, holding her baby and leaving her two older children in the apartment. After walking toward them, Blanca realized they had guns. She pled with them not to hurt her or at least to let her put her baby down. After she put the baby down, they shot and killed Blanca. The police took her two older children, and to this day, Juana doesn't know where they are. Blanca's husband at the time took the baby and left before the police arrived. Juana remembers the day she learned about her daughter's death: "I was working over there, in the restaurant Bernal, when I received the call. I knew when they told me that I had a phone call, that it was going to be bad news about Blanca. The same men who had killed my son Yoni had killed my daughter Blanca as well."

After the deaths of her children, Proyecto lawyers filed a new claim for political asylum for Juana in 2000, compiling a wealth of new evidence, including a newspaper photo from Guatemala City of Blanca lying dead outside her apartment. They also provided sheaves of evidence from human rights groups such as Americas Watch about the intense level of political violence in Guatemala. In a rare case of justice, Juana was granted political asylum on September 7, 2001.

I've given Juana's story a structure now that did not exist that day in her backyard. As Juana tells it, the past of Guatemala is part of the present of Harlingen, and she goes back and forth almost seamlessly, moving between the lives and deaths of her children and the abuses of her husband. This must all seem strange and somewhat removed to Otto, who has been staring off in space for most of this story. He just shrugs when I ask him if he'd ever want to visit Guatemala. Yet he has clearly been listening. When Juana is trying to remember the ages of her five children, including the two who died, she stumbles over Yoni's age: would he be twenty-six or twenty-five now? "Twenty-six," says Otto without hesitating. Although she's scared of the ongoing violence, Juana does want to return—for a visit. She wants to see her son, Frederico, and his two children, the older of whom is named Yoni. She starts crying when she talks about her desire to investigate the disappearances of Blanca's two older children.

Although it would seem that Juana's situation is much improved now that she has won asylum, her situation is still somewhat precarious. She's eligible for legal permanent resident (LPR) status but can't afford the fees: $255 for application, $200 for the medical exam, and $55 for fingerprints. Without LPR status, Juana can't travel back to Guatemala, and if she does, she may well have trouble reentering the United States, this very provisional home.

Money is very tight. Although she now has work authorization, Juana hasn't been able to work since she broke her ankle when she tripped off the poorly constructed ramp that connects their front door to the dirt ground. The landlord isn't sympathetic, and has been bothering her to pay the rent for the last two months. But otherwise, Juana says she is at peace with her situation. "Better to be alone than with that man," she says, referring to her husband, from whom she says she hasn't heard since he was deported. "I'm happy here with my son." She turns and looks over her shoulder as a car rumbles up in the alleyway. Otto leans over the window and talks with two other teenage boys. "I'm leaving," he calls, and we say good-bye. He smiles slightly before he slips inside the car, and they're gone.

Each time I get in my car to drive to the next woman's house, I'm struck by how this seemingly simple act of mobility, of having a car and a driver's license, is a privilege connected to legal status. It allows me to connect to them in ways that they cannot connect to one another. Yet car mobility is basically an autonomous and lonely practice. I've spent many hours driving, alone or with Alex, to meet his father at some halfway point between houses. I remember one cold and snowy Thanksgiving, meeting him at the end of the long weekend in a hotel parking lot in Iowa City. Bundling up seven-year-old Alex in a blanket, tucking him into the back seat of the car, surrounding him with little toys and candies to distract him from the pain of saying good-bye to his dad. Setting off on the four-hour drive back home to Champaign as his dad heads to Minneapolis. Alex is happy to play with the little science kit I've found; he's intrigued by the plastic test tube. Then silence. Then crying. "My finger's stuck, Mommy." I glance back and sure enough, his middle finger is squeezed tightly into the test tube. He's getting desperate and I'm reaching back over the seat, trying to pull it off, trying to keep my eye on the road at the same time. Then he says, "Mommy, why are you driving in the ditch?" Fortunately, the ditch is a fairly level grass median separating the four-lane highway, and I can bring the car to a slow stop without too much trouble. There we sat for a few minutes, Alex still pulling on the test tube and me taking a deep breath, turning around, and giving the tube one hard pull. It pops off. Alex rubs his finger. "Is your finger still there or did it come off with the test tube?" I ask. He holds up his middle finger and it looks like he's flipping me off. We laugh, perhaps for different reasons, and start on our way home.

4

Puerto Rican Chicago

Gentrification lurks around the corner of Chicago's Humboldt Park neighborhood. Driving west on Division Street, one sees the signs—a yuppie bakery, an upscale restaurant, well-dressed people getting their Starbucks coffee before catching the "el" to work, just a fifteen-minute ride to downtown. Then pass under a forty-five-ton steel Puerto Rican flag, stretching from one side of the street to the other. The feel of the neighborhood shifts. Lightposts are adorned with wrought iron banners depicting Taino Indian hieroglyphics and Afro-Caribbean masks. Puerto Rican grocery stores and restaurants, a Dominican cultural center, and Latin music stores line the street. In one lot stands a statue of Don Pedro Albizu Campos, a famous Puerto Rican independence fighter of the early twentieth century, and a *casita*, or "little house," built in his honor. Roughly ninety new businesses have opened since this one-mile stretch was declared the Paseo Boricua in 1996, thanks to an antigentrification campaign by Puerto Rican activists, with the assistance of former alderman (now U.S. congressman) Luis Gutierrez and his successor, Billy Ocasio. The city of Chicago supported the effort, even paying for the steel flags that mark both ends of the Paseo. The steel pays homage to the thousands of Puerto Ricans who moved to the South Side in the 1940s and 1950s to work in the steel mills of the Windy City.

At the heart of the Paseo is the Café Colao, owned and operated by Wanda Colon, a forty-year-old single mother of three. The café is usually host to a lively mixture of community organizers, neighborhood folks, homeless people, high school kids, and twenty-something punks. José Lopez (Wanda's uncle), the director of the Puerto Rican Cultural Center (PRCC), may be found baking flan in the back or sitting on the patio, perhaps strategizing with a union organizer about a nationwide campaign to get out the Latino vote for the 2004 presidential elections. For nearly thirty years, the PRCC has worked at the grassroots level to sustain a Puerto Rican community, and they've connected that effort to an ongoing campaign for the independence of Puerto Rico from U.S. control. The café bears testimony to this struggle: signs on the wall proclaim "Fuera Marina Vieques" (U.S. Marines Out of Vieques) and "Mi Tierra No Se Vende" (My Land Is Not for Sale). Portraits of famous Puerto Rican independence leaders, men and women, also adorn the walls, and a Puerto Rican flag flies in the window.

Wanda, who arrives at work by six every morning, runs the café with calm efficiency. She holds her baby girl, Mia, on one hip while ringing up a purchase on the cash register. She takes the orders and runs the espresso machine, knowing before her customers say a word whether they want an espresso or cappuccino, and how many spoonfuls of sugar she should mix in, and whether to speak to them in English or Spanish. In the summer, Wanda's fifteen-year-old son Damian helps out, taking orders, handling a delivery, and caring for his baby sister. When both Wanda and Damian need to take care of customers, Wanda's mother, visiting from Puerto Rico, takes Mia, who through all the passing around maintains a slight smile, as if amused by the adult hustle and bustle. "She has been my blessing—since I brought her home, she has never been fussy," says Wanda. "I went through so many hardships while she was inside of me—I just believe my grandmother sent her to me, to give me peace."

Retaining control of the neighborhood is critical for the survival of single mothers like Wanda. She needs her family and her people to keep the café running and to help her care for her children. She depends on the neighborhood as much as it depends on her. As entrepreneur, activist, and mother, Wanda is a domestic intellectual who occupies a powerful position within the community, helping to consolidate its cohesiveness. Owning stores and houses, controlling the neighborhood, holding cultural festivals—these are clearly necessary for a community to form and develop an identity of self-determination that counters the years of prejudice and poverty Puerto Ricans have encountered in Chicago. Activism here involves paying careful attention to the relationship between sites—the home, the neighborhood, the city, the United States, and Puerto Rico. Puerto Ricans are a diasporic population, one whose identity has historically been shaped by physical movement between the island and the mainland as well as by a continual flow of cultural exchanges. As Juan Flores describes it, "For peoples caught up in circulatory, back-and-forth migratory motion and thereby subject to the constant renewal of personal and historical ties, culture is experienced as dramatic movement and change, adaptability and resilience" (74).

Puerto Ricans were basically resettled in Chicago by the U.S. government in the 1940s and 1950s, recruited to work in the steel mills and factories during the boom economy of World War II. In the movement between Puerto Rico and Chicago that came to characterize families' efforts to make money and yet stay together, it was difficult for Puerto Ricans to consolidate in one area. Added to that were the pressures to assimilate and the developers that kept driving up the costs of property and forcing people to move west, away from downtown. It has been no small victory, then, for the Puerto Ricans to have claimed this space.

When Wanda looks out on Division Street, she sees that much work is still to be done. "You know what I call this street? The boulevard of broken dreams, like the actor—what's his name? James Dean, you know, the rebel without a cause. That's what I call Division Street. They have a lot of dreams, hopes, and goals and all that, but they've become products of the environment." Wanda points one day outside the café, to a beautiful young girl she has been telling me about, a sixteen-year-old named Kaela who lives next to the café and who just had her second baby, a boy named Jeremiah. His brother Justin is seventeen months old. Kaela is holding the baby and talking, angrily, to a young man whom Wanda identifies as the father of Kaela's first child. It's hot and the baby is crying and Kaela turns and walks away, pulling Justin along behind her. Wanda shakes her head and wipes a table with a damp cloth.

A few steps in the other direction is the PRCC's Family Learning Center (FLC), a state-certified school where mainly young single mothers go to get their high school degrees. The center offers free child care in the same building, helps the students with transportation, and provides job counseling. Some classes address the immediate needs of young women's lives—parenting, sex education, job internship programs. Having these needs met, the women are better able to complete coursework than they might in a public school setting. The curriculum is designed around the history, culture, and politics of Latin America, so students learn where their families came from, what brought them to Chicago, what alliances might develop between Puerto Ricans, Mexicans, and African Americans (all of whom attend the school, even though it's predominantly Puerto Rican). Students participate in other PRCC programs, helping to organize cultural and political events, putting on plays, reading poetry, learning Puerto Rican dances.

By creating a community of support that emphasizes how each single mother deserves help in raising her child, the FLC rearticulates the concept of "dependency" that is so operative and stigmatizing in the lives of single mothers all over the country, but especially so for Puerto Rican women who are subjected to the stereotype of the "welfare queen." This rearticulation occurs first by acknowledging that dependency is in fact a problem—not an individual problem but rather a condition that is the product of being a colonized people whose culture and history have been rendered inferior and whose economy has been monopolized by the U.S. government. "Inferiority" and "dependency" are not intrinsic to individuals or groups but rather products of identifiable historical, economic, political, and cultural conditions. When these conditions change—when, for example, neighborhoods, schools, and cultural centers become spaces controlled by Puerto Ricans—then dependency is replaced by the recognition that all members of the community help out one another in order to survive and thrive as a people. The community that has grown out of the PRCC's work is the solution to welfare dependency—not marriage, minimum-wage jobs, or sheer willpower. Other single mothers, teachers, and activists in the neighborhood help raise children in communal spaces, providing a powerful alternative to the mainstream insistence that single mothers make it on their own to prove their worthiness as mothers.

In this politicized space, there is considerable potential for young mothers to emerge as domestic intellectuals engaged in the struggle for the freedom of Puerto Rico, or working on Latino electoral campaigns, or educating people in the neighborhood about safer sex and HIV. That doesn't always happen, however, and I don't think it needs to happen in order for single mothers to emerge as domestic intellectuals. The domestic intellectual may not be a singular voice or role model but rather a collective position, a collaborative effort where a group often stigmatized in national debates on welfare demonstrates its independent existence, its ability to negotiate everyday life.

In Solidarity

I moved to Chicago from the U.S.-Mexican border in the late 1980s to start graduate school and immediately began looking for activist groups to join. I found Prairie Fire, a group of Anglo activists that grew out of the Weather Underground and since then has worked on a number of political issues including support for Puerto Rican independence, feminism, and gay rights, and opposition to U.S. militarism throughout the world. Prairie Fire offered an intellectual and activist space for working through the questions of white privilege. It was a space that complemented and often went beyond the academic theories of postcolonialism and feminism that were also shaping my ideas. Acknowledging the history of U.S. colonization in Puerto Rico and the need for self-determination, Prairie Fire knew that its work was in support and solidarity, never calling the shots but neither withdrawing from a commitment to work for the liberation of Puerto Ricans. Prairie Fire organizes public events, for example, on the injustices suffered by Puerto Ricans imprisoned for inordinately long sentences for beliefs and actions connected to the independence struggle. Other Prairie Fire members work at the PRCC's alternative high school, which teaches kids about their histories, language, and culture, restoring much of the confidence sapped by a public school system that never recognizes Puerto Rican identity outside of gangs and welfare. I taught a literature course for a year at the school; it was a place of belonging, even though I didn't fully belong. It felt like the right place to be, and the movement between the graduate seminar and the center felt right—they were informing each other, and I was being taught and teaching at the same time.

Now, more than a decade later, I return as a single mother, looking in new and arguably more urgent ways for community, aware that it exists here at the center, but not for me. I'm very aware of my own nostalgia for my time in Chicago, when I was part of the Prairie Fire community, and how the emptiness of academia has made me long for those days again. I'm back here in the spring of 2003, drinking espresso in the café, interviewing Wanda and the students. The FLC has just moved from its long-time location in an old brick building several miles from here, where I taught, to the Paseo Boricua, as part of the effort to transform the area. The alternative high school and cultural center will move into a building not far from here. Everything seems to be coming together. I wish I could stay, come here with my child and be part of this space; I'm overwhelmed by this desire to belong. And one day I ask Marísol Morales, FLC director, "Do you think I'm romanticizing this community?" She answers indirectly: "All of us who live and work here have a really concrete understanding of community. You can find it everywhere and everyone knows what it is. But at the same time, there's a lot of negative things that occur, the fucked-up shit, like the hypes (drug users) helping us move stuff in (to the new space). They may be eyeing our shit, but you have to give them credit for helping."

The PRCC has survived everything from FBI raids in the 1980s (the agency was convinced the high school was training terrorists) to budget crises. They have held together, no doubt, because of a passionate belief that Puerto Rico should be free from U.S. control. More than a dozen Puerto Ricans have gone to prison because of this belief. Yet the PRCC has also survived because of the recognition that the politics of liberation and independence, if articulated in the abstract, may not serve the needs of students for whom daily life consists of gang warfare, poverty, and teen pregnancy. As Marísol puts it, "It's not about training more *independistas*. It's about being twenty years old and reading at a fourth-grade level." Rather than working from the revolutionary objectives of liberation and nationalism, then, the PRCC works from the ground up, asking how the experiences of coming from a colonized and diasporic people plays out in Chicago, and how the center can restore a sense of history and cultural pride so as to change the conditions of everyday life. Says José Lopez, "The movement, from the 1960s, was always grounded in grassroots organizing—bilingual education, (protesting) police brutality, better health care. We didn't start out demanding Puerto Rican independence, even though we believe in independence. The independence mentality comes to the fore with consciousness raising about why we're here—that the Puerto Rican migration is the product of the overall situation, of colonization."

The PRCC's rhetoric and material practices exhort independence and autonomy, self-reliance and self-determination, at both individual and group levels. In articulating the connection between the individual and the group, the PRCC offers an alternative to the conservative belief in individual agency, an alternative that still acknowledges the importance of a belief in oneself. It's a definition of self-sufficiency that is disarticulated from individual autonomy, linked rather to an individual's place within a community and to an awareness of how gender and ethnicity are constructed by larger structures. This is how to acquire agency—to understand how subjects are shaped in their movement between places, within structures.

I hope to show in the rest of this chapter how the PRCC has worked to increase the agency of single mothers through its careful attention to spatial issues—to how pregnant and maternal bodies occupy space, and what needs to be done to increase their mobility. As Pierre Bourdieu suggests, understanding how to produce social change involves the ability to see how bodies are placed, and how that place is shaped by larger social relations that extend beyond the immediate place—relations that are often naturalized such that they are not visible as social forces. "Social space translates into physical space," he says, "but the translation is always more or less *blurred*," masking power relations that shape the space. The PRCC and its Family Learning Center clarify those blurred relationships.

I want to situate the PRCC and the FLC within the context of the neighborhood. It is clear through the story of Wanda Colon how one single mother's life gets shaped by this space and the community's antigentrification efforts. Wanda's story, seen in the wider historical struggles of Puerto Ricans in Chicago, illustrates another important point about space: one cannot afford to act outside the imperatives of capitalism. As Bourdieu says, "The ability to dominate space, notably by appropriating (materially or symbolically) the rare goods (public or private) distributed there, depends on the capital possessed" (127). For Wanda and others in the struggle for space, capital is not just possessed by the individual (although that is one important component). Wanda owns her café, but she owns it as part of a community-orchestrated effort to make sure property stays in the hands of Puerto Ricans. Gentrification succeeds when it masks the inequities of the marketplace, when the general public sees gentrifiers as "fixing up" a neighborhood. Capitalism takes for granted that those with money will buy desirable property, and that neighborhoods benefit from this influx of resources. The PRCC has revealed that what gets elided in gentrification are the other kinds of investments in the neighborhood—community engagement, children in public schools, attendance at churches, construction of cultural centers and events. These elements also contribute to the vitality of a neighborhood. They allow more people to occupy the space, in more variegated ways, than the market, yet they cannot exist outside that very market.

Paseo Boricua, at the Café Colao

The verb "colar" literally means to filter liquid through something, as in the filtering of coffee. But it has many other meanings as well. Meredith Rúa uses it in her analysis of the blending of Mexican and Puerto Rican identities in Chicago to indicate the continual process of identity construction, as subjects pass through spaces where ethnic identities are negotiated. It's a useful way to think about what happens in this café each day; it's where identities are filtered, so to speak, through the conversations and meetings that occur here. When Wanda bought the place from her aunt in March 2002, she changed the name from Bakery Borinquen to Café Colao, shifting from a Puerto Rican name ("Borinquen" refers to the indigenous population of Puerto Rico) to a more hybrid term, reflecting the growing complexity of the neighborhood's Latino population (and consumer base, for Wanda is a savvy businesswoman). People interact, argue, build alliances, care for babies, ask for money, post fliers. On a summer day in 2002, a young filmmaker from Columbia College is shooting a scene from *Boricua,* his three-part video representing different aspects of Puerto Rican identity. "Could everybody please be quiet?" says the director's assistant to the café crowd, some of whom look a bit skeptical at the request yet nevertheless are impressed enough to acquiesce. An elderly Latino man, long gray hair slicked back, dressed in a suit, pushes his *paleteria* cart down the sidewalk, past the café. A short while later, another cart passes, this one, named "La Flor de Michoacan," is pushed by a middle-aged man, maybe from Michoacan, Mexico, accompanied by his family, it seems—a woman and two young boys, perhaps wondering why they must spend their day helping their parents selling ice cream treats, perhaps strategizing a way out of work and toward play.

The verb *colar* can also mean "to empty. To lie, defraud or to covertly pass something. To pass on or pass something through a tight place. To pass on as true something that is false. To drink wine. To enter a place surreptitiously and without permission; to cut in line or to move up your turn in a line, etc. To make a mistake. To fall in love" (qtd. in Rúa 123). These are also apt associations for Wanda. She intended to run the bakery with the father of Mia, a man whom she says "swept her off her feet." At the age of thirty-seven, she fell in love for the first time in her life. Yet it turned out to be a lie, and a mistake. He often accused her of infidelities, when he was the one being unfaithful. He became abusive, even when Wanda became pregnant, at age thirty-nine, with his child. "What enabled me to end it was the biggest slap in the face that a woman can actually go through. Even when I was pregnant, he was still accusing me of being unfaithful. Then, he got another woman pregnant." She points out toward the street. "A young little trash from Division Street who said we would never be together. I don't blame her, I blame him. But he allowed it—he denies it, he still denies it . . . but I know it's true. He never recognized Mia, and now I wouldn't allow it. That's when I decided to do this [run the café]."

In some ways, pregnant teenagers are a reminder of Wanda's youth. She became pregnant at seventeen and decided to marry Luis, the father, despite her misgivings, because he was a good man and because some members of her family, especially her grandmother, pressured her not to get an abortion and to recognize that Luis would be a good husband. But Wanda almost immediately began to question her decision: "After I had my first son—the year after—I said what am I doing. This is not for me. I just felt like my life had stopped. I felt I wasn't going anywhere. Oh my God, I'm married, I have a kid, doing the housewife thing, working, being a mother. I just felt there was a void."

Wanda began work as a retail clerk, then went to school to earn an associate's degree in retail management and eventually became a clothes buyer for some of the department stores on Michigan Avenue. Her ambition and restlessness were a source of constant tension in her marriage, prompting three separations and, finally, a divorce when Wanda was thirty-five. At that point, she also grew tired of the shallowness of the Michigan Avenue crowd. Hungry for more meaningful work, wanting to return to the community that was an integral part of her upbringing, she worked for a year as the accountant for the PRCC's AIDS awareness project, then for a year for Billy Ocasio's successful campaign for city alderman. Then she decided to buy the café and become her own boss, remembering what her mother had told her years before: "Take care of yourself. Don't be dependent on anyone." In her new role as entrepreneur, Wanda becomes integral to community activism, helping to resist gentrification: "I want to see the community progress, and I want the people who have moved out to see that you can come back and patronize the places you used to visit—even buy places."

The community is composed of many different identities, not all of them eager to belong in the same manner. Moving back, says Wanda, has required her to become "ghettofied," to talk to the gang bangers, drug users and prostitutes on their own terms, which in turn means they'll look out for her, even letting her know when a flower pot gets stolen from the patio: "You have to speak to people on their terms, because if you come with the attitude that 'I don't want you hanging out here,' forget it. You won't have a place." For example, when Wanda wanted to prevent gang bangers from smoking pot around her patio, she approached the leader and said, "As a sister, I'm coming to you with the utmost respect, and I hope that you have the same respect. I'm starting off here with this business, and it's really not good for my business to have you here smoking pot. He said, 'You know what, sister, you have a deal.'"

Control of the neighborhood is critical for single mothers like Wanda because family and friends live in the area, and they often provide an important source of child care. About 60 percent of Puerto Rican births in the United States in 1995 were to single mothers, although it's important to note that some of those mothers live either with their children's fathers or with extended family.[1] Gentrification drives up the cost of housing and causes families to disperse. The threat of neighborhood dispersement is a smaller-scale, albeit just as significant, version of the displacement that Puerto Ricans have dealt with due to U.S. colonization and economic influences on the island since the United States took control of Puerto Rico after the 1898 Spanish-American War. Puerto Rico became a protectorate. U.S. corporations moved in, and the island was a direct colony until 1952, when Congress granted it limited self-rule in the form of commonwealth status. It remains in the status today, although there is much debate, both on the island and on the mainland, about whether Puerto Rico should remain a commonwealth, become a state, or gain its independence. Puerto Rican activists in Chicago and elsewhere have argued that it is still a colony and that the island deserves its independence. Says journalist and historian Juan Gonzalez: "Puerto Rico remains the biggest, the most lucrative, and the oldest colony in the United States in an age when colonies were supposed to have disappeared" (247). Puerto Ricans on the mainland occupy an especially complex position, both citizens and foreigners, able to travel back and forth "freely," yet many times forced to move because of poor economic conditions in Puerto Rico, where most of the wealth has gone to the coffers of U.S. corporations. The entire island is basically a free-trade zone, with companies exempt from federal taxes and many environmental regulations (Gonzalez 232).

Beginning in the late 1940s, Puerto Ricans were encouraged through various government programs and offices to migrate to the mainland, primarily to New York at first, then increasingly to Chicago. Governmental migration offices were set up to oversee the massive migration. Flores calls these years the beginning of the "modern Latino diaspora": by 1960, more than one million Puerto Ricans were on the mainland (81).[2] The resettlement "was part of a larger planned migration strategy in Puerto Rico aimed at resolving the island's 'overpopulation problem' and advancing its new industrialization program" (Pérez 48–49). The U.S. government apparently felt Operation Bootstrap, the U.S. industrialization program on the island, would fare better if there were fewer workers—potentially unemployed and unhappy—on the island. In Chicago, men went to work in the steel mills and women in the garment factories and as domestic labor. Chicago and Puerto Rico were linked, as family members gradually arrived to join others.

What happened to families when they moved to Chicago? There was intense pressure to perform as model citizens, distancing themselves from African Americans and Mexicans. It was difficult under colonization on the island to retain culture and language, but it was even more difficult in the United States, given the lack of established Puerto Rican communities and pressures to assimilate. In an attempt to control the new population, the city of Chicago did its best to prevent Puerto Ricans from forming communities. The director of the Commonwealth of Puerto Rico office in Chicago, for example, urged "Puerto Ricans not to settle down with any Spanish-speaking people, but to distribute themselves all over the city in Polish, Italian, Czechoslovak and other areas" (qtd. in Ramos-Zayas 48). Families were often divided, with some members still on the island. Puerto Rican women in Chicago had to both hold down domestic labor and factory jobs and raise their children: "Like other poor and minority women, they were expected to work; but they were also upheld as the ideal of family and female virtue. Their propensity to work in the informal sector—mainly caring for relatives' children—often obscured their waged labor, reproduced the myth of breadwinning fathers and nonproductive mothers, and reaffirmed their popular image as mothers wholly dedicated to their nuclear families" (Pérez 55).

Puerto Rican barrios did manage to form on the near west and north sides of Chicago, but almost immediately they struggled to maintain the cohesiveness of their communities. Beginning already in the 1960s, neighborhoods were assailed by gentrification, poverty, and de-industrialization, destroying neighborhoods and with it family cohesiveness. The image of the dedicated mother was replaced by the stereotype of the welfare queen. The Puerto Rican neighborhoods became what they still are today—Humboldt Park, Logan Square, and West Town, although the latter two have largely been gentrified by now. Social protests came to Humboldt Park in 1966. The Division Street Riots were set off when a police officer shot a young Puerto Rican man and the police used attack dogs on the crowd. Quickly, Puerto Ricans lost their "model minority" status, becoming—in the minds of the authorities and the public—the African

Americans who were also protesting police brutality and racism at that time. Two important developments followed from the events of 1966: community groups began addressing poverty, housing, discrimination, and police brutality, and the media began focusing on the problems of gangs, drugs, welfare dependency, and violence in the community (Pérez 57). Some of this coverage, continuing throughout the 1970s, was sympathetic, but all of it focused on the *problems* of the Humboldt Park and West Town neighborhoods, as in this example from the *Chicago Tribune* quoted by Pérez: "Language problems, lack of jobs, and massive cultural shock often shatter Puerto Rican families" (57). This characterization was part of the increasingly popular "culture of poverty" theory, put forth in two widely acclaimed books: *Beyond the Melting Pot* by Nathan Glazer and Daniel Moynihan, and anthropologist Oscar Lewis's *La Vida* (described in the introduction). On the other hand, families did indeed become more unstable into the 1960s and 1970s, as gentrification pushed the community westward and led to some dispersion, and as deindustrialization produced widescale unemployment and poverty.

In addition to the Young Lords, other activist groups formed in the 1960s and 1970s, responding to social issues in different manners. The Young Lords, for example, developed day-care centers, demanded low-income housing, and challenged displacement (Ramos-Zayas 53), even as they espoused a nationalist agenda. These second-generation Puerto Ricans didn't plan on returning to Puerto Rico, but they were fervently patriotic. After the Young Lords dispersed in the mid-1970s, a group with a similar belief in the combination of grassroots activism and nationalism emerged—the Movimiento para la Liberacion (MLN). José Lopez was the executive secretary. They started the Puerto Rican Cultural Center, which has been working steadily since then to organize Puerto Ricans around common cultural, political, and economic struggles. Their center works as a central meeting place and includes the FLC, the day-care center, a library, and an alternative high school named after Pedro Albizu Campos, the leader of the armed revolutionary movement in Puerto Rico during the first half of the twentieth century.

By the 1990s, a renewed wave of gentrification was threatening the Puerto Rican neighborhoods, especially West Town, bordering on Humboldt Park. In the 1990s, "West Town experienced a loss of 24.7 percent of its Latino population while the white rate increased by 7 percent. . . . In 1990, there were 54,361 Latinos in West Town, constituting 62 percent of the residents. By 2000, their numbers decreased to 40,920 or 46.8

percent of the population. . . . The number of white residents increased from 44,728 to 50,887 for a total gain of 6,159 white residents" (Pérez 12, drawing on U.S. Census Bureau statistics).

Several nonprofit organizations formed to counter gentrification, including the Humboldt Park Empowerment Partnership, a coalition of more than eighty community organizations and business leaders. They came up with a strategic plan in 1996 for attracting investors, especially Puerto Ricans; building affordable housing; and developing cultural landmarks. "The rationale behind these initiatives," says Nilda Flores-Gonzalez, "is that in order to keep Puerto Ricans from selling their property to speculators and developers, and in order to encourage Puerto Rican professionals to move into the neighborhood and bring their capital with them, Puerto Rican goods, services, and culture have to be provided there" (13). Separately, Alderman Billy Ocasio brought together a group of community activists, government officials, and architects and came up with the idea of the Paseo Boricua.

Everyday Nationalism

The PRCC may have a radical reputation in some Chicago circles, but what has won over the neighborhood and the students is its commitment to the everyday. It's what Ana Ramos-Zayas in her study of Puerto Rican Chicago calls "nationalism as everyday social practice" (4). This is obvious when I visit the FLC one hot day in late July 2002, when the PRCC is still housed in an old warehouse on Claremont Street. Inside the building, six young women, all single mothers, are attending summer school, gathered around a table in a room made bearable by a large fan in the corner. One of their teachers, Michelle, is giving a lecture on the Bill of Rights, writing key points on the board, and the women are taking notes, occasionally interrupting her with questions and launching into discussions on related issues, such as, Is the death penalty cruel and unusual punishment? Michelle lets the women offer opinions; they talk to one another in both English and Spanish as she writes more points on the board. "Serial killers should die," says one student. "They're crazy—they can't be rehabilitated." Another disagrees—they still shouldn't be killed for what they've done. The incongruities of the situation are striking at first: a lesson on the U.S. Constitution at a center where nationalist Puerto Rican ideology, anti-colonization efforts, and pro-independence sentiments are regularly expressed and theorized. Yet the class is also testimony to why the FLC succeeds in graduating more than 90 percent of its students and finding them jobs. Programs serve the immediate, everyday needs of people in the community, including single mothers who have dropped out of high school and need to earn a high school diploma under the curriculum requirements of the state education system. However, this mainstream objective is pursued within a space that mainly defies the mainstream belief that success is based on assimilation, asserting rather that success comes with pride in ethnicity.

This pride in Puerto Rican identity is exactly what Albizu Campos High School and all the programs of the PRCC try to foster, recognizing that education about history and culture needs to be combined with material support on a basic, everyday level. A nationalist politics works only if it has practical effects, as Ramos-Zayas argues in her analysis of the success of Albizu Campos high school:

> There is a powerful irony in the fact that a pro-independence ideology, which encourages critical appraisal of U.S. policies toward Puerto Rico and of the myth of the "American Dream," actually encourages high school students to pursue mainstream mobility routes, such as abandoning gangs, finishing high school, and enrolling in college. One would think such nationalist ideologies and identity politics would instead create resentment and anger, and encourage program participants to reject U.S. institutions. However, the opposite seems to be the case: high-risk Puerto Rican youths—including gang members and teenage mothers— are being drawn into the alternative high school, peer counseling initiatives, and the community building process sponsored by pro-independence activists. I argue that it is precisely the identity politics behind the oppositional education programs that explains why these students defy the odds and remain interested in schooling. (165–166)

As such, the identity politics derived from a nationalist ideology is diffused through different PRCC programs and becomes integrated into everyday life, in some ways losing its political force but in other ways becoming more important, as is obvious when visiting the single mothers who attend the Family Learning Center (which is separate from the high school).

In my interviews with the single mothers at the FLC, few of them mention anything about Puerto Rican nationalism or aspire to become full-time activists at the center. They want to go to college, or cosmetology school, or enter a computer training program. While sometimes they stay connected to the PRCC, they may leave and never return, indicating the temporality and fragility of community. The politics takes place at the level of the everyday, where they are learning to take care not only of their own children but also of their classmates' children, and, furthermore, then to have enough energy and self-esteem to care for themselves. As Patricia Hill Collins puts it, when mothering is shared by like-minded people, it becomes a political act, through which "vulnerable members of the community . . . attain the self-reliance and independence essential for resistance" (233). As such, young mothers become domestic intellectuals, articulators and practitioners of collaborative families.

Somos la Fuerza

The cover of the Family Learning Center's 2001–2002 yearbook shows a photo of a pregnant Latina with a Puerto Rican flag painted on her stomach. She smiles, hands spread across her breasts, as if claiming the flag and her baby as simultaneously her own, as together constituting her pregnant body. Above the photo is the yearbook's title—"The Birth of a New Beginning"—and across the bottom are the words of Puerto Rican poet Julia de Burgos: "*Somos la vida, la fuerza, la Mujer*" (we are the life, the force, the woman).

One might read the cover as an articulation of a pro-natalism that characterizes many nationalist movements and has prompted feminist critique for the ways in which a heterosexual family undergirds nationalism, seemingly freeing "the people" while relying on continued secondary status for women. Pro-natalism has been part of the movement for liberation in Puerto Rico, as articulated in the early part of the twentieth century by the most famous liberation leader, Don Pedro Albizu Campos. The pro-natalism, however, must be put in an important context: the U.S. government's sterilization campaigns on the island, which independence leaders and subsequent generations of activists have seen as an attempt at genocide.

Shift the struggle from Puerto Rico to Humboldt Park, from 1919 to 2002, and the image of a pregnant woman with a flag painted on her body both draws on and rearticulates this history of colonization. To say that single mothers represent hope, a new beginning, is to challenge the stereotype of welfare dependency. To give birth is indeed to reproduce the nation as it takes shape in the diaspora, in this community that raises children together, and in doing so builds alternatives to welfare and other forms of dependency. The young woman is clearly in control of herself, graduating from high school and looking to a future where she and her child may see the independence of Puerto Rico. The personal and the political intersect, or perhaps the distinctions between them are not even an issue. Adults who work at the PRCC consider themselves like parents to the young people at the high school and at the FLC. Lourdes Lugo, principal of the high school, regularly opens her home to the teenage girls who are having trouble in their own homes. She explains:

> One of the great advantages of being single and being a member of the PRCC, working in the high school, is that it gives me the possibility of helping other families raise their kids. I'm not a parent. I probably will never know what the pain of a parent feels like. But I can definitely be helpful in the process—if I can be the channel between a mother and a daughter who can't talk to each other. Or have the child in my house for a few weeks and bring them back. I'm part of a community of raising children. A lot of people call me Mom—former students, people I've worked with, lots of people.

The rearticulation of "mother" and "Latina" through an identity politics that is not strictly nationalist (since not all the students are Puerto Rican) defies the stereotypes of the young and shamed welfare mom. As Lysette Rivera says in her yearbook testimony, "My accomplishments are learning a lot about motherhood and learning how to solve problems in the Latino community. I have also picked up the ability to learn how to cope with my problems. Even though my life wasn't all that good this year, I learned to be strong and to go on with my life." Lysette's ability to connect her identity as mother with her identity as Latina, and her problems as an individual to solutions within the context of a Latino community, exemplify what the FLC aims to do—provide a space where these articulations can be made. In their writing classes, one assignment asks the students to write letters to their children about what it could mean to be a member of a new Latino generation. Rosalyn Santiago expressed her concerns that her son Daniel would be confused about his identity, because she is Puerto Rican and Mexican and his father is Mexican:

> I am not sure what you would consider yourself, but you should be proud of your ethnicity. I am proud of my ethnicity, and I consider myself an American Latina. Danielito, don't let anyone see you as less just because you come from two different cultures. It would be interesting for you because you will have the opportunity to learn from both of them. I am starting to learn from my cultures. Always remember you should be proud of who you are, and where you come from.

Ana's Story

After her four hours of summer school, Ana goes to work at the receptionist desk. Her son Nathaniel sits in a chair next to her, happily sucking on a Hi-C from Subway. He takes a long drink from the straw, pulls the straw out of the plastic lid, then manipulates the straw back into the hole, laughing at his own dexterity. When Ana gets busy taking phone messages, another student picks up Nathaniel and cuddles him, then sits him down on the couch in the waiting room, right outside Ana's office. She changes Nathaniel's diaper. Nathaniel continues his straw game as one of the high school teachers sits down next to him, engaging him for a few moments before Ana is free. It's clearly a routine that everyone is used to—an extended family of sorts caring for Ana's child as she works a few hours after her classes. Soon, Ana's mother will come to pick up Nathaniel and care for him until Ana gets off work at 6 P.M. Ana uses the money she earns from this summer job to pay for diapers, clothes, and other small items for her son.

Ana was born in Mexico and moved to Chicago when she was two; she herself was raised by a single mother. In fact, she remembers the day her father left her:

> My dad left me when I was about four. I was going to be five. I remember him being abusive to my mom. And I remember when he left—I had just gotten out of the bathtub, and he told me he was never going to be back. I remember that really clear, like yesterday. My brother had just been born. My brother never got to see him.

Ana's mother worked very hard to support the family, working in a sewing factory and selling Mary Kay cosmetics.

Ana got pregnant age at seventeen. She and her boyfriend were living together, and they weren't using birth control. "Our baby was conceived out of love," she says. "His dad really wanted a baby. I didn't want to have children because we barely had money for each other—we were still going to high school. He wanted a baby so much that I finally said yeah— I didn't want him to think that I didn't love him enough to give him a baby." Although her boyfriend wanted to get married, Ana thought she was too young, and she wasn't sure about him: "I didn't want to get divorced right away. I told myself if he really loves me, this can wait. As you can see it didn't work out, and I'm glad I didn't."

Ana had to drop out of high school as a junior during her pregnancy, and after Nathaniel's birth she and her boyfriend moved in with his parents. Although her boyfriend was supportive during her pregnancy, they began arguing after the birth, in part because of the tensions involved in living with his family, where the living room became their bedroom and the care of the baby became everyone's business. Her boyfriend also became jealous when Ana began classes at the FLC, usually refusing to care for the baby even though he could see Ana trying to finish her homework, do the housework, and take care of the baby. Then he became abusive, says Ana, "pushing me around, yelling—screaming at me in front of my child. And I didn't think that was a good environment for him. And he didn't seem to care. He didn't want to go to counseling—I just got up and left. By the time he got home from work one day, all my stuff was gone. For a long time, I felt like going back to him. Now I'm glad I did what I did. I'm real glad."

Ana had plenty going for her, including a very strong single mother of her own with whom she now lives—enough to defy the seeming inevitability of the culture of poverty theory. But the FLC has also helped her carve out a good life for her and her son that does not require them to make it on their own. On the one hand, she is very independent, determined not to rely on another man or on welfare; she receives only medical benefits and has not applied for food stamps or cash benefits: "I haven't asked for anything else because I think I should do it on my own. I should try hard to do it on my own. I think I should do everything for my son. If I see that I really, really do need it, I probably would ask." On the other hand, Ana depends on her mother and the FLC's teachers and fellow students; she has assembled an alternative family. "My mom is my queen," she says, listing all the reasons she admires her hard-working mother, who owns her own home and car. Indeed, her mother's success is one reason Ana doesn't feel embarrassed to be a single mom:

> There's a lot of people who say, "Oh my gosh, she has a baby and she's not even married." I say, "No, I'm not. I'm not going to make a wrong decision." There are people who think it's not right to have a child and not get married. But why am I going to go through all of that. My mom is my woman figure. I have thought to myself: if she could do it, I could do it. My son's dad used to say to me, "You're not going to do it without me," and my mom used to tell me that my dad would tell her, "You guys are going to die because you don't have me to support you." And I told my son's dad, "You know what? You see my mom having her own house, her own car, living well, you know. What makes you think I'm not going to make it?" I just let him know that yes, I'm going to make it without him.

Ana left her boyfriend when their baby was six months old, due in part to support from fellow students: "I see other women coming out of abusive relationships. I think, if they can do it, I can do it."

The FLC believes in the possibility of "self-transformation," as Marísol Morales describes it: we have "tried to create a space" that "respects all of the women's right to transform themselves and their situation and create a better reality for themselves and their children." The self cannot be transformed, however, simply by exhorting women to try harder. As such, the center offers single mothers a material place where they can integrate different components of their selves, unlike President Bush's exhortation that work will make you "respectable," without regard to the difficulties of managing school, child care, work, and transportation. Tuition and child care are free. Morales regularly arranges rides for students for whom transportation is an issue. A daily "unity" meeting gives the young women a chance to talk about problems in their lives. The curriculum offers an integrated analysis of different aspects of identity: write about being a mother; learn about the culture of Puerto Rico through classes in *bomba* (a traditional Puerto Rican dance), in which mothers dance with their children. The self grows stronger when seen in its relation to other people, places, and structures. Exhorts Morales to the students in a message in the yearbook: "Be self-reliant phenomenal women. Be your own heroines and above all else, live and help to live."

The FLC provides options for the students so that marriage just becomes one option among several rather than the most viable form of support. As twenty-year-old Janet, a recent graduate of the FLC, says, "I've learned here never to count on a man. He can buy me this and that, but don't count on him." Neither does Janet, however, assume that she must do everything on her own: "Being a mother by yourself is something that you need a lot of support for." Working through her identity as a teenage mother at the school helped Janet realize that her father was wrong when he tried to convince her to get an abortion because being a young mother would ruin her chances of finishing school. Actually, she says, she lacked confidence in her ability to finish high school before she got pregnant, and then dropped out when she was three months pregnant. When she got pregnant, her father pressured her to have an abortion because he didn't want her to give up on her studies and dedicate herself only to being a mother. Now, she feels she has proven that she can do both, and she doesn't regret having Teodoro, although she wants him some day "to realize I went through a lot for him." She wrote in the yearbook after graduating in 2002: "I made it! I'm finally graduating with the class of 2002. I finally proved my parents and family wrong about me graduating." She is about to begin training to become a bank teller. Although she has a good relationship now with her baby's father, who supports them, she wants to be financially independent.

The FLC recognizes that teenagers don't know how to be mothers, but that they can learn, and that learning works best when it takes place across the curriculum, encompassing both the practical and the emotional. As Janet says, "Being a teen and being a mother is different. As a teen, you only think about yourself. As a mother, you're not like that anymore." Says Erica, "I didn't know how to care for a child. They helped me understand how I felt." In the parenting class, Erica recounts how she learned to read to her daughter (now one year old), to discipline without spanking, to express emotions, and to help her learn how to walk. Confidence in one's mothering is also built through cultural affirmations. One night a week, for example, they read their poetry at the Café Batey Urbano, a neighborhood café owned and run by Puerto Ricans.

The program's staff also provides information so that, hopefully, the women won't become pregnant again unless they want to. Information about bodies is put in a context about gender and empowerment, and many of the students say it is the first time they have ever had access to sex education. Janet was seventeen when she got pregnant with Teodoro, now two years old. "In school, we did talk about safe sex, but mainly in terms of AIDS. But my mom only told me 'take care of yourself,' nothing about women's stuff. Only 'don't let no guy touch you or take advantage of you. Guys are only liars—they only want one thing." Erica remembers that at her high school, "everybody would just make a joke about it [birth control]. If you took a condom, they would look at you like you were a slut. Mostly everyone was scared to get one—the guys would, but the girls wouldn't."

Marísol Morales describes the misinformation and myths about sex:

> Parents don't talk to them. Boyfriends provide an escape from the insanity they face with their families. They end up getting pregnant. Birth control is not something they feel is realistic. Boyfriends won't use condoms and they don't know how to ask. They feel like—I'm just going to be with him, they don't think, well, he's not just going to be with you. Men won't use condoms because they say sex doesn't feel as good, and they claim that it means their women don't trust them. The girls tell me that their guys say "pregnant pussy is the best pussy." They believe the guy will want to stay with you if he has sex with you when you're pregnant.

The students process the information in a daily discussion group where they talk about men, relationships, and everyday struggles.

The school also attends to the material issues that make education difficult, issues that would make it virtually impossible for them to attend a regular public school. The free child care is obviously the most important element, but the FLC also figures out transportation for the students, especially during the winter. Erica recounts how, when she didn't have transportation during the cold winter months and was reluctant to take her daughter out, Marísol would pick her up for school. The center helps the women find jobs; for example, Erica is going to work as a secretary for a progressive law firm when she graduates in a month.

As I prepare to leave the neighborhood to return to Pennsylvania, I look for Kaela, who has been evading my interview attempts. She wanders into the café one morning and agrees to talk for a bit. She answers tersely, ready to leave as soon as we begin. She repeats a cliché about single moms, perhaps mocking my question, referring to herself as "a kid with kids" and to the father of her first child as "like a kid himself." Was she using birth control either of the times she got pregnant? "Yes, but it didn't work," she says, shrugging her shoulders. Is there any stigma attached to being a single mom? "No—all my friends are single moms." Do either of the fathers help with child care? "When it's convenient."

Kaela has lived on Division Street for four years, after leaving her parents' home in the suburbs of Chicago, due in part to arguments with her mother, who now lives in Pennsylvania. She moved in with her grandmother and aunt and still lives with the latter in a small second-floor apartment. Her aunt helps with the children, but mainly, says Kaela, it's up to her. Financially, her father contributes $100 a week and buys things for her and the babies. Living on Division Street has been a mixed experience. On the one hand, Kaela says she has learned a lot about being Puerto Rican; she went for awhile to Pedro Albizu Campos High School before she had to drop out, when Justin, a sickly baby, developed a groin injury. Her Spanish has improved, and she wants to raise both her children to be bilingual, to feel pride in being Puerto Rican. She does feel part of some kind of community, and people on the street clearly know Kaela and her children—they care for both of them as Kaela talks to me. Yet the violence and danger of the street is overwhelming, Kaela says, and she hopes not to raise her children here. She wants to return to the suburbs.

Kaela's situation points to one of the central questions confronting the PRCC, especially in relation to its youth program: how to inspire enough pride in Puerto Rican identity, enough anger about racism and colonialism, so that young people want to stay and build up the neighborhood and not move to the suburbs. What forces can counter adolescent desires for clothes, music, cars, and the other things that obviously represent pleasure and success? These issues are especially powerful for young mothers, who need even more support to counter the isolation of long hours spent with children. Even Wanda, whose café is one center of the activist community and who grew up in a supportive family, says she often feels "pretty much alone" in raising her kids. A connection to her people is what helps her survive, she says:

I feel pride in who I am. I was fortunate to be taught about the plight of the Puerto Rican people—there's a lot of ignorance in Humboldt Park.

After 9/11, for example, a lot of Puerto Ricans were sporting the American flag. They haven't read the history (of U.S. colonization of Puerto Rico). I was fortunate enough to have long talks in the kitchen with my grandmother. She was born in 1916 and has seen everything. Being a Puerto Rican is knowing your history, your culture, knowing where you come from. . . . My children are sooooo Puerto Rican!

PART III

Keyword: Ethics

The denunciation of single mothers has in the past relied on an intensely moral discourse of shame: the shame of getting pregnant "out of wedlock," of not being able to support your baby, or having failed in your marriage.

The intensity of these judgments has faded for many single mothers, yet the threat is always lurking, just around the corner, in the form of politicians, social scientists, and others who continue to argue, in various ways, that the two-parent family is the best structure for raising children. The most vociferous of these voices are the family values politicians, following in the footsteps of Dan Quayle. He claimed credit in his 1996 book, *The American Family: Discovering the Values That Make Us Strong,* for helping to create a national consensus, extending to President Clinton, on the importance of family values, best demonstrated through what he calls "the intact family," or "the only truly functioning family. Fathers do matter. Families are the basis of our society. We must support the unified model of father, mother, and child. On this, we're all allies. Strengthening families should not be a political issue" (2). Although Quayle has lost some support, there are now less media-hungry but still influential voices acknowledging that the intact family is no longer the norm while at the same time mourning its demise. Looking for easy explanations to troubled youth, for example, social commentators are quick to point to the high divorce rate. Looking for reasons for the high divorce rate, social commentators are prone to blame "selfish" women. Nationally syndicated newspaper columnist Cal Thomas, for example, professes deep concern about what he believes to be a disdain for marriage and blames "contemporary culture," mentioning as a specific example *Sex and the City* for encouraging women to value personal happiness over commitment to marriage.

The "intact family" bases its moral vision on an isolated and idealized domestic sphere. In this world, certain universal truths such as mothers' sacrifice are grounded in biological essentialisms about gender and sexuality. There are no choices—or at least, there are only bad choices. Conservatives may advocate choice in the market but are appalled by the possibility that people might choose to inhabit different kinds of families. This is a very convenient strategy, for if the "intact family" is maintained or achieved, no further inquiry need be made. The private sphere remains private, and all the skeletons remain in the closet. Family values proponents can claim the moral high ground because they never acknowledge the complexities of parenting, the simultaneous and sometimes contradictory impulses to care for your children and for yourself. Expressions of desire—at least on the part of mothers—are indications of selfishness.

Foucault gives us one way to understand the articulation of sacrifice and morals. As I discuss in the "Everyday Life" section, he traces the historical shift, in Greco-Roman times, from the practice of "care of the self" to the Christian mandate to "know thyself:"

> First, there has been a profound transformation in the moral principles of Western society. We find it difficult to base rigorous morality and austere principles on the precept that we should give more care to ourselves than to anything else in the world. We inherit the tradition of Christian morality which makes self-renunciation the condition for salvation. . . . "Know thyself" has obscured "take care of yourself" because our morality, a morality of asceticism, insists that the self is that which one can reject. (1997, 228)

The good mother—the moral mother—knows that in order to be perceived as good, she must renounce her desires. Knowing oneself requires the rejection of bodily desires, of self-love. The mother must sacrifice all aspects of herself in order to care for her family, and in doing so, she shows herself to be defined through her relations to others. Notice how this mandate lets everyone else off the hook for caring, since care of others, both inside and outside the home, is the mother's job—this is one criteria of an "intact family." The bad mother is selfish and thus suspect in her ability to care for others. The bad mother becomes the object of moral denunciations. Everyone feels free to judge the bad mother.

The challenge for domestic intellectuals is to resist this pressure to sacrifice oneself in order to avoid becoming the object of shame. We must help create the conditions in which all single mothers live free of the pressure to marry or remarry to avoid stigma. In the next two chapters, I argue that in the realms of divorce, assisted reproductive technologies, and adoption, there is a complex mixture of forces that, on the one hand, allows women the choice to raise children without fathers and, on the other hand, quickly reasserts the ability of a father to restore order and normalcy if anything should go wrong—for example, if the mother is unable to demonstrate her self-sufficiency. In custody decisions, the best interest standard for determining where children should live after divorce often relies on traditional gender roles such as stay-at-home mothering even as divorced mothers are expected to provide substantial financial resources. Sociological research and popular advice books on divorce also assume the importance of the father in the "normal" development of children, especially sons. In the realms of assisted reproduction and adoption—both of which carry enormous potential to rearticulate the family away from essential gender roles—there is still a bias toward heterosexual couples.

How can domestic intellectuals move from the realm of morals to that of ethics? Morals are absolute, universalized, and formed in a social vacuum. Ethics, by contrast, are relational, complex, and material, formed in response to particular needs in particular places and times. Foucault argues that care of the self is an ethical practice because it leads one to care for others; indeed, it is impossible to truly care for others if one does not take proper care of oneself: "The care of the self is ethical in itself; but it implies complex relationships with others insofar as this ethos of freedom is also a way of caring for others" (287). But Foucault elides one important question: What are the conditions that facilitate care of the self? By not addressing these differential conditions, Foucault cannot be positing a truly ethical position, for it will turn out that only fairly wealthy people can afford to care for themselves. Care of the self becomes a consumer choice.

This articulation of choice to consumption is a central concern of feminists who argue that the two realms are antithetical. In the final chapter, I consider the commodification of assisted reproductive technologies; the ability to produce a baby without having sex distances us considerably from the "intact family," but the potential for rearticulating gender roles has been limited by the sheer expense of infertility treatment. The cost of adopting a baby is also prohibitive for some single women. Nevertheless, because domestic intellectuals work from within existing conditions, we cannot simply stand outside the marketplace and critique its reliance on consumer choice. We have to find ways through commodification, by shifting the focus from a politics of choice to a politics of access. How can we expand all women's access to reproductive technologies, whether they seek contraception, fertility treatment, or adoption?

Women's mobilities and agencies are critical to contesting the "intact family" in which only mothers do the work of caring. To shift from morals to ethics requires us to value this work and the reciprocal relationship in which it takes place—and, indeed, to make the relationship more reciprocal by providing support for the caregiver, so she can do the work of caring with more joy and pleasure. "Care of the caregiver" is critical to care of the dependent, as Eva Feder Kittay argues. One cannot convincingly argue for the care of dependents, such as children, without also addressing the care of the caregiver. Speaking of her daughter, who has cerebral palsy and requires around-the-clock care, Kittay says that "to advocate for my daughter without also advocating for those who are entrusted with her well-being is at once unjust and uncaring toward the caregiver. It also fails to accomplish its original aim of assuring a good and fulfilling life for my daughter" (1999, 260). This is what it means to value reciprocity and relationality—to see that both people (or many people) in a relationship are in some way dependent on others.

Traditional gender roles need to change in order to accommodate this expanded sense of relationships. In the chapter "Mothers and Sons," I use Nancy Chodorow's influential 1978 book, *The Reproduction of Mothering,* to show that much legal, sociological, and popular research still relies on the gender and sexual roles she critiques. In fact, the growing number of single mothers has in some venues prompted a resurgence of the fear of the overprotective mother who does not allow her son to develop his independence. Drawing on this feminist work and my own experiences raising a son, I ask how a single mother can raise a boy who will share equally in the work of caring, who will not assert his complete autonomy from women and children, who will value interdependency. Foucault's notion of ethics may not lead to interdependency; in fact, it seems premised on an autonomous and implicitly masculine self who is mainly concerned about his own everyday pleasures.

An ethics of family acknowledges the contradictions and difficulties of taking care of oneself and one's children. In many ways, single mothers as domestic intellectuals are ideally positioned to articulate this ethics of dependency. As an alternative to the moralisms of the intact family, whose obligations are only to itself, single mothers recognize the ongoing and always incomplete work of caring. As an alternative to the liberal belief in the rational subject able to fully express his or her needs, the ethics of dependency acknowledges that there are times when needs cannot be clearly expressed. Babies and even older children often cannot say what they need. Mothers must anticipate needs. What comes to be known as "mother's instinct" is actually the result of years of routinized behavior, in which thinking about others becomes a practiced way of approaching the world. What single mothers need, then, is a network of support in which others' thinking about them is equally automatic, more a product of routines, habits, and bodily movements then rational reflection and consideration.

Obligations to others cannot be completely fulfilled because that would assume that at some point in time, one ceases to be responsible to others. Bill Readings argues this point in his articulation of an ethical university: "Indeed, the assumption that we can pay all our debts is fundamentally unethical, since it presumes the possibility of overcoming all responsibilities and obligations, achieving 'freedom' from them. Autonomy, as freedom from obligation to others, holds out the impossible imagination of subjective self-identity" (186). The domestic intellectual presents an alternative to autonomy because she constantly pursues these obligations, never expecting to retire to her home, having fulfilled her obligations to others, and never fearing that she will be alone, without help in meeting her own needs and those of her children. We can't know in advance what our children will need, or what a neighbor or lover or friend will need; we have to remain open to the ongoing needs of kinship. Says Readings:

> To put this another way, such a community would have to be understood on the model of dependency rather than emancipation. We are, bluntly speaking, addicted to others, and no amount of twelve-stepping will allow us to overcome that dependency, to make it the object of a fully autonomous subjective consciousness. The social bond is thus a name for the incalculable attention that the heteronomous instance of the Other (the fact of others) demands. (190)

The heteronomous Other is not just one's child, but other people who need our help at different points in life—aging parents, unemployed friends, neighbors who fall ill. And we will at various points in our lives also need assistance. The domestic intellectual articulates this position exactly: the ongoing search for reciprocity that extends far beyond one's immediate household and children. In the final chapter, I explore how this search for reciprocity requires us to think about mothers in the United States and in other countries who are forced to give up their babies for adoption. By thinking relationally and reciprocally, we can produce a community of single mothers, united not by geographical proximity but by the pursuit of conditions that facilitate care of oneself and one's children.

By expanding an ethics of care beyond the mother-child relationship, beyond the "intact" household, single mothers as domestic intellectuals began to dismantle the very category that constituted us. We avoid the moralistic claims that come along with a strict and essentialist formulation of identity politics, as I argued in the introduction. Although the moralisms of identity politics are different (and in my opinion less contaminating) than the moralisms of a Dan Quayle, they are nevertheless judgmental and exclusive. A moralistic identity politics holds that no one is as worthy as a "single mother" because he or she has not sacrificed sufficiently. It turns single mothers into martyrs and returns us to the position of the sacrificing self. It alienates allies who may not be single mothers but who may be sympathetic to the ethics of dependency.

The category "single mother" at this point in history is politically and socially necessary and effective, as long as we keep it flexible and open to conflict and contradictions, to the endless pursuit of our obligations to others. We can do incredibly important work as single mothers. At the same time, we should not make it exclusive but rather gradually expand its parameters to include all those interested in the mutual project of sharing in the joy and work of mothering. When the identity "single mother" is no longer necessary for doing this political work, we as domestic intellectuals will have succeeded in our project.

5

Mothers and Sons

How does the son of a single mother become a successful man? It's not easy, if you listen to a number of voices from across the political and social spectrum. In independent filmmaker John Singleton's 1991 *Boyz in the Hood,* ten-year-old Tre's mother, played by Angela Basset, brings her son to live with his father after he gets into trouble at school; she fears that she will be unable to keep him from joining a gang. "I can't teach him how to be a man," she tells his father, played by Laurence Fishburne. "That's your job."

"Single-parent families are the source of the saddest and most destructive part of our society's two nations," says sociologist James Q. Wilson in his widely reviewed book *The Marriage Problem* (131). "The children of single moms," he says, "are more likely than those of two-parent families to be abused, to drop out of or be expelled from school, to become juvenile delinquents, to take drugs, and to commit adult crimes" (8). Without fathers at home, sons become unruly: "Fathers are part of the first line of defense of a family, guarding their wives and children from unsavory lures and dangerous predators. The police are a backup force when adult protection is inadequate. But without a father, the family is less safe and the streets more threatening. Energetic, sexually active, unsupervised males fill the streets; many have impregnated women but few have married them."

In the parenting section at the mega-bookstores, advice books on how to cope with divorce worry that boys will not develop "normally" if they grow up only with their mothers. Says Evelyn Bassoff in *Between Mothers and Sons: The Making of Vital and Loving Men:* "The most obvious explanation for the poorer adjustment of older boys who are raised exclusively by their mothers is the absence of a viable connection to their fathers. Mothers can nurture, teach, discipline, and provide financially for their sons, but they cannot, of course, model male behavior" (117). She

173

recounts a story initially told by Robert Bly about a boy named Kevin whose parents divorced when he was twelve; he lived with his mother. Kevin had a dream about running with a pack of "she-wolves" through a forest; when they came to a riverbank, they all looked in the water and saw their faces. "But when Keith looked in the water, he saw no face at all." Bassoff quotes Bly: "When women, even women with the best intentions, bring up a boy alone, he may in some way have no male face, or he may have no face at all" (118).

I'm playing catch in the street with seven-year-old Alex. I throw balls high into the air, over his shoulder, grounders to his right and left. He scrambles all over, scooping them up, squeezing his glove, firing the ball back. A neighbor, an older man who has surely seen us play before, stops to watch us. "Who taught that boy how to play?" he asks.

The very visibility of mothers raising children alone prompts a denial, one especially vehement for mothers of sons, since mothers of daughters maintain the traditional assumptions about child development. This may be more true for adults, less so for children who are slower to rely on gender stereotypes. Even at twelve, Alex's friends are ready to accept me on their basketball team. I'm helping coach an informal league and often play in the full-court scrimmages, as does the male coach, father of another player. After a few outings in which I prove myself, the boys call out when teams are being chosen: "We want Alex's mom on our team!" They say nothing about the other coach, one boy's father, who tires quickly and doesn't have my prowess with the left hand.

As the oft-cited statistic goes, one in two marriages in the United States ends in divorce. In about 90 percent of divorces, mothers are awarded either sole or primary residential custody of the child(ren). What is produced is a family structure that both diverges from and relies on the nuclear family, as mothers are awarded custody precisely because they have always been the primary caregivers. Mothers also bear the burden, then, of the conservative backlash against the breakdown of the nuclear family norm, for it becomes our responsibility to prove that divorce will not harm our children and, indeed, the nation. A convergence of forces has produced this backlash—the fathers' rights movement, which cuts across race lines to include the Million Man March and the Promise Keepers; general defenders of family values like James Wilson; and more liberal but still socially conservative politicians like Bill Clinton who have enacted policies, such as the 1996 welfare reform act, that attempt to legislate marriage, especially among poor people.[1]

Even among less blatantly conservative voices, there remains concern about the welfare of children of divorce; some studies identified as among the more "optimistic" still sound dire. *For Better or for Worse: Divorce Reconsidered* by E. Mavis Hetherington and John Kelly, was reviewed by the *New York Times* as one of the more measured investigations, yet the authors' study, following 121 families, mainly white and middle class, from 1973 for thirty years, found that divorce raises the risk of serious problems for young adults from one in ten to one in four. Another way to put it: "80 percent of children from divorced homes eventually are able to adapt to their new life and become reasonably well adjusted" (228).[2] I suppose this is meant to be reassuring, but the qualifications are striking: "eventually," "reasonably," and what about the remaining 20 percent? The problem here is that kids of divorce are measured against an unstated norm—the kids from the nuclear family, whose lives aren't even studied, and thus we are led to presume, certainly erroneously, that 100 percent of kids from "intact" families are "well adjusted."

Feminists have applauded no-fault divorce for removing the burden of proving that differences are irreconcilable. No-fault divorce, available in all states by the early 1970s, has helped women get out of bad relationships, start over, raise their children without a "patriarch." Yet this freedom is not pure freedom because so many sectors of society and sources of power remain deeply invested in gender and sexual norms that often preclude forms of support that could take shape outside those norms. Divorce in most locations may no longer be shameful, but there is still considerable pressure to prove that your children will turn out as well as the kids of the nuclear family next door. Despite the implementation of supposedly gender-neutral standards for determining child custody, numerous scholars have shown that legal discourse still relies on conventional assumptions about husbands and wives, fathers and mothers. In many respects, for mothers who want custody of their children, this is a desirable bias at the outset. Yet its implications are more complex. As I will show in this chapter, divorced mothers are often held to the impossible standard of the stay-at-home mom who also is the primary breadwinner for her family. And they are not really "free" from the relationship with their ex-husbands, even when the men play a relatively small role in children's lives. A wide variety of discourses and institutions, both academic and popular, persist in asking: "How does the absence (or presence) of a father affect a child?"

Given the retention of these familial assumptions and the fact that women after divorce have a much higher poverty rate, it is not surprising that the remarriage rate in the United States is so high. Until remarriage happens, life may be difficult, especially in the absence of a support network. In addition to the economic hardships, there will always be societal forces that fear the dominant mother, especially the mother of a son. These are not impossible to counteract, but she must work hard to present herself as someone other than the overprotective mother who will impede her son's "normal" development. Some divorce manuals sound the alarm that single mothers will become too dependent on their children for emotional fulfillment. Hence, we see another permutation of the pressure to be self-sufficient: don't depend on your children, especially your sons—for your identity/source of love. It's more acceptable, even expected, for mothers to stay close to their daughters, for that fulfills traditional gendered expectations.

Divorced single mothers find themselves in a difficult situation: on the one hand, they are expected to be both mothers and fathers to their children for most of the year and to spend extra time with them to guarantee domestic stability, to counter what James Wilson predicts: "In single-parent families, the mothers are less likely to have meals with the child, to impose chores, to read to their children, or to enforce rules governing watching television than would be the case in two-parent families" (10). On the other hand, mothers may also be blamed for spending too much time with their children, for not letting their sons grow up. The good single mother is willing to let her son go, like Angela Basset's character in *Boyz in the Hood,* or to remarry to provide the appropriate masculine role model. Many people consider it impossible for a single mother to become a masculine role model, so a boy feels pressured to look elsewhere in order to become masculine in the conventional sense (heterosexual, competitive, aloof), to reject his mother because she represents the feminine, that which threatens to domesticate and pamper.

Here's the question: How does the single mother get around the instantiation of gender roles—often by the state, through divorce and custody? If to become a domestic intellectual is, in part, to step outside the traditional gendered and sexual expectations for raising sons and daughters, how does one carry through on these possibilities? Critical to answering these questions is figuring out what role fathers should play after divorce. I don't want to argue against their participation in child raising through time with kids and child support payments—both forms of assistance go some distance toward redefining gender and sexuality. But I do want to ask how discourses of divorce—legal, social scientific, popular advice books—greatly inhibit the formation of alternative family structures in which more than two adults are responsible for the raising of children. To lay the groundwork for demonstrating how these traditional family norms are still present in divorce discourse, I will provide a brief summary of Nancy Chodorow's *The Reproduction of Mothering,* a seminal feminist text in explaining how boys and girls grow up to be men and women. For me, the central ethical question that emerges from this text is still the one that we should ask of mothering: How can the close relationship between mother and child serve as the basis for an ethical politics? How can what Eva Kittay calls "the potency of bonds; the relaxed boundaries of the self" (36), which are so often stigmatized, become the way we—especially boys—come to think of relations to others throughout life?

Gender Performance

Judith Butler became famous for saying that gender is a performance, but perhaps Nancy Chodorow said it first, when she laid out her object relations theory, an explanation of the psychological and social forces that shape gender development in childhood and adolescence. "Ongoing social structures include the means for their own reproduction," she said, "in the regularized repetition of social processes, in the perpetuation of conditions which require members' participation, in the genesis of legitimating ideologies and institutions, and in the psychological as well as physical reproduction of people to perform necessary roles" (205). Girls are raised by women, who teach them how to act in caring and nurturing ways, and thus they are likely to want to become mothers, to get gratification from that role. Boys are also raised by women, but they are taught by numerous sources to distance themselves from that love, to prove their autonomy and independence by identifying with the father, an idealized and often absent figure. As Chodorow puts it, "Mothers are seen to represent regression and lack of autonomy and boys learn to dissociate themselves from Mother—they learn they must reject dependency and deny attachment and identification" (155). This arrangement is not only a relational but also a spatial and material issue, produced by mothers' much larger role in child raising and housework and the tendency for fathers to work and play more outside the home. Because of the absence of the primary role model, attaining masculinity is a vexed and often confusing process.

This is an old narrative but one that still carries much weight in the United States. One might think that single-mother families would represent alternatives to that narrative, and in many ways, as I've shown throughout this book, we do. In this chapter, however, I focus on how discourses of divorce, from the legal system to sociological studies of its effects to popular advice books and media representations, reproduce normative gendered and sexual expectations. Furthermore, these discourses have material effects in mothers' lives—quite often, income drops significantly, isolation intensifies, and mothers take on even more of the burden of their traditional roles in the form of constant responsibility. The danger is that gender roles become even more entrenched. This is not to say that individual single mothers live out these subject positions in their entirety but rather to comment on the constant pressures to come up with creative alternatives on one's own while also helping children cope in the "real world" outside the home, where one has little influence. Schools, for example (at least in many locations in the United States) continue to assume a heterosexual couple raising children, as is manifest in the many forms that come home with spaces for "mother" and "father." Many of Alex's teachers have called me "Mrs. Juffer" (at which point I look around for my mother) when I have volunteered in their classrooms and instructed their students to do the same, even when I ask to be called "Jane." "Will your husband be coming to the parent-teacher conference?" is a question I have been asked almost every year at the first meeting with the new teacher.

Much of this chapter will focus on sons, and here I must confess that this emphasis is in part due to my personal experience raising a boy. I also believe, if it's possible to state something distinct from my experience, that societal pressures on boys to prove their masculinity apart from their mothers are of particular intensity, though daughters of single mothers face other expectations. The same studies that express concern about boys achieving masculinity, for example, fear that girls growing up without a father will become promiscuous in their search for a replacement figure. My focus on boys, though not to the exclusion of girls, is more strategic than anything, and is meant to point to the feminist potential of raising boys differently.

The absence of a father from the everyday task of parenting means the mother does not demonstrate her reliance on or obedience to a man, for example. She does the work of both father and mother, both cooking (loosely defined) and checking the oil (an easier task). Yet one might also ask this: In the families of divorce, given the child's movement between households, does the father become an even more desirable object of identification than in married households, by virtue of the fact that he is still present but tantalizingly so? Does the father who takes the children on Saturdays for a day of fun make the mother seem more of a taskmaster who insists that homework get done and instruments get practiced? Does the increased amount of time that the son spends with his mother make him more eager to leave, even when that time is good?

Chodorow's theory draws on psychoanalysis, but she distances herself from the biological essentialism of Freud. For her, it's all about socialization. What are the effects of children's close attachment to their mothers? Perhaps the most significant effect is that girls perceive themselves relationally, whereas boys come to see themselves as autonomous beings. "From very early on, then, because they are parented by a person of the same gender . . . girls come to experience themselves as less differentiated than boys, as more continuous with and related to the external object world and as differently oriented to their inner object-world as well" (167). The boundaries between girls and others are less rigid, more permeable. "Girls' identification processes, then, are more continuously embedded in and mediated by their ongoing relationship with their mother. They develop through and stress particularistic and affective relationships to others" (176).

These other relationships include the father, whom the daughter learns to desire in a way different from the desire for her mother: "A girl does not turn absolutely from her mother to her father, but adds her father to her world of primary objects" (167). She learns to idealize him, as boys do, but because she does not identify with the masculine, she learns rather that men are more free, mobile, and attractive because of that freedom: "Although fathers are not as salient as mothers in daily interaction, mothers and children often idealize them and give them ideological primacy, precisely because of their absence and seeming inaccessibility, and because of the organization and ideology of male dominance in the larger society" (181).

Proper heterosexual identity is attained when the daughter learns to transfer her love of her father to another man—her husband—and to continue to think of herself as a mother, sacrificing her own desires for the needs of others. The cycle continues when her more emotionally independent partner doesn't fulfill her needs, and she turns instead to her children as her primary relational source: "By doing so, she recreates for herself the exclusive intense primary unit which a heterosexual relationship tends to recreate for men" (202).

The world of boys is much different. Whereas the "basic feminine sense of self is connected to the world, the basic masculine sense of self is separate" (169). Because fathers are less present, boys tend to identify more with a cultural stereotype of masculinity, whereas girls tend to identify more with their actual mothers (176). A boy's identification processes, says Chodorow, "are not likely to be so embedded in or mediated by a real affective relation to his father. At the same time, he tends to deny identification with and relationship to his mother and reject what he takes to be the feminine world; masculinity is defined as much negatively as positively" (176).

Because boys are raised mainly by their mothers but expected to learn masculinity through a largely absent father, gender socialization is more fraught for boys than it is for girls, says Chodorow: "Masculinity becomes an issue in the way that femininity does not. Masculinity does not become an issue because of some intrinsic male biology, nor because masculine roles are inherently more difficult than feminine roles, however. Masculinity becomes an issue as a direct result of a boy's experience of himself in his family—as a result of his being parented by a woman" (181). He must dissociate from the very person he loves most, he must learn to deny his feelings of love and relationality or risk being called a "mama's boy," a "sissy," a "wuss." "A boy represses those qualities he takes to be feminine inside himself, and rejects and devalues women and whatever he considers to be feminine in the social world" (181). It's confusing for boys: Why must you devalue the very person you most love, why is this love coded as "dependency," feminine? This dilemma is captured by the South African writer J. M. Coetzee in his memoir of his boyhood. He says of his mother:

> His mother loves him, that he acknowledges, but that is the problem, that is what is wrong, not what is right, with her attitude toward him. Her love emerges above all in her watchfulness, her readiness to pounce and save him should he ever be in danger. Should he choose (but he never would do so), he could relax into her care and for the rest of his life be borne by her. It is because he is so sure of her care that he is on his guard with her, never relaxing, never allowing her a chance. (122)

Coetzee's *Boyhood* is filled with such painful ruminations, the young boy trying to understand why he should identify with his gruff and unpleasant father, whom he despises. The narrative illustrates Chodorow's point about the difficulty of attaining masculinity in households where mothers and fathers occupy traditional roles: "The exclusive responsibility of women for children exacerbates conflicts about masculinity in men. As long as women mother, a stable sense of masculine self is always more problematic than a stable sense of feminine self. Yet cross-culturally, the more father-absence (or absence of adult men) in the family, the more severe are conflicts about masculinity and fear of women" (213).

If boys do not successfully differentiate themselves from their mothers, they may not become "proper men"—that is to say, they might not be fully heterosexual in the ultra-masculine sense. The belief in the Oedipal complex governs this set of expectations: "The major goal is the achievement of personal masculine identification with their father and sense of secure masculine self, achieved through superego formation and disparagement of women" (165). Having learned to disdain women, the boys-become-men repeat the cycle: "In adulthood, he will seek relationships with women for narcissistic-phallic reassurance rather than for mutual affirmation and love" (195).

The implications for mothers are that we continue to do the work of caring, both in the home and outside, and this caring is then denigrated as women's work: "Women's mothering, then, produces psychological self-definition and capacities appropriate to mothering in women, and curtails and inhibits these capacities and this self-definition in men. . . . This set of expectations is generalized to the assumption that women naturally take care of children of all ages and the belief that women's 'maternal' qualities can and should be extended to the non-mothering work that they do" (208). Mothering often isolates women in their homes, or in the frantic juggling of the double shift of home and work, making it difficult for them to have the kind of social and leisure lives that most men enjoy. She in turn becomes more "dependent" on her children: "That women turn to children to fulfill emotional and even erotic desires unmet by men or other women means that a mother expects from infants what only another adult should be expected to give" (212). By contrast, says Chodorow, "In a society where women do meaningful productive work, have ongoing adult companionship while they are parenting, and have satisfying emotional relationships with other adults, they are less likely to overinvest in children" (212).

Perhaps this formula seems too rigid—we all know parents who raise their children differently, men and women who share to varying degrees in parenting, fathers who are caring and nurturing and mothers who are the breadwinners. Yet we can also see how psychoanalysis and its variations have informed judicial and popular beliefs about how children should develop. Later, for example, I'll consider popular literature on coping with divorce, where one can find both helpful information and egregious assertions about the dangers of mothers and sons. Here's one example from Bassoff's *Between Mothers and Sons:*

> The strong father, by disapproving of the "mama's boy," also discourages the adolescent boy from getting too cozy with mother. What Freud did not say, and what I think may be equally as important, is that the father's presence also assures the son that mother will not have to turn to the boy for the sexual and emotional fulfillment that she finds with her husband; in other words, the son is let off the hook because his father is "taking care of business." Without the paterfamilias, the threat of an eroticized relationship between mother (or other females in the household) and son becomes greater; in the absence of the strong husband/father who gratifies his wife's sexual appetite, the boy may imagine, sometimes with good cause, that his mother hungers after him. (120)

Television often reproduces the idea that boys in single-parent families should take on the role of the "man of the house." On the sitcom *8 Simple Rules,* Kate is a mother of three teenagers, a fourteen-year-old boy and two girls in high school. This example is slightly different because Kate's husband died a year ago, but it nevertheless illustrates the pressure on boys to become men. It's Thanksgiving, and she's trying to make a big dinner for the family. She arranges for her son Rory to go to a hockey game with a male friend, and at the game, the friend advises him: "You're the man of the house now that your dad's gone. That's not just a saying." Rory takes him seriously and upon returning to the house, scares off his sisters' boyfriends, telling one that his sister has mono and luring the other outside with the promise of a game of catch. The girls eventually figure out what he did and tell their mother, who asks her son what he was thinking. He says, "I was trying to protect them." Kate smiles tenderly, but the smile fades when Rory adds, "I was afraid they were going to turn into big fat whores." She tells him, "Don't take on this responsibility. You're the son. I'm the parent. I'll take care of the girls." The episode ends with them all sitting down to Thanksgiving dinner; they all turn to stare at the empty seat at the end of the table. Kate says to Rory, "Will you cut the turkey?" These texts and many others constantly return to the question: How can a son mature without his father present? Kate is sympathetic because she tells her son not to take on the father's role yet also encourages him to try it out—not to discipline his sisters but to carve the turkey.

What should be the role of the father after divorce? What best serves the children? The need to determine the "best interest of the child" now governs custody decisions, and I want to turn to the issue of how this nebulous standard is adjudicated. Although the "best interest" standard has been lauded as gender neutral—in part, the product of feminist efforts— I show that many judges still rely on traditional gendered and sexual assumptions. We might say that divorce has lost its stigma precisely because the legal system still relies on these norms, and thus divorce doesn't represent a serious threat to notions of family. Mothers are still expected to be nurturing, yet not too nurturing; to demonstrate constant care without "smothering"; to be sexually pure in order to avoid confusing their children—this is especially the case for lesbian mothers but also for mothers who do not remarry and may be considered "promiscuous"; to put their children's needs ahead of their own, even though they must work to support them—careers cannot come first. In many ways, then, custody decisions reproduce the gender roles described by Chodorow. Women are more defined by their relationships to their children, with all that entails—more everyday responsibility, anxiety, worry, exhaustion, and lack of mobility. Men are more autonomous, with all that entails—less everyday responsibility, anxiety, worry, exhaustion, and more freedom to move for work and leisure.

In short, thirty years after no-fault divorce was instituted across the country, women are still more likely to be perceived as at fault for children's problems, more responsible for their "normal" development. Perhaps that's what we want, for few of us can imagine not raising our children. Yet somehow we must find a way to redefine the system, such that boys can be loving and nurturing and affectionate for their entire lives, without needing—any more than girls—to distance themselves from mothers, and girls can feel strong and independent and autonomous and receive help in the labor and joys of caring for others. Perhaps this redefinition can occur within the terms of heterosexual couples, but I also find that the entrenchment of these terms across many discourses inhibits the possibilities for new gender performances to take hold. Again, I believe the answer exists outside the parameters of the nuclear family, in the creation of extended support networks that alleviate pressures on any single parent.

In the Best Interest of the Child

Ostensibly, the gender essentialism that for most of the twentieth century informed custody decisions has dissolved, replaced by standards of gender neutrality that treat fathers and mothers as equal partners. There has also been a move toward equal treatment of gay and lesbian parents, as judges have rejected a categorical per se dismissal of homosexual parenting and instead adopted an individual-case basis, again determined by what is considered in the best interests of the child. On the surface, it would seem that marriage as the primary institution implementing the gendered norms of Chodorow's theory is losing its hold. As one legal scholar put it, "Modern law has dismantled the legal regime premised on marriage" (Carbone 1).

However, even if the most firmly encoded elements of the family as institutional norm have become less visible, many legal scholars agree that they remain in the form of judicial interpretation. For example, one study showed that despite the fact that all states have adopted gender-neutral custody laws, many judges give preference to mothers in custody decisions.[3] Gender bias also shows up in cases where fathers pursue custody or a modification of original agreements. In these situations, women are more likely to be held to traditional standards of mothering; women have lost custody for putting children in day care to pursue careers, for example, while men who remarry have won custody based on arguments that their new wives can take care of their children. Another problem, or another way of stating the problem, is that gender neutrality in the law doesn't acknowledge the work women do in the real world. This argument has been made perhaps most adamantly by feminist legal scholar Martha Fineman: "There are more and more empirical studies that indicate that mothers' relative positions have worsened in our new ungendered doctrinal world" (1995, 26). Fineman faults feminists for focusing on gender neutrality and positing mothering as an essential role that holds women back: "Much reformist rhetoric directed at family law constantly reaffirms the notion that the disabilities and disadvantages of

Mother must be overcome—the family refashioned so that the individual woman is left unencumbered" (1995, 74). This position ignores the everyday reality that women still do bear the brunt of child care, says Fineman. Also, what she calls the "neutering" of mother strips mothering of all of its positive characteristics, making "'Mother' an empty legal category, robbing real-life mothers of the protection of their specificity" (1995, 67). In this context "caretaking is devalued and biological and economic connections are deemed of paramount importance" (1995, 70). Fineman calls for "an affirmative feminist theory of difference" (1995, 41) that would shift the legal focus from the heterosexual couple to the mother-child dyad as the basis of legal theory.

Finemen's position has the advantage of answering the question: What role should fathers play? Quite simply put, they shouldn't play any role. It gives us a way out of the inevitability of gendered reproduction by eliminating the father. Yet it carries other risks: it does not say who will help the divorced mother, and how children who are still raised in a world where fathers matter will cope with the loss of a father. Of course it doesn't acknowledge that some fathers are loving, good people who should play a large role in their children's lives. It could essentialize women once again as mothers whose primary identity is their relationship to their children.

Other feminists have made arguments for joint custody in which gender roles break down as both mothers and fathers care for children. Carol Stack and Katharine Bartlett wrote a feminist defense of joint custody in 1986, arguing that "joint custody stakes out ground for an alternative form of parenting . . . these rules promote the affirmative assumption that both parents should, and will take important roles in the care and nurturing of their children" (qtd. in Carbone). The question remains, however, as to what role fathers actually play when awarded joint custody: some would say it merely returns us to a day when fathers exercised legal control but contributed little time and energy to child care.

In the early history of the United States, children were considered paternal property and fathers were invariably awarded custody, even in cases of demonstrated cruelty. Neither children nor mothers had rights, nor was children's well-being considered an issue worthy of consideration. Gradually throughout the nineteenth century, the Industrial Revolution produced a separation of work and home. Children lost the economic value they had held for agrarian families. Mothers became the nurturing protectors of hearth and home and were seen as best suited to raise children. Courts began to base their custody decisions on the "tender years presumption" that children needed their mothers, and that mothers were best suited to care for children unless they were proven to be morally unfit or impure. The "tender years presumption" was obviously based on traditional gendered roles, as Chodorow would describe them.

"Tender years" guided custody decisions for almost a century, and some legal scholars would argue that it still governs many judges' assumptions that mothers are better suited to raise children, especially young children. But the automatic granting of maternal custody has been replaced over the last thirty years by a seemingly more gender-neutral consideration, referred to as the "best interest standard." During the 1970s and 1980s, "societal pressure for sexual equality and gender neutrality, the growing fathers' rights movement, and feminist ideology weakened the hold" of tender years, and most states replaced the guideline with the "best interests of the child standard" (Jacobs 3).

The best interest standard has been widely criticized for its vagueness. Critics agree that it is a nebulous concept, highly contingent on judicial interpretation of what are many times complicated situations involving mothers, fathers, and children of various ages and situations. "Because the standard provides no objective basis for judicial choices, best interest decisions depend on the character, value, and prejudices of the presiding judge" (Dolgin 1). Some legal scholars speculate that the standard remains because its very indeterminacy provides the flexibility necessary to accommodate the shifting form of the American family; it allows judges to claim that they adhere to one standard—the best interest of the child, which appears inherently moral. Despite the fact that it provides very little direction and often is more concerned with adults than with children, says Dolgin, the standard has "provided comfort to a society and a legal system beset with unending and bewildering changes in the character of family" (7).

In other words, the focus on children and morality in the midst of social change allows judges to rely on a conservative family norm without calling it that. Not surprisingly, the best interests of the child are met by a "middle-class, comparatively mainstream" situation (Dolgin 3). Determining what's in the best interest of the child necessitates an inquiry into the lives and personal characteristics of the two parents, which can lead to stereotypical assumptions:

> For instance, courts have denied custody to a parent because that parent
> was involved in a same-sex relationship or an interracial marriage.

These and other behaviors viewed by a court as socially marginal may become determinative in custody decisions. They may preclude judicial review of the child's larger situation. This in turn minimizes the likelihood that the best interests of the child will in fact be met. (Dolgin 3)

The vagueness of best interests seems most often to work against mothers, argues Susan Beth Jacobs. Even though mothers continue to get custody in the vast majority of cases, in cases where fathers contest or seek custody, she says, mothers are losing due to "inappropriate criteria caused by gender bias unrelated to the best interest of the child in the areas of economic resources, employment, traditional family values, and morality. Thus, the best interest of the child standard is an indeterminate, vague standard in which judicial subjectivity and gender bias often penalize single mothers and children, resulting in custody decisions that discriminate against mothers" (2). Adds Jacobs, "When fathers want custody, they stand a very good chance of getting it." Women are also likely to make concessions about things such as child support based on their fears of being found wanting by judges and thus risking modifications in custody. The areas of vulnerability include the following.

Judges impose unfair standards when it comes to work. Courts have awarded custody to fathers who have sought custody on the basis of higher incomes, yet they have penalized mothers who have gone to work to support their children on the grounds that mothers should be home with their kids. Judges have sometimes failed to take into account the reasons why mothers have a harder time making enough money to support their kids—such as dropping out of the job market precisely so they could spend time at home when their kids were young. Furthermore, women who have put their children in child care or who have had to work long hours have sometimes lost custody, but fathers are not considered to be "bad dads" when they have hired child care. Jacobs says that working mothers are "measured against" a "traditional mother standard," and "fathers are measured against a 'traditional father' standard": "The traditional father is not expected to know or participate in traditional mothering skills such as cooking, cleaning, taking the children to the doctor's office, or chauffeuring children to activities. Thus, any effort the father makes to do these ordinary household tasks is seen as remarkable" (5).

Perhaps the most publicized case illustrating this double standard occurred in 1994, when a Michigan county circuit judge, Raymond Cashen, awarded custody of three-year-old Maranda Ireland to her father because her mother, Jennifer, used day care while attending the University of Michigan. The couple had never married, but the father, twenty-year-old Steven Smith, lived with his parents, and he argued that his mother, a full-time homemaker, could care better for Maranda than could a day-care provider. Said Judge Cashen, "There is no way that a single parent attending an academic program . . . as prestigious as the University of Michigan can do justice to their [*sic*] studies and the raising of an infant child" (qtd. in Jacobs 1). Better for the child to be raised by blood relatives, he said. The case had entered court when Jennifer, who had been raising Maranda on her own, sued Smith for the weekly $12 child support payments he had failed to pay.

Judges have sometimes awarded custody to fathers who have remarried on the grounds that "the father's ability to provide the children with a husband and wife relationship" was in the child's best interest, particularly because the new wife was willing to stay home with the children and thus provide a "more stable environment" (Jacobs 9). Jacobs describes several such cases, including one in which part of the evidence at trial was the "father's photo album containing photographs of his home and family life with his new wife. The court held that it was in the children's best interest to live with the father and stepmother" even though the judge acknowledged that the mother had been the primary caretaker and that the children were thriving (Jacobs 9). The court was critical of the mother because she supplemented her income with welfare and wanted to move to be closer to her parents.

By contrast, judges have not considered mothers' family or friends as appropriate caregivers. The expectation that mothers assume the role of primary caregiver and demonstrate their self-reliance may have especially harsh implications for mothers in cultures where communal child care is a common practice. In her study of 240 Canadian child welfare cases, for example, Marlee Kline found that "when a First Nation mother is receiving ongoing help from extended family members, that contribution is often ignored or regarded negatively" (132). This disregard of cultural traditions can have devastating effects for First Nation mothers, who are often unable to regain custody of children put in temporary foster care with non-Native families even after they have shown they can care for their children with the help of family and friends.

In cases where nonmarital, sexual relationships are taken into account, mothers are much more likely to be penalized than fathers. The Uniform Marriage and Divorce Act holds that "parents' sexual behavior is only relevant if it adversely affects the parent-child relationship," but Jacobs found that—again, due to the vagueness of the best interest standard—some judges are prone to rule that mothers' nonmarital relationships are harmful to the moral development of her children, even though they cannot "delineate exactly how the child has been harmed." This bias is especially evident in the case of lesbian mothers, who face a judicial system still imbued with the stereotypical notion that gays and lesbians are defined by their sexuality. Julie Shapiro documents numerous cases in which lesbian mothers have lost custody due to judges' beliefs—either stated or implied—that their "immoral" behavior was harming their children. In one Illinois case, the original court ruled against a heterosexual father's attempt to win custody of his three daughters from their mother; the father said he thought homosexuality was wrong and acknowledged that he had arranged for the children to receive counseling after his ex-wife told him she was a lesbian. But the Illinois Court of Appeals reversed the decision; although it did not explicitly state that the reason for reversal was the mother's sexuality, it characterized the mother's "decision to acknowledge to her family that she was a lesbian as her 'pronouncement of her gay lifestyle,'" suggesting, as Shapiro notes, that she was selfish (17–18).

It would seem that "best interest of the child" requires the mother to renounce her own desires and needs. Yet in reality, mothers who are able to take care of themselves, to lead healthy and fulfilling lives, are better mothers than those who sacrifice everything for their children. The complexities of this negotiation between one's own needs and the needs of the child are often lost on judges, however. Where does a mother's interests leave off and a child's begin? This dilemma is illustrated by the issue of mobility: What happens when the mother, who is most likely the custodial parent,[4] wants to move to another state with her child(ren) to take a job or pursue a new relationship? Some states require a woman to seek permission before moving, and although most states are not that explicit in their demands, courts may reconsider custody any time there is a "material change in circumstances," such as an interstate move (LaFrance 7). The result is that mothers who want to move risk reopening the custody decision; in modification hearings, fathers could make cases for custody revisions. Many times, the fear of revised custody prompts mothers to forgo the move before even going to court.

In his study of mothers' movements after divorce, legal scholar Arthur LaFrance found that "many women, as they contemplate interstate relocation, find their former husbands seek to prevent such a move. Moreover, the former husbands are frequently successful, particularly in the trial courts" (2–3). Does pursuing a career, a job that will lead to a good life for her children, mean the mother is being selfish, pursuing her interests instead of the children's? Clearly not, say feminist legal scholars. Yet the fathers' rights movement has had some success in arguing that it is not in the children's best interest to be uprooted. The inability to move is one reason the poverty rate for single mothers continues to be high, as both jobs and remarriage are likely to increase household income. At a time when people move frequently—across states, not just to a cheaper neighborhood—for career reasons, only half as many households headed by women move interstate compared to those headed by men (7).

In relocation cases, the vagueness of the best interest standard renders mothers vulnerable, for often their entire lives are reduced to the singular question of whether moving is in their child's best interest. "In relocation cases, state courts proceed as though they may reopen and reconsider custody without regard to the full personhood of the custodial mother and without regard to the custodial parent's reliance upon the terms and finality of the original custody judgment as a predicate for indurating and expanding her life" (LaFrance 7). Lower courts often present mothers with a choice that is not much of a choice: "She may move without her children or she may stay and keep her children" (12).

When mothers make an argument about the complexity of "best interests," they run up against judges who see their lives more reductively:

> Courts do not confront the loss of education, the loss of employment, the loss in community or social opportunity, or the impact of these losses on the emotional capability of the custodial mother to maintain a home in a community under circumstances she may deplore. If she speaks in anger, frustration, depression, disappointment, and sadness, she is viewed as non-cooperative. The father who brings litigation to block a mother's relocation is viewed as advancing his legitimate interest, seeking admirably to remain in the lives of his children. The mother who resists, if she insists she does not want to stay, is considered as selfish and indifferent to the children. Many custody statutes specifically identify "non-cooperativeness" as a negative factor in deciding the best interests of the children; an assertive woman may, therefore, be deemed an unfit custodian and lose her children. (LaFrance 13–14)

How can a mother teach her son that women are independent and autonomous when the courts will not let her pursue a career, when it asks her to decide between a fulfilling job and raising her child?

The Nexus Rule

The legal system has wrestled with how to apply the best interests standard in cases involving gay and lesbian parents. Legal scholars generally agree that judges are increasingly claiming to examine each case on its own merits, a practice that commentators have called the "nexus test." As its name suggests, the nexus test allows judges to determine what is in the best interest of each child, given the particular circumstances of the family, and thus seemingly removes the immediate onus previously attached to gay parenting; it "requires individualized analysis of conduct in a particular case and its effect on the particular child with the ultimate trial result left to the trial judge's discretion" (Shapiro 2). The nexus test replaces a per se rule that would place all gay and lesbian parents in one category, ready to be judged unsuitable parents: "Courts have been increasingly unwilling to adopt rules which explicitly disadvantage all lesbian or gay parents involved in custody cases. Instead, many courts have endorsed a more individualized approach, one that is linked more directly to an analysis of the best interest of the child" (2).

The nexus test, in combination with the best interest of the child standard, requires judges to ask: Given the particular conditions of each parent's relation to the child, does the parent's sexuality have any adverse impact on the child? Seemingly, this could represent a victory for gay and lesbian parents, as the nexus test does not categorize and requires proof of harm in individual cases. Yet the nexus test has not assured fair treatment—like the best interest of the child standard, it allows the judge considerable leeway, which means he or she is free to assert traditional family values, without proving a nexus between sexual orientation and harm. The test is not consistently applied: "Instead, many courts appear to engage in a free-form assessment with neither analytic rigor nor guiding principles, with results that are, even for family law, disturbingly arbitrary. Many gay and lesbian parents still lose custody or face restricted visitation simply because of their identity or conduct, without regard to its impact, or absence thereof, on their children. Countless more live in understandable fear that if they turn to the courts to seek custody or visitation, they will be treated harshly" (3). As a result, many lesbian and gay parents begin custody negotiations from a weak position.

We see again how Chodorow's theory of reproduction is relevant here. Judges deploying the best interest standard rely on conventional assumptions about mothers and fathers: How can a boy become properly heterosexual if he is raised by a lesbian mother or a gay father? Girls would be hampered as well, according to this logic. There appear to be no appropriate models for identification. Furthermore, judges often speculate about the harm a child may suffer because of lesbian/gay parents, based on their assumptions that "children of lesbian or gay parents may be stigmatized, embarrassed or subjected to teasing by their peers due to their parents' sexuality" (9). As Shapiro notes, "since bias against lesbians and gay men is widespread, virtually any court can invoke the specter of bias and accompanying stigma, label it 'harm,' and use that basis to deny custody. This process effectively circumvents the protections offered by the nexus test" (9). She cites several cases in which judges awarded custody to heterosexual fathers because they assumed the children would be teased and ostracized if they lived with their lesbian mothers, even though no evidence of harm was presented. In one Kentucky case, the court of appeals appeared to rely heavily on this psychologist's statement when it denied a lesbian mother's request for custody:

> Without question, in my opinion, there is social stigma attached to homosexuality. Therefore Shannon will have additional burdens to bear in terms of teasing, possible embarrassment and internal conflicts. Also, there is excellent scientific research on the effects of parental modeling on children. Speculating from such data, it is reasonable to suggest that Shannon may have difficulties in achieving a fulfilling heterosexual identity of her own in the future. (Qtd. in Shapiro 10)

Courts are especially likely to penalize gay parents who are open about their sexual preferences, which, as Shapiro notes, produces effects that are certainly not in the child's best interest: being discreet about sexual identity leads to isolation, "cutting them off from their most significant sources of support" (11). Ruthann Robson describes the cases of several lesbian mothers who, for the sake of retaining or regaining custody, basically renounced any public expression of their sexuality—and sometimes private expression as well. In a Virginia case, *Doe v. Doe,* Jane Doe struggled to retain visitation rights to see her son, who spent eight weeks with her in the summer as well as some holidays; his father's new wife wanted to adopt the eleven-year-old son and terminate Jane's parental rights because she was a lesbian. A Virginia trial court agreed, but the Supreme Court of Virginia reversed the decision, saying that although Jane's relationship with her partner was "unorthodox," in all other matters of conduct, she was exemplary, and in terms of her parenting, she exhibited a "selfless wisdom." Furthermore, the court noted that in "determining her fitness as a mother and the future welfare of her son, we are not unmindful of her testimony that should it become necessary for her son's sake, she would sever the relationship with the woman with whom she now lives. There may come a time when the welfare and best interest of her son require that she honor this commitment" (qtd. in Robson 108–109). To assert her rights to live with a partner would have made Jane a selfish and thus unfit mother.

Deessentializing Fatherhood?

There's another way in which the judicial system seems to be moving away from essentialist notions of gender but in a manner that sometimes results in a reinforcement of those very roles. In the last decade, an increasingly vocal "fathers' rights" movement, in combination with the move toward gender neutrality, has led to more joint custody decisions, with fewer mothers automatically winning sole custody. Furthermore, more courts have been willing to recognize a father's ties to his children even when he was never married to the mother, a significant shift from earlier decades. A series of Supreme Court cases have ruled that a father's "ties to his children could not constitutionally depend on whether he married their mother" (Carbone 1). However, it is not enough merely to prove paternity: fathers must show involvement in their children's lives. Supreme Court Justice Stevens said in one case, "When an unwed father demonstrates a full commitment to the responsibilities of parenthood by coming forward to participate in the rearing of his child . . . his interest in personal contact with his child acquires substantial protection under the Due Process Clause. At that point it might be said that he acts as a father toward his children" (4).

These developments seem like a good thing, from the perspective of feminists who have argued that fathers should be more engaged with housework and child care. Some studies show that when fathers share legal custody, they are more likely to be involved in their children's lives (see Seltzer 135). Yet many feminist legal critics are suspicious, arguing that joint legal custody gives women and men equal rights but does not recognize the fact that mothers continue to bear the brunt of the workload: "Fathers are given support and reinforcement for being volunteer parents, people whose duties toward their children are limited, but whose autonomy about parenting is broadly protected. Mothers are defined as draftees, people whose duties toward their children are extensive, but whose autonomy about parenting receives little protection" (Czapanskiy, qtd. in Carbone 8). The problem, says Martha Fineman, quoting Anne Marie Delorey, is this: "Joint legal custody gives rights and responsibilities to mothers, but it gives rights without responsibilities to fathers. Mere legal control of children is simply an assignment of power, and when this type of power is given to fathers, judges are merely reinforcing patriarchal power" (83). So the father has significant legal power but is not very involved in everyday care. It is important to note that joint legal custody is different from joint physical custody, and that the latter is still fairly unusual: in the former, parents share legal decisions but there is still a primary residential custodial parent, most often the mother. In the latter, parents share physical custody, although it appears that in many of these situations, the child still spends more time with the mother.

Joint custody also shows that despite the seeming move away from the married/divorcing couple and toward the child as the center of the law, the focus remains on the relationship between the parents, because that relationship is critical when judges determine whether and how shared custody will work. Custody disputes have become the way parental relationships continue to dominate divorce—how parents relate to each other informs custody decisions as judges determine what arrangement is in the best interest of the child. In many cases, such as domestic abuse, this examination is a beneficial one. Furthermore, there is potential for truly shared parenting conditions, but only if the father demonstrates his commitment to sharing all aspects of parenting. This leads us to the solution proposed by legal scholar Karen Czapanskiy: "Biological parents would acquire equal decision-making power only when they have demonstrated equal responsibility for the child's well-being; in the more customary case where one parent has assumed primary responsibility, that parent's wish . . . should receive greater deference" (qtd. in Carbone 18).

Another dilemma arises in the case of child support payments. On the one hand, fathers' contributions to a child's financial well-being are not only legally required, they seem ethically requisite. Yet many divorced mothers don't receive them: over $84 billion of child support arrears are owed in the United States, and only 56 percent of custodial parents have some type of child support order in place and functioning (Swank 1). The support can make a big difference in kids' lives—"for divorced custodial parents, child support payments make up between 26 and 29 percent of family income" (2). On the other hand, the state's desire to force fathers to pay child support is often connected to the government's reluctance to provide any kind of welfare, and sometimes produces a relationship between father and mother that the mother would rather not have but is forced to continue because there are no other options. Hoping to lower the welfare rolls, Congress passed in 1992 the Child Support Recovery Act, whose main objective was to track down "dead-beat" dads. The 1996 Personal Responsibility Act ("welfare reform") also included dramatic measures to collect child support: "The act required employers to report new hires in an effort to track delinquent non-custodial parents; allowed the state to seize assets, request the denial of the issue or revocation of passports, and revoke professional and drivers' licenses to collect child support arrears" (3). It comes as little surprise that the same critics who urge tougher collection methods ultimately endorse fewer divorces and stronger commitment to marriage as the solution: "Having more couples who are likely to produce children and get and stay married would reduce the number of child support cases. The difficulty, of course, is how to encourage couples to get and stay married" (Swank 9).

We return to the dilemma I discussed in the introduction to this book: How much should single mothers turn to the state for help, when inevitably that help turns into a form of regulation and surveillance? Furthermore, how do we distinguish between the kinds of fathers' rights movements that seek to share equally in parenting and those that seek to restore patriarchy, led by the likes of William Safire, who said in a 1994 *New York Times* column: "Let me tell you what fathers want. We want our intrinsic authority back." Yet as divorced mothers we often turn to ex-husbands for support, and many of them are good and loving fathers. This seems necessary if, as feminists, we want to break out of the gender socialization described by Chodorow. The irony is that then, once again, we are back to a nuclear family model—in varying degrees of dispersed location.

Life after Divorce

Judicial opinions both produce and reflect societal attitudes about divorce. As I argued above, the best interest standard allows judges to present themselves as flexible and progressive while simultaneously enforcing, if they wish, traditional gender roles. The courtroom is also a site where sociological studies on divorce become the means for arguing what this best interest might be, and inevitably best interest will involve a determination of how the mother and father are getting along after separation. Thus, whether these studies are marshaled for the mother or father, they rely on the maintenance of a relationship between the couple.

In turn, divorce studies often become the basis for popular books, such as James Wilson's *The Marriage Problem,* which reports on these studies as if they were objective even though he relies heavily on the more pessimistic investigations. These books make their way into the "parenting" section at Barnes and Noble and Borders, where they clamor for attention next to more sympathetic advice books on how to help kids cope with divorce. One finds a range of opinions, yet almost all are premised on the nuclear family as the norm, with the question repeatedly asked: How do kids fare without fathers at home? It's not surprising, then, that even the most optimistic studies find that fathers' involvement is critical to kids' well-being, and that even the most well-adjusted kids of divorced parents don't do as well as kids in "intact" families. It makes sense that the absence of a father would negatively affect a child—because it is still so widely assumed that a child should be raised by a mother and a father. No one bothers to ask: What if we stopped asking about fathers? What if we started asking about other people's involvement, about communal living, community support?

Nevertheless, my book is about everyday realities, and some of the studies and advice books deal sympathetically with the reality that for most families, divorce *is* painful, and life after divorce *is* a struggle. Just how much of a struggle life after divorce is depends on how much of a struggle life *before* divorce was—and there's no objective equation for determining how much "struggle" warrants divorce. Marriage advocates urge couples to stay married no matter what, for the sake of the kids and themselves. "Adults may prefer to be joyously in love, but children don't much care whether parents zoom to heights of romantic ecstasy or not. Your children don't care whether your marriage feels dead or alive, empty or full. As long as Mom and Dad don't fight too much, they thrive under the love, attention, and resources two married parents provide" (James Wilson 144). They add: "Even the unhappiest of couples who grimly stick it out for the sake of the children can find happiness together a few years down the road" (148).

In social conservatives' views, divorce becomes a scapegoat and marriage the panacea for all social ills. The better studies attempt to disarticulate poverty from family structure, arguing that poverty, not single mothering, makes life difficult for children. There is nothing inevitably broken about divorced families, and many mothers do just fine raising kids on their own, say Mavis Hetherington and John Kelly: "If someone creates a Nobel Prize for Unsung Hero, our nominee will be the divorced mother. Even when the world was collapsing round them, many divorced mothers found the courage and resiliency to do what had to be done. Such maternal tenacity and courage paid off. Despite all the emotional and financial pressures imposed by marital failure, most of our divorced women managed to provide the support, sensitivity, and engagement their children needed for normal development" (229–230). What's striking is again the sense that even these sympathetic authors expect mothers to manage on their own, in heroic fashion, to deal with the following issues.

Many women's income drops precipitously after divorce. While the decline varies significantly, the poverty rate of female-headed households is 31.6 percent, compared to 5.2 percent for nuclear families. Divorce accounts for 60 percent of those female-headed households (Boney 66). Custodial mothers earn 50 percent less than men, mainly because they often take lesser-paying jobs in order to accommodate child-care needs (66). The loss of income may be combined with other financial anxieties, such as loss of health insurance, inadequate child care, holding more than one job, and working nontraditional hours. A mother may be able to spend less time with her children, or feel distracted by household chores when she is home. After divorce, women must do the work previously done by two people. Even if the father was not an equal partner, she must do the jobs he used to do, which may well involve learning new tasks such as car and yard maintenance. Routines change. "Divorce destroys the reassuring rhythms and structures of family life, especially those that give a child's life order and predictability," say Hetherington and Kelly. "When one adult is suddenly doing the work of two, household disorganization and overload often ensue. Pickup meals, irregular dining hours, erratic bed-, play and reading times all increase during the first year after a divorce. The children of newly divorced mothers are also more likely to be late for school and less likely to have help with homework" (46). For many mothers, an entirely new schedule with the ex-husband also must be developed and constantly revised-drop-offs and pickups, visitations and vacations. This involves constantly talking to the ex, which may produce more stress and conflict.

Just at the moment when mothers could use the help of friends and family, they have often lost the social networks they had while married, if husbands' friends and relatives were a large part of this network. The family may have to move to a cheaper neighborhood, and the kids may have to change schools. Despite the fact that divorce is common, many social events are formed around married couples. Single women may be seen as disruptive, threatening, or just out of place.

New relationships introduce new elements of stress. When and how to introduce the new boyfriend or girlfriend to the kids? How will he/she get along? When is it right to begin dating, to have someone spend the night, to take a trip? What role should the new person play in the kids' lives? At the same time, the ex-husband remains a part of the scheduling. How will the ex-husband and the new partner get along, if both become involved in child care?

Many single mothers feel guilty, blaming themselves for the difficult living conditions. Even if they believe that the divorce was better for everyone, that doesn't prevent them from feeling responsible for sadness or anger their children may be feeling. These feelings may be exacerbated by family members, religious beliefs, and social institutions that produce, for different reasons, the idea that the mother has in some way failed. Mothers are more prone to guilt than fathers, mainly because of the gender socialization that Chodorow describes, in which women feel more responsible for providing love, affection, constant care, and stability. Guilt and insecurity hamper clear thinking about the everyday issues of parenting. Care of the self, as I describe it in chapter 1, becomes more difficult, and sacrifice for the sake of children seems more compelling. This is especially true in the realm of sexuality, where divorced mothers may be particularly reluctant to get involved with someone new out of a desire to protect their children from another adjustment. They may also be sensitive to charges of "immorality," which, as I note above in relation to legal discourse, are much more likely to be leveled against women than men. Divorce advice books aren't especially helpful here. On the one hand, they often urge mothers, especially mothers of boys, not to rely on their sons to fill the place of the absent father. On the other hand, they warn against any behavior that might be construed as "promiscuous." Bassoff, for example, urges mothers not to become dependent on their sons but also not to let their sons see them as too sexual: "If a mother is casual about the men who share her bed, she may be casual about all other intimate relationships—even the sacred mother-child relationship—and teach him that love bonds, rather than being permanent and precious, are transient and replaceable" (Bassoff 143).

Despite their efforts to acknowledge changing family structure, the studies and advice books reproduce gendered norms. For example, they acknowledge that divorce often isolates mothers and then warn divorced mothers that their sons will be more troubled without their fathers and encourage them to work extra hard to make sure that male role models are present. Rather than focusing on the possibilities of mothers raising sons for redefining gender, experts seek ways to reinforce the roles Chodorow described, as in this advice from Hetherington and Kelly:

Our work suggests that one reason why young boys have more difficulty in adjusting to divorce is that they get less emotional support from their overstressed mothers, who find that the combination of demandingness, opposition, noisiness, and physicality makes a young son more exhausting and difficult to parent than a daughter. The loss of another male presence may further complicate adjustment; the lack of a father or other intimate male adult seems to affect young boys more. Preadolescent boys often benefit from the continued involvement of a caring, authoritative, non-custodial father, stepfather, or grandfather. (xx)

By contrast their study found that girls adjust more easily to divorce than boys. This conclusion is also suspect, however, because it does not reflect on the gender norms it invokes: "Until adolescence, girls are less demanding and resistant, easier to parent, and thus apt to receive more maternal support. Additionally, the vast majority of children are likely to find themselves living with their mother after divorce, and the close, companionate mother-daughter relationship common in many of these homes helps to protect girls, who are also less vulnerable to the disappearance of a father than boys are" (149).

In the face of all these difficulties, many women will seek to remarry. The failure rates for remarriage, however, are 60 percent, often due to difficulties as stepchildren and stepparents try to figure out their relationship to one another. Few social scientists have the imagination to see outside marriage as a solution—that perhaps the solution is not two parents but two or more people raising kids. The question for divorced mothers is how, in the midst of balancing work and home, one finds support networks; often, the task of forming communities falls to the single mother who best understands the need for support but who has the least time for the difficult task of organizing.

Notes from Home

"Home starts by bringing space under control," said Mary Douglas (qtd. in Morley 16). For mothers struggling to restore or maintain a sense of stability and security for their children after divorce, bringing space under control becomes difficult, even as the home becomes even more of a haven from the outside world, the stable site when children must travel back and forth between houses. If the mother has moved or lost friends, if she is busier juggling work and child care, then this home becomes more isolated, the paths between sites more difficult to traverse. The single mother experiences an intense loneliness, much as that described by second-wave feminists like Betty Friedan and Jane Lazarre, but a loneliness made more intense by the lack of a partner. In *The Mother Knot*, Lazarre, who was married, writes about the loneliness of her life with baby Benjamin, the "interminably interior days" (85), the "long solitary days" of "apparent inactivity" (45). She describes how spending so much time alone with her child destroyed her self-confidence, made her wonder whether she was going crazy and whether her child was normal (85).

There are fewer paths connecting home to elsewhere. Children may not want to leave home and mothers may succumb to that desire. Here are some journal entries, beginning in Alex's fourth year. I'm surprised, reading back, how quickly I became nostalgic for the nuclear family. I was tired and lonely, writing a dissertation, teaching, raising Alex. I clearly felt tied to the home in ways that I never had before divorce. Much as Alex did, I found comfort in the routine, our life together in a tiny house in Urbana. At the same time, it often felt very isolated.

APRIL 10, 1995

I'm more confined to the house since our separation than I was before. I do more child care—forty-five to fifty hours a week, not counting sleeping hours. I don't even think about going out at night, having a social life like most grad students do. When was the last time I heard music, danced, had a beer? We walk back and forth between our house and Carol's, jumping in puddles. Getting thoroughly muddy. The other day, Sally stopped to drink out of a puddle and peed in it at the same time. We looked at each other horrified for a moment, then burst into laughter. Sally wagging her tail, pleased she could humor us. Returning home from Carol's, I sit down at the computer desk, surrounded by stacks of notes and books. Thinking this dissertation must somehow get done but feeling like I'm writing for no one. Should go to a conference—isn't that what we're supposed to do? A trip out of town seems unlikely. I know Steve would take good care of him but I simply can't go. I want to provide Alex as much of a stable home as possible to make up for all the moving around he has to do, from here to Steve's to Carol's houses. So when I'm with him, we often stay here—where he wants to be.

August 5, 1995

Spent last day nursing Alex through a head injury after collision with Silas. He fell asleep immediately, then said his tummy hurt. Dr. Gilpin said to go in—possible concussion—so a trip to the ER. Alex threw up once in the hospital. They said wake him up every two hours during the night. But I didn't have to because he threw up at least that often. Poor thing—gulps, heaves, his little body. Moving from bed to futon to couch, there's a pile of vomity laundry stacked up in the basement. I feel shaky this morning, ready to burst into tears.

August 24, 1995

Eating a Healthy Choice dinner (chicken teriyaki) as I watch Dan Rather on the CBS evening news. One hour before Alex comes home. I like watching the evening news, it reminds me of my dad laying down on the sofa after dinner to "watch the news," then falling asleep. My sister, mom, and I would laugh as we cleaned up and he snored. Could I really be nostalgic for this family experience? Tonight there's a story about a woman who lost her two sons, ages two and three, in the Oklahoma city bomb blast. She had had her tubes tied and thus was despondent that she couldn't have any more children. But then an artist who painted the sons as angels (after the blast) introduced her to a doctor in Austin, where, at no cost, in a complicated operation, she had her tubes untied and fertility restored. The reporter applauds the potential restoration of motherhood and the actual restoration of family: turns out the woman and her husband were divorced in December but now plan to remarry. They want to have eight children and she believes she will be reunited with her two dead sons in eternity. I have to laugh, it's so sappy, yet it makes me a little sad, too. The house feels empty tonight and much as I look forward to our bedtime routines, I also miss Steve's laughter, his big generosity.

MARCH 21, 1996

Alex is growing up so quickly—has become very animated and gestural. Happy. So much has happened to me in the last months—feeling isolated, worried, lonely, cynical about academia and the job market. Fearful about the future, possibilities for happiness.

But these are generalizations.

Alex has learned how to play Crazy 8. I deal the cards and he spreads them out, using his body to shield my view. Then he quickly forgets, leaving them in open display and announcing, "I have diamonds and spades but no clubs or hearts." I let him win, wondering if these concessions will come back to haunt me in some unforeseeable way.

He's constantly devising new games and new rules for those games. He's an improviser, a bricoleur. Wild but not unresponsive, most of the time, to my requests. We curl up in bed at night to read stories. He curls his fingers into my hair and I gently untangle them when he drifts off to sleep. Return to my computer to try to write a few more pages.

16 JUNE 1996

A trip to Italy without Alex. Terribly hard, at times, sobbing on the plane. Wonderful at other times, relaxing, on the beach, in the cities, sipping a cappuccino rather than gulping it. Alex, fishing with Steve. He'll be home today, finally, in a few hours. He has, by Steve's account, had a wonderful time, as Steve told me on the phone today—no meltdowns, no counting of days, wonderfully adjusted to all the new people and situations. He stopped just short of saying "he didn't seem to miss you at all." Part of me, especially in Italy, was relieved that Alex was doing well, having fun—mainly playing with lots of kids. Perhaps it means I'm doing a good job, preparing him well for new situations, moving him toward independence. I get at least partial credit for that. I also wonder, though, to what degree he needed to get away from me for awhile. Too much time together isn't good for either one of us. Steve, with fewer child-care hours, less work, is better able to engage in pure sheer fun. Is this the way it will always be? Of course I want Alex to have lots of kids to play with; that and the fishing and swimming may have been the primary reasons for his good time—not necessarily being with Steve or away from me. Makes me think already, at 5 1/2, he needs me less than I need him. It's due in no small part to the enormous amount of physical and emotional work I've done the last six years—from conception to now, when I have given every ounce of energy I have to his needs. And already he can move on, away from me, in part because of my devotion, leaving me to probe my own identity/dependency. Makes me want to have another child—to do what—to continue to bolster my mothering identity? Shouldn't I look for other routes? But I am, of course. It's just that mothering is so secure, so safe, so exhausting but so dependable—until you separate/divorce and your child leaves with the other parent. How could it be that he does fine without me? What if some day he wants to spend more time with his dad? A boy and his dad?

13 DECEMBER 1997

Steve's move to Minneapolis makes holidays so crazy, complicated. Now it's time to figure out Christmas, and I'm remembering Thanksgiving—meeting in Iowa City, halfway between here and Omaha, so Steve could go with Alex to visit his family. Me driving with Sally across the frozen Midwest, thermos of coffee in hand and Ani DiFranco on the tape player. Driving back, Alex is upset, crying that his daddy lives so far away. He's sitting in the back seat and I'm trying to drive and comfort him with assurances that he'll see Steve soon, at Christmas. We'll get our Christmas tree soon. It will snow and we'll go sledding and make hot chocolate. My boyfriend James will have us over for dinner, and I know he has a surprise present for Alex. The crying stops for a second. There's silence. Then Alex says, "I have an idea. Why don't James and Mary live together and you and Steve?" Oh, hon, that's a good idea, but I don't think that will work, I said, faced with the prospect of explaining different kinds of love. Happy that he saw we all cared about one another and him, but heartbroken that he was taking it on himself to solve the problem of distance. Later I wondered: perhaps he doesn't understand the difference because I have so carefully shielded him from any display of sexuality in front of James. He never sleeps over at our house and we rarely even kiss in front of Alex. It's funny—because I sometimes dress provocatively in defiance of the norms of mothering and sexuality yet I lead the most cautious of sexual lives.

10 MAY 1999

Yes! A job, and a good one at that. Two-two teaching load, $49,000, a department where I can teach cultural studies. But telling Alex was awful.

He burst into tears when I told him. "Where? Pennsylvania? I'll never even learn how to spell that word." I tell him he will make new friends, have a new house, see his dad a lot. I discover that I need permission from the state of Illinois to move, even though Steve lives in Minneapolis. I have to get a lawyer and he informs me that we need to prove the move will be in Alex's "best interest." How could it not be, I ask? I'll be making a good salary, good benefits, it's a great town for kids, not that different from this one. I've spent almost nine years in graduate school working for this chance. Yes, yes, says the lawyer, it will all be fine. But I worried aloud to my lawyer: What will the judge think about my book on pornography? The fact that I don't have a partner/new husband whereas Steve is remarried and settled, close to family? He is somewhat reassuring but can't say for certain that those things won't matter. Depends on the judge. A conservative judge could choose to emphasize that we are moving more than 1,000 miles away from family and friends, and that these are more important factors than my career. I find myself answering to a governing body that knows nothing about me, my child, the particulars of this situation. Midst the requirements of the state, though, what emerges is relief—that what matters to both his father and me is Alex maintaining a close relationship to his dad despite the miles.

10 OCTOBER 2001

I still think that money doesn't matter as much as Steve and Alex being close. When Steve visits, the three of us share the house, almost like nothing ever happened. We go to Alex's basketball and soccer games, go out to eat together, laugh and tell stories, watch the Cubs on TV. They do things alone together—and as I watch them drive away, off on a big hike or a fishing expedition, I think—there they go, father and son. That's a good thing. That offsets but doesn't completely erase the anxiety of making ends meet—paying a $1,200 mortgage, saving for A's college, paying off student loans, switching money between credit card companies to try to lower my monthly payments.

NOVEMBER 2002

Windswept fields. Gettysburg, PA, home of the famous battle. Feels like we're in the South. An appropriate place, I guess, for the battle of the eleven-year-old boys' soccer teams. I was happy for Alex when he made the "elite" travel team, but now I'm not so sure. Wandering up and down the fields yesterday, listening to coaches scream instructions at young boys, whose faces are tight and drawn, serious, intent on winning. They seem too young, skinny legs, scraped knees, wide eyes. Our team is good, perhaps they'll win the tournament. The coach is determined, I can tell. He has been quiet all season, maybe because they've won all their games handily. First round yesterday he lost it, screaming at the referee, at the kids, at Alex, directions about where to position on the field, when to pass, when to shoot. I can't stand it. Find a place for myself apart from the parents, who have also become much more vociferous. A mother of one of the players who doesn't start tells me that his brother is much better, a star on the high school team. I wonder if that's why his father doesn't come to this son's games. Is he embarrassed? Alex doesn't start either, but I'm glad, much as I want him to play. Too much pressure for boys. These are his role models, this is the community where he learns gender? Make a mistake, get pulled. Fail to run hard, get berated. Score a goal, become a hero. Do nothing, escape both wrath and glory.

SEPTEMBER 1, 2004

Alex is now thirteen. This book is almost done. I can say this with certainty: Alex is a sweet boy even though he wouldn't want me to say that out loud. He loves his half-brother, who just turned one. He likes our little friend Amelia, age two, who comes to play every once in awhile so her mother can perhaps get some writing done. He still loves animals. He high-fives his friends on the soccer field after they score a goal. He hates George Bush and the war in Iraq. He cares about me. When we were driving cross country, more than twenty hours, to visit my parents in Iowa this summer, and I was so tired, he helped me look out for cops. He asked me, "How ya doin'?" OK, I said, I think I can make it a few more hours. "You're my hero, Mom," he said, patting my back.

6

Choice

"Choice" is the key word in Gloria Steinem's explanation of why single mothers represent a threat to conservative forces as we enter the twenty-first century. On an Oxygen channel documentary on single mothers, Steinem says, "Positive choice is new. It would be OK if those women had been cast aside—left, widowed, divorced. It's OK for women to be victims. It's not OK for us to affirmatively choose what we want to do."

The documentary follows a support group for women who have already become or who want to become single mothers. What is striking, however, is the lack of choice they feel, from the attempt to become pregnant to the work of raising a child alone. The frustration prompts intense emotions, from Janet, who cries when she can't get pregnant through artificial insemination, to Karen, who is sad that her daughter's father doesn't want to be part of her life. Lori gives up on artificial insemination and adopts a baby girl from China, happily so, but then struggles as the doctors discover a tumor on the baby's leg. At one point, all the women sit around discussing whether their children will feel a loss at not having or knowing a father. There is one dispassionate voice: the doctor, who warns about the risks that fertility hormones might cause ovarian cancer.

None of these single mothers or mothers-to-be seems to be exercising much of the choice that Steinem celebrates. Instead, the road to mothering is arduous and filled with obstacles that many women could not overcome. Still, by the end of the documentary, each woman is pregnant, has had a baby, or is on the verge of receiving an adopted baby.

Feminism has helped make single mothering a respectable choice. Given the history of demonization of single mothers precisely because they seem to have made the choice not to marry, this is a considerable achievement. It corresponds with other Second Wave demands for the freedom to control one's body and future, through the choice of where to work, who or whether to marry, and whether to have a baby. Yet there are problems with hinging a politics on choice: What about women who can't choose? And who does *really* choose, in the unfettered and autonomous sense in which the concept is often invoked in the United States?

Reproductive freedom for much of Second Wave feminism meant the choice to have sex without having a baby. Now we might say that reproductive freedom includes the choice to have a baby without having sex. Assisted reproductive technologies and adoption deessentialize motherhood and fatherhood, distancing these roles from the realms of biology that, as we saw in the last chapter, still seem so powerful in determining the lives of single mothers and their children. The potential of reproductive technologies was recognized by Shulamith Firestone in her 1970 *The Dialectic of Sex: The Case for Feminist Revolution,* in which she called for the development of birth technologies such as ectogenesis (babies in test tubes, to be reductive) that would free women from the "tyranny of reproduction." What if sexual procreation were no longer the basis for family? The more technology is used to assist reproduction, the less one thinks of birth as natural, grounded in gendered and sexual essentialisms. As anthropologist Marilyn Strathern describes the potential of assisted reproductive technologies, or ARTs: "Procreation can now be thought about as subject to personal preference and choice in a way that has never before been conceivable. The child is literally—and in many cases, of course, joyfully—the embodiment of the act of choice" (1992, 34).

The issues raised here extend beyond the family, beyond the question of whether to have children or not. They encompass the boundaries of the cultural imaginary and the basis of social relations, so much of which are structured around the idea that "family" is inevitably determined. "If till now kinship has been a symbol for everything that cannot be changed about social affairs, if biology has been a symbol for the given parameters of human existence, what will it mean for the way we construe any of our relationships with one another to think of parenting as the implementing of an option and genetic make-up as an outcome of cultural preference?" (Strathern 1992, 34–35).

Single mothers who use ARTs thus become domestic intellectuals who offer new, nonbiological conceptions of family and new ways of thinking about caring and nurturing. They represent the emergent possibilities of all kinds of alternative families. Single mothers who adopt also move away from essentialisms grounded in biology, as their families have no connections to the body or biological similarity. Both options present the possibility of dispersed motherhood—as more than one mother can be identified (the genetic and the gestational mothers, for example, and the birth and the adopting mothers). If dispersed motherhood extends beyond conception into child raising, it produces the kinds of communities grounded in an ethics of reciprocity and caring that allow single mothers to raise children outside of traditional gendered and sexual expectations.

Despite all this potential, or perhaps because of it, there are powerful institutional forces that seek to restore heterosexual and coupled norms. Family law, as we saw in the last chapter, is grounded in a family composed of one father and one mother, and is often unequipped to deal with the multiple possibilities generated by assisted reproduction. Single mothers, especially women who openly identify as lesbian, are not granted the same access as heterosexual couples when they seek assisted reproduction or adoption, even though conditions have improved considerably in the last decade. Assisted reproduction is often very expensive and rarely covered by insurance policies, which, if they cover the process, likely do so only for married couples. Some infertility clinics still openly deny treatment to single women and lesbian couples, and some have less obvious policies that produce the same effects. Sometimes, if you're wealthy enough, you can buy your way through the system. ARTs have become a consumer choice, as has adoption. Adoption agencies often put single mothers low on the list of prospective parents, and it can also become very expensive, especially when mothers turn to international adoption.

Furthermore, ARTs and adoption both raise ethical questions about global sisterhood. As middle-class and wealthy women are treated as consumers, with the possibility of buying a baby, other women throughout the world and in parts of the United States don't have access to birth control or abortion and may be forced to give up their babies for adoption. Whose choice should be given primacy in these situations? Is the mother who gives up her baby for adoption a "bad mother"? And what about the children for whom choice is an even more vexed category? Addressing their most immediate needs seems opposed to the longer-term issues of dislocation and cultural removal.

The problem with "choice" is that it quickly slides into personal responsibility and individual wealth. If it was your choice to have a child, then it must be your responsibility to care for her/him, and if you can't, then you must be a bad mom. The ethical challenge for feminism, then, is to work toward the conditions in which all women enjoy reproductive freedoms, including the choice to become a single mother and raise your child in a situation which is, as much as possible, a life of freedom.

Single Mothers by Choice?

There is a crucial difference between rights and choice, argues Rickie Solinger in *Beggars and Choosers,* her powerful critique of liberal feminism's reliance, since *Roe v. Wade,* on a politics of choice. In the battle for reproductive freedom leading up to Roe, activists deployed the language of rights, premised on the idea that access to abortion should not be contingent on how much money one has. *Roe v. Wade* guaranteed women the right to abortion without regard to whether they could afford to pay for one or not. Increasingly, however, the movement has shifted its rhetoric to one of choice—the pro-choice movement—a rhetoric that articulates with consumerism. Says Solinger:

> In a country weary of rights claims, choice became the way liberal and mainstream feminists could talk about abortion without mentioning the "A-word." Many people believed that "choice"—a term that evoked women shoppers selecting among options in the marketplace—would be an easier sell; it offers "rights lite," a package less threatening or disturbing than unadulterated rights. (2001, 5)

This rhetoric of choice did little to counter—indeed, became complicit with—federal and state legislation to limit the use of public funds such as Medicaid to pay for abortions. Numerous Supreme Court decisions upheld these cutbacks. Women's access to abortion has been further restricted by other legislation, including "parental notification rules for teenagers, mandated waiting periods, counseling sessions, education/propaganda requirements . . . bribe programs that give women money if they get sterilized, and federal contests to reward states with low abortion rates" (Solinger 2001, 33).

The autonomous subject seemingly transcends these material conditions; she is the citizen-consumer-subject, like the televisual single mothers described in chapter 1. I am not ready to give up on the category of "choice," however. If we can contextualize it, return it to the social formations that parcel it out differentially, I believe it still to be a valuable alternative to the lack of options that historically has confronted women in relation to their bodies. As this chapter should make clear, I see multiple possibilities in the deessentializing of family, and little way around commodification. The practical, everyday realities of living under liberal capitalism needn't preclude us from pursuing greater access for all single mothers to the material resources that facilitate choice. The relational issue becomes the key nexus: When does one group's pursuit of choice limit another group's access to resources? In the case of Single Mothers by Choice (SMC), the United States's largest support group for single mothers, there *is* a danger that their insistence on the right to choose to be single mothers is contingent on at least a rhetorical denial of the capacity of other single mothers to choose.

SMC founder Jane Mattes, who started the group in 1982, three years after she became a single mother, credits feminism for removing much of the stigma of single mothering. "There are probably a number of reasons for the increase in older single women having babies, but I believe that the one that underlies them all is the women's movement," she says (12). Foremost among the achievements of feminism, Mattes says, was the right to abortion, which helped legitimate single mothering by expanding the whole notion of choice and fertility. Furthermore, the feminist critique of dependency on men suggested women needn't wait for a husband to start a family. They don't even need a relationship or a sexual encounter; half of SMC members get pregnant by donor insemination. The women's movement also helped make women financially self-sufficient, enabling them to support children on their own.[1]

The denial of dependency suffuses SMC's rhetoric. On the one hand, group members are very proud of their identities, and they are quite particular about the definition of a single mother: "A single mother by choice is a woman who decided to have or adopt a child, knowing she would be her child's sole parent, at least at the outset." This conscious decision sets the SMC apart from other, less decisive (hence, more dependent) single mothers. Perhaps most importantly, SMC distinguishes itself from low-income mothers, citing statistics that document their middle-class incomes and educations, their well-planned decisions: "We often plan for a baby for several years, just as many married couples do, putting aside a portion of our earnings, buying a house in a neighborhood with a good school district, sometimes even changing jobs or careers in order to have a more flexible schedule or do less traveling or attend fewer evening meetings in order to be able to spend more time with our baby" (Mattes 11). In aligning themselves with married couples, SMC reveals the extent to which they aspire to a norm of self-reliance, buying into the myth that married couples are more economically self-sufficient than other families. Although they don't think of it as state aid, married couples benefit from entitlement programs like FHA loans at below mortgage market rates, employer subsidized health benefits, and marriage relief tax deductions.

SMC also distances itself from the "stigma" of divorce and the body of research, analyzed in the last chapter, that predicts children of divorce will be damaged in some way. Divorced women don't often make the choice to become divorced and thus are unprepared for the consequences:

> Because of the high rate of divorce we have all seen women who had not planned or been prepared to take on the responsibility of being single parents being forced to do so. In many cases they have managed to develop the skills necessary to cope with the job. It is not surprising, then, that a mature single woman would feel that if she decides to become a single mother she can do at least as well as, if not better than, someone who was unexpectedly left with the task at the end of a bad marriage and an upsetting, life-disrupting divorce. (Mattes 13)

In fact, divorced women are not even eligible to become SMC members unless they have more children as single mothers after they're divorced: "The reasoning behind this is that there are other groups for divorced moms that can offer support on typical divorce issues, such as child support and visitation, more effectively than we can, as these are not issues with which a single mother by choice has to grapple" (SMC Web site).

An SMC is a reasoned and deliberate individual, for "the core essential attribute of a person in the state of dependency is the absence of the capacity to make sensible choices" (Solinger 2002, 62). This deliberation ideally starts before women have even decided for sure to become single mothers. The group presents itself as offering a space for a deliberated choice; it says that "half of our members are 'thinkers.'" Mattes's guidebook emphasizes careful planning: "Make a decision," she says, presenting detailed advice for every step of the decision-making process. Are you really ready to become a mother, to sacrifice much of your freedom? Are you financially stable? Do you have a support group for difficult times, like children's illness? Like the popular discourse analyzed in part I, her book emphasizes that mothering is a matter of self-surveillance. Prospective mothers are encouraged to complete a "self-examination" questionnaire: "Only you can answer these questions" (22).

Having deliberated, one can then proudly present oneself to the world as a "single mother by choice." In telling people you're pregnant, say this: "I'm very happy to tell you that I have decided to become a single mother—and I am pregnant!" (Mattes 94). SMC urges mothers to be proud of their "unconventional" routes to pregnancy: "Insemination indicates to the world that you clearly chose from the beginning to become a single mother. Some SMCs feel strongly that they do not want there to be any reason for people to think that their pregnancy was accidental" (40). If one makes the right choice, then presumably one has control over the effects. Your kids, for example, will have less difficulty than kids from families who were caught unawares: "Teen-aged children of never-married mothers evaluated in a recent study have been shown to have a better adjustment than those from either divorced homes or stepfamilies, despite the fact that overall the divorced and stepparent families had higher incomes" (16).

Yet SMC cannot police the boundaries of choice as much as they might like. Anecdotes in Mattes's book and on the Web site reveal the ambiguity of many women's "choices." Women who found themselves accidentally pregnant and then decided to keep the baby, for example, are allowed to be SMC members. Choice is complicated as well by the struggles many women have in trying to get pregnant through reproductive technologies. They may give up, or turn instead to adoption. Some situations Mattes describes reveal that their members are not that different from mothers who didn't make a deliberate decision. Her advice addresses common conditions: how to deal with teachers who ask where your child's father is, how to counter loneliness and isolation, how to find time for a social life, and so on.

In its emphasis on choice, SMC undermines the potential for alliances with other single mothers as well as the possibility that their work might help change the political-social conditions shaping mothering and the general act of caring for others. This is not to say that members of SMC will not be good mothers. It is to note, however, that in endorsing the liberal rhetoric of choice based on personal responsibility, they demonize "dependency" in the same manner as does liberalism/neoliberalism. Theirs is a counterproductive and contradictory rhetoric: they reject the support for caring that they and other mothers could use because they fear being stigmatized as dependent. They attempt to transcend social conditions rather than arguing for the resources that would help themselves and many other single mothers. They miss a crucial opportunity to make an ethico-political claim based on their mothering, to intervene in liberalism's dismissal of caring as a reciprocal process. Single mothering may be a right that is now available to all self-sufficient women, but only in the terms of a liberal discourse that does not recognize the right to support. Feminist scholar Robin West explains the contradictions in liberalism's discourse of rights:

> Caregiving labor is an essential, foundational, precondition of liberal society, but the market and political economy long associated with liberalism leave those who provide the care vulnerable. . . . It would be fair to surmise, given this state of affairs, that in a liberal world that depends crucially upon caregiving labor, and employs rights to assure the conditions of liberalism, that rights to care . . . would be given a very high priority. Nevertheless, and without a doubt, the traditional liberal answer to the question posed herein has been a resounding "no." Rights, in liberal societies, protect individuals' autonomy, will, choices, plans of life, contracts, property, and conscience. Women give birth to and then provide care to children who mature into those rights-bearing autonomous adult individuals and then often provide the care for those adults when they have reached an age such that they yet again require full-time caregiving assistance. But no regime of rights protects caregivers or caregiving labor. Rights have never been viewed, within liberalism, as a source of support for caregivers. (90)

Rights are available only to those with the money to purchase them, returning us to the category of consumer choice.[2] The danger in positing single mothering as a choice, a lifestyle, is that it removes mothering from social contexts—all those single mothers who can't prove they made the right choice are castigated or ignored because they are seen as individuals responsible for their decisions: "So long as women are free to choose to become or not to become mothers, and free to choose whether to do so within or outside of marriage, then their relative impoverishment and lack of support . . . is simply of no moment" (West 92). In this discourse, state assistance is not a right, it's a charity that a respectable mother shouldn't pursue. Never does SMC mention the possibility of seeking different forms of state aid, such as food stamps or Medicaid. Within consumerism, there is no inequality: "Choices that impoverish us—so long as they are free—do not make us unequal. They just represent our preferred styles of life" (92). Yet as West notes, caregiving is not like other forms of labor—once you're a mother, you don't simply choose not to do it, to change jobs, or to ask for more pay.

Rights are about the right to be left alone. SMC buys into that liberal assumption when it emphasizes that single mothers should be prepared to raise their children alone, and that, in fact, proving that one can do so legitimates one's choice—indeed proves that one has made a choice. This is surely a contradictory position for a support group to adopt. "Rights limit our obligations," says West, "they do not create obligations, and they assuredly do not protect us within relationships created through those obligations, or more specifically protect us against the exploitative potential created by our obligatory commitments" (105). In its insistence on autonomy and distance from obligations to other kinds of mothers, SMC may contribute to the conditions in which some single mothers are rendered more vulnerable, less able to fulfill their obligations to their children.

Sisterhood Is Global

Women's struggle for reproductive choice throughout the world has involved a battle against patriarchal control of reproduction. Access to contraception is still a major issue for poor women, who are outside the policymaking process when it comes to the development and dissemination of contraceptive methods. Too often, governments use contraception to control women's fertility and sexuality rather than to empower them (see Fathalla). As recently as the 1960s, 20 percent of the American public supported compulsory sterilization of unwed black mothers (Fathalla). In 1974, the Department of Health, Education, and Welfare decided to develop a federal funding plan for reimbursing states for sterilizing poor women (Solinger 2001, 11). Many women who become single mothers throughout the world are not in the position to have made that choice.

Seeking an ethical position in relation to reproductive technologies and adoption should prompt us to ask how access to these choices in the United States is shaped by denial of access to poor women in this country and in other countries. Although the relationship cannot be reduced to one of dominator/victim, there are clearly situations where one group's agency is enhanced by another group's lack of agency. For example, the infertility clinics that treat wealthy white couples often buy their drugs from Mexican factories, "where the predominantly female work force is poorly paid and part of the target audience for public population control campaigns" (Cussins 69). The fact that there is so much money to be made in infertility treatment prompts one to ask whether scientists and researchers are spending too much time on in vitro and embryo transfer research at the expense of examining the causes of infertility, which is most common among low-income women (see Wajcman).

The emphasis on the possibilities generated by assisted reproduction also can make adoption seem like a less desirable choice, and adoptive families less "natural" because they do not rely in any way on biology. Adoption is not without its connection to global inequalities. There are fewer and fewer babies to adopt in the United States because of birth control, abortions, and the fact that more single mothers are keeping their babies. That has led many people—couples and singles—to seek transnational adoptions. Some critics say this sets up an exploitative condition in which poorer countries are forced to "sell" their babies. How can one say that women without the means to raise their children are making a choice when they give them up for adoption? Some feminist critics, such as Rickie Solinger, insist that as long as there is so little economic and social support for single mothers, many women will feel pressured to give up their babies for adoption, and in this context, adoption is "about the abject choicelessness of some resourceless women" (2001, 67). These pressures come in part from conservatives who posit adoption as the acceptable alternative to abortion. Recall that in the mid-1990s, Newt Gingrich and his allies in the Contract with America proposed that children of poor mothers be sent to orphanages, neatly "solving" the problems of illegitimacy and welfare.

If one wants to fully attend to structural inequalities, one should consider the fact that the U.S. government is responsible for much economic and political devastation throughout the world. In Latin America and parts of Asia, where many U.S. couples now go for adoptions, the United States has caused or contributed to decades of devastation. Free-trade policies have also rendered many countries economically vulnerable. By the 1980s, says Solinger, 70 percent of babies brought into the United States for adoption were from four countries—South Korea, Colombia, India, and Mexico; most of the rest came from El Salvador, the Philippines, Honduras, Sri Lanka, and Guatemala (2001, 25).

Disturbing as these situations are, the everyday realities remain: What about the children? Furthermore, many of the adults looking to adopt are sensitive to global politics and want to incorporate that sensitivity into child rearing. They want to form alternative families—single mothers, gays, and lesbians who are also marginalized in the United States. Is it sufficient for adoptive parents from the United States to do whatever they can to acknowledge the differences in power, what Doreen Massey describes as a power geometry, in which different social groups' levels of mobility are contingent on other groups' lack of mobility? Can we switch from a politics of choice to one of access, the latter being more attentive to power? Who possesses reproductive freedom? Who doesn't? How do we expand access to both birth control and reproductive technology?

The questions raised by assisted reproduction are part of a larger debate within feminism about technology. Simply stated, some feminists have taken a doomsday view of technology, arguing that it is a product of patriarchy, deployed to control women's bodies. On the other extreme, there are those who celebrate technologies' possibilities for freedom from biological mandates. Fortunately, many feminists have done important work across disciplines to show that there is nothing *inherently* evil or liberating about technology, that its potential is closely linked to structures of control. As E. Ann Kaplan and Susan Squier argue, "Technology has no more of an inherent essence than does 'nature' or its principles: gametes, embryos, animals, human beings. However, technology—now most often 'managed' by mainstream institutions and biomedical forces—needs to be opened up to, and its control shared by usually marginalized communities whose bodies and lives are most affected by technologies" (12).

Babies without Sex

What are all the ways a woman can now become pregnant without having sex? There's the relatively low-tech route of donor insemination. A woman can buy sperm from a sperm bank or get it from a willing friend. She can have a friend inseminate her (the turkey baster method) or she can go through a doctor. Women who have trouble getting pregnant can use in vitro fertilization, in which their eggs are extracted and fertilized with sperm; then the embryo (or more likely, embryos) are reimplanted. If their eggs are not viable, they can buy donor eggs. If their uterus is not viable, they can hire a surrogate mother. We live in an age of dispersed parenting. It may no longer be possible to identify a singular mother or

father. If one woman is the genetic contributor of the egg and another ges-
tates the baby, who is the mother? If a couple uses sperm from an unknown donor because there is a problem with the male partner's sperm,
are there two fathers? One might also count all the people who assist in
the process, including nurses and doctors; as Strathern argues: "Dispersed kinship is constituted in dispersed conception; it includes those
who 'produce' the child with assistance as well as those who assist. As a
consequence, there exists a field of procreators whose relationship to one
another and to the product of conception is contained in the act of conception itself and not in the family as such" (Strathern 1995, 352). Family is being deessentialized, distanced from the problematic gender roles
which so often come to seem grounded in biology and bodies. The origin
of the sperm and egg come to matter less: "The technologies are, so to
speak, indifferent to the social origins of egg and sperm, the persons from
whom they come, even to where gestation takes place" (355).

The freedom from intercourse is a freedom from origins. One might
imagine eggs and sperm freed from bodies, from the direct path of penis-
vagina intercourse: "Gamete traffic materially incorporates new routes of
relation and kinship as well as revolutionizes the signification of reproduction" (Farquhar 23). Men who donate sperm and women who donate
eggs are not responsible for the babies produced. The previously natural
act of procreation has been denaturalized, rendered open to manipula-
tion, made part of the "free" market system. Mothering, traditionally defined by both its genetic and gestational capacities, has been split into two
roles via assisted reproduction. By the end of the 1990s, says Charis
Thompson,

> it was already a commonplace that a woman can share bodily substance
> with a fetus to whom she is not genetically related. As a result of donor
> egg IVF and gestational surrogacy, the overlapping biological idioms of
> shared bodily substance and genes come apart. The maternal genetic
> material, including the determinants of the blood type and characteris-
> tics of the fetus, is contributed by the egg, which is derived from the
> ovaries of one woman. Nonetheless, the embryo grows in and out of the
> substance of another woman's body; the fetus is fed by and takes form
> from the gestational woman's blood, oxygen, and placenta. It is not un-
> reasonable to accord the gestational mother a biological claim to moth-
> erhood. (178)

The potential for dispersed mothering is threatening to many people, however. In her ethnography of fertility clinics, Thompson found that most clients were eager to "disambiguate" mothering—to define who is the real mother in egg donor and surrogacy cases. This was particularly true in instances where women received eggs from relatives. Thompson recounts one case, for example, in which a couple, Michael and Kay, had a long history of infertility. Michael's sister Rachel agreed to be a surrogate mother and be implanted with the embryo produced by in vitro fertilization of Kay's eggs and Michael's sperm. During the two-hour period in the clinic after implantation in which Rachel had to remain in a prone position, the two women joked about whether the baby might look at all like Rachel, even though she/he would belong genetically to Kay and Michael. Thompson recounts and comments on their conversation:

> They resolved the question by accepting that if Rachel had an effect on what the baby looked like, it would be because she had provided a certain environment for the baby to grow in, not because she was part of the baby's "nature." Rachel's role in the pregnancy was thus returned safely to the realm of caregiver and provider of a nurturing environment. Their narrow geneticization of incest prevented biological embodiment of the brother's child from being incest. (184)

Rachel did become pregnant and gave birth, so it could be said that the sister and brother had a baby, but the family was very careful to say that genetics defined mothering in this case.

Other women embrace the idea of shared motherhood, especially when they come from cultures where this idea is already accepted. Thompson describes the case of an African American woman who wanted to use an egg donor from her community: "She said that using a donor was not as strange as it might seem, as it was like something 'we've been doing all along.' When I asked her what she meant, she explained that in African American communities, it was not unusual for women to 'mother' or 'second mother' their sister's or daughter's or friend's child(ren)" (182). There was nothing unnatural about accepting another woman's egg: "Shared mothering was not presented as necessarily involving a natural kinship rift; indeed, it was presented as a practice that preserves racial identity and integrity" (Thompson 196). In another case, a fifty-one-year-old Mexican woman who had four children from a previous marriage got remarried and decided she wanted to have children with her new husband. She used eggs donated by her daughter to conceive a baby. Thompson found again that the family drew on existing social practice to explain the situation, in this case "the prevalence of generation-skipping parenting (where a grandparent parents a child socially and legally) in the communities with which (the mother) was familiar" (186).

In all these cases, whether the involved parties acknowledge it or not, technologies are unraveling the binaries that have shaped the family. The distinction between nature and technology blurs, as technology is used to achieve what couldn't naturally take place yet which turns out to be natural—a baby. "Reproduction becomes a technological achievement rather than a natural sequence of events. Kinship is no longer defined against 'natural,' 'biological' facts; nature and technology have become mutually substitutable" (Carsten 174). This naturalization of technology is critical to its social legitimation, given the potential for linkage with such practices as cloning and genetic engineering that still meet with widespread public skepticism.

Reproductive technologies also make public, to some degree, the private act of procreation. This "making public" may provide an answer to the concerns of feminist and queer theorists who have argued that the heterosexual nuclear family enjoys a privacy and freedom denied to gay and other marginalized relationships (see my summary of Warner and Berlant, introduction). No longer are babies made only in the privacy of the bedroom, under the auspices of "love" and "intimacy." They are conceived in the clinic, in a situation involving the exchange of money and the rendering visible of the most private of acts. The procreative process has become a "collaborative process that takes place in the public spaces of the laboratory and the clinic" (Grayson 100).

However, collaboration is not a purely progressive political practice. Making procreation a public business also brings it into the realm of regulation, raising many questions about who controls women's bodies. Should the state have a role in determining what happens in fertility clinics? On the one hand, greater state regulation might lead to more equal conditions of access, something I discuss more in the next section. RESOLVE, the National Infertility Association, has argued before Congress for state and federal legislation that would require insurance companies to cover infertility treatment. Yet the possibility of state regulation of women's bodies is certainly one of which to be wary. There are no guarantees that regulation would lead to greater access for single mothers and lesbians, just as there are no guarantees that regulation would lead to stricter monitoring of the short- and long-term effects of fertility drugs on women's bodies. It's a difficult situation, recalling the questions about the state that I discussed in the introduction. How much energy should be put into efforts to convince the state to make infertility treatment a fairer and less risky procedure? What other options do we have?

At the moment, subjecting fertility to state, legal, and economic (free-market) regulation means subjecting women's bodies to institutions that are still largely invested in the heterosexually coupled nuclear family. The assisted reproduction business at almost every turn favors the couple: the clinic themselves, insurance policies, the legal system, and public opinion. All of this renders doubtful, again, the idea that choosing to have a baby with the help of reproductive technology is really a choice.

"Enterprise Culture"

How is the deessentializing potential of assisted reproduction recuperated into naturalized notions of gender and sexuality?

First, most infertility clinics favor heterosexual couples; the business puts most of its energy into helping these couples, most of them married, have their own biogenetic child. The Centers for Disease Control estimates that 16 percent of reproductive health-care providers in the United States routinely refuse to offer treatment to single women (Ginty), a disconcerting statistic that probably does not account for many cases. Anecodotal accounts of bias are common. The Women's E News service, for example, told the story of Melinda Milsaps, a nurse whose own employer—Shands Healthcare and Faculty Group Practice in Gainesville—would not allow her access to artificial insemination because she was single. Five other clinics also refused her care. She sued Shandy and lost in federal court (Ginty). In Britain as well, it's still a question as to whether single mothers using donor sperm are as "qualified" as married women. A study by the Family and Child Psychology Research Center in London set out to find, in part, if children of single mothers using donor insemination (DI) were doing as well as two-parent families using DI and found, to their seeming surprise, that they were. Still, the lead researcher, Dr. Clare Murray, said the families would need to be followed up: "It's not clear, for example, how the children of solo DI mothers will react to the knowledge of their conception and whether or not the absence of a father will affect their psychological development as they grow up." ("Why Women Opt").

In the United States, some clinics are only licensed to use their frozen sperm for couples in which the husband's sperm were deemed the problem. Even those who may treat other people if they want prefer heterosexual couples. Charis Cussins found in her ethnography of infertility clinics that in the medical staff's deliberations about whom to accept as a patient, it is "thought to be preferable to evince a stable family environment, and that is almost always interpreted to mean that anyone seeking treatment should be heterosexually partnered, although not necessarily married" (72). Clinics sometimes rejected couples who argued in their counseling sessions because it seemed there wouldn't be a stable environment after the birth (Cussins 74).[3]

Heterosexist norms also manifest themselves through insurance policies. Only one-fourth of health plans offered at companies with ten or more employees offer coverage for fertility treatments, according to RESOLVE. Fifteen states have laws mandating insurance coverage for some level of infertility (Curphey). However, coverage applies only if the woman has been diagnosed as infertile, and the standard medical definition of infertility is failure to conceive after one year of unprotected intercourse, a definition that can be used to exclude lesbians and single women. RESOLVE government affairs director Erin Kramer told a Women's News reporter that most states and a majority of clinics "feel that a woman does not have a fertility problem if she does not have a male partner" (Curphey).

Without insurance, the costs can be prohibitive, especially for single women. Artificial insemination at a clinic ranges between $200 and $500 per attempt, plus $200 to $400 per vial of donor sperm. There are additional fees for consultations, exams, and handling of the sperm. The overall chance of conception using frozen sperm is 8 to 15 percent per cycle. The total cost can easily rise to $5,000 or more. If women can't afford this, they may have unprotected sex with men, risking sexually transmitted diseases. Much more expensive is in vitro fertilization, which costs between $25,000 and $75,000 (Ginty), depending on how many attempts a woman makes, and there is just a one in four chance that it will work over the period of a year. There is virtually no public assistance covering assisted reproduction, leaving many women without the option.

Assisted reproduction has become part of Enterprise Culture, says Marilyn Strathern. Those who seek assistance are not considered sick or disabled but rather "customers seeking services," enabled by these new technologies to "achieve desires that they could not achieve unaided" (1992, 35). Reproductive services constitute a "business that caters to those who will make a business out of being a family" (35). Having a baby via assisted reproduction is becoming hip, stylish, part of one's self-fashioning. In the last decade, hospitals and HMOs have begun to advertise infertility services; "infertile couples are perceived as an underserved, infinitely expandable market, a market willing to supply substantial out-of-pocket funds when denied access by insurers or managed-care organizations" (Moore 81). The overt marketing removes some of the stigma of infertility treatment, as does the fact that more women in their forties and even fifties are bearing children, including high-profile women like actress Geena Davis (48 at the time her twin sons were born) and Elizabeth Edwards, wife of the senator and 2004 vice presidential candidate John Edwards, who had children at the ages of forty-nine and fifty-two.

Consumer choice is also a way to demonstrate active citizenship. To choose to become pregnant because you are financially responsible shows that you are worthy of full participation in society. A consumer society posits that if you have money and you want something, you can get it. The pursuit of a baby through technology in turn demonstrates that one intends to be a parent, and this intention suggests one is prepared to be a good parent, as opposed to women who get pregnant by accident and don't have the financial means to support the child. Once couples set out to have a child, then, it is hard for them to turn back, and the infertility business capitalizes on the endless production of desire. Says Strathern, "When initial treatments fail, others may be suggested, and intending parents may thus be led into relocating what it is of themselves they reproduce. If finally what remains intact is the intention or desire to have a child, then that desire is what the child 'reproduces'" (1995, 355).

Ultimately, if you have enough money, being a single mother will not keep you from finding a clinic that will serve you. Members of Single Mothers by Choice report that "in general the medical profession is fairly positive about mature, responsible single women trying to get pregnant by insemination" (Mattes 29), with some exception in more conservative areas. The typical "mature" single mom who seeks assisted reproduction is the successful career woman who finds herself in the somewhat ironic position of having spent too much time becoming independent of husbands. Writing in the magazine *Bust* about this situation, Rose Tattoo says: "We wanted equal work and pay, and we're still so busy trying to prove we deserve it that we forgot to procreate until it's too late. We liberated ourselves right out of two-income comfort and somebody at home to play child-rearer" (54). At thirty-eight, Tattoo began considering donor insemination, determined to become pregnant at thirty-nine. She visited the California Cyrobank, where she found that she could buy sperm that had cleared all medical tests and go through the insemination process (including doctor visits, drug treatments, vitamins, and other procedures) for a cost of about $2,000 a cycle. Optimistic that she would conceive, Tattoo nevertheless encountered women her age who could not; they are confronted with the possibility that their money may not be able to buy them what they want.

The industry confronts this challenge head-on. Doctors can continually present new suggestions for treatment, new combinations of hormones. One doesn't feel coerced but rather presented with the opportunity to fulfill desire. In her ethnography, Cussins discovered a "culture of perseverance" in which women were willing to embark upon another "combination of hormones, another cycle of artificial insemination, another go at IVF." Over the course of months of interviews and observations, she found only one woman who stopped treatment for nonmonetary reasons.

Women continue treatment even when they know the odds aren't great. It's all about risk management:

> The existence of new technological options takes away the choice simply to accept infertility. In the face of a possible treatment, however unsuccessful, infertility becomes a tentative condition. In turn, there can be no "peace of mind." New technological options produce a forced choice; once a choice exists it must either be pursued or refused. (Franklin 108)

Debby, one of the featured women in the Oxygen documentary on single mothers, says assisted reproduction is like gambling: "I feel like a gambler at Atlantic City," she says. "What if it's the thirteenth try? This next quarter is going to be my jackpot. I said I was going to try for a year and this will be my twelfth try. But what if it's my thirteenth?" The documentary follows Debby throughout the different phases of treatment—at the doctor's office being inseminated; getting shots of fertility drugs from a friend in her home; calling a friend, close to tears, to say that she has gotten her period. She spends $18,000 and struggles to keep up her resolve. More than anything, however, she wants to give birth, and it is only with considerable reluctance that she decides to adopt a baby girl from China.

Finally, it must be said that the potentially denaturalizing realm of reproductive technology can powerfully essentialize motherhood. There is simply no excuse not to do everything possible to have one's own baby. New technologies can reinforce "pro-natalist values and practices, which ensure that women who fail to bear children face constant reminders of the extent to which they fall short of hegemonic ideals" (Stanworth 291). Some women become desperate, making them vulnerable to coercive physicians who urge costly and risky procedures. Already, there is evidence to suggest that physicians turn too quickly to fertility drugs. For example, during in vitro fertilization, women are given drugs that stimulate egg production, on the theory that multiple eggs fertilized with multiple sperm and implanted as multiple embryos will be more likely to produce a pregnancy. However, some research has shown that in vitro fertilization is just as likely to succeed when only one egg is harvested, then fertilized and implanted. In this case, women need not take the drugs that have unpleasant side effects and perhaps even more devastating long-term implications.

The Rule of Intentionality

The legal arena is another realm where the nuclear family is being reinvoked in response to the threat that "family" is losing its coherence. At the heart of the question is whether these new kinds of families should in fact be treated as a kind of business, under the rubric of contract law, instead of under the traditional rubric of family law. It is becoming clearer to even conservative judges that family law may not work if the "family" is no longer the traditional mother and father and that perhaps another foundation of liberalism could stand in its place—contracts. As with consumerism, contract law is based on choice and intentionality. There's an ostensible clarity to contracts—courts can "simply" decide if all parties consented to the terms of a voluntary agreement. If a woman signs a contract saying she will carry a child for a couple and, at the end of nine months, give up the baby she has gestated, the contract should stay in place, even if the surrogate mother changes her mind. Yet contract law seems inadequate for capturing the social conditions that facilitate an individual's choice. It also may be inadequate for determining the best interest of the child: What if the contract honors a parent who no longer wants to be a parent? The court would then not be looking out for the child's best interest by awarding custody to a reluctant parent.

In the past, some courts have been reluctant to acknowledge the commerce in babies. In the famous Baby M. case, for example, William Stern contracted with Mary Beth Whitehead to bear him a child by being artificially inseminated with embryos produced by his wife's egg and his sperm. He agreed to pay Whitehead $10,000 for having the child, then terminating her parental rights. In 1989, the New Jersey Supreme Court ruled, however, that the contract violated the state's adoption laws prohibiting the sale of children. Yet just two years later, in another celebrated case, another court, this one in California, used contract law to uphold a contract when the surrogate mother changed her mind and wanted to keep the baby she had carried for a married couple. The case, *Johnson v. Calvert*, reveals the degree to which contract, couched in the terms of "intentionality," relies once again on a kind of choice linked to class privilege as well as to the court's desire to reinforce heterosexual parenting. The ability to demonstrate ownership of property indicates one is responsible, capable of owning children, as if they were cars or houses.

Anna Johnson was a single black woman who agreed to serve as the gestational surrogate for a couple—Mark and Crispina Calvert (Crispina was Filipina, Mark was Anglo). At the end of the pregnancy, however, Johnson decided she wanted to keep the baby, marking "the first time that a surrogate mother without a genetic link to the child she had carried fought for custody of that child" (Grayson 99). Johnson lost three court cases, up to the California Supreme Court (*Johnson v. Calvert*), and the U.S. Supreme Court refused to hear the case, assuring the Calverts full custody of the baby boy. Both Anna Johnson and Crispina Calvert claimed to be the baby's natural mother. In deciding in favor of the Calverts, the lower courts relied on biological/genetic arguments to rule that the couple were the natural parents, as they had produced the egg and sperm. The California Supreme Court reached the same decision but relied more on intentionality than biology, interestingly acknowledging that both mothers had biological claims to the child. However, given the fact that California law recognizes only one mother, they had to decide. They turned to the parents' intentions, settling the case by referring to the contract. As legal scholar Deborah Grayson analyzes the case: "For this court, in instances where genetic consanguinity and childbirth do not co-incide in the body of one woman, the woman who intended to procreate the child and to raise it as her own is the natural mother" (105). Note the court's desire to reinstate a "normal" family by identifying a "natural" mother. Justice Kennard, the only woman on the bench, dissented because she didn't think children should be equated with intellectual property, and, she argued, "both the genetic and gestational mothers have sub-stantial claims to legal motherhood" (Grayson 105).

The rule of intent relies on the same assumptions of equality that con-sumer choice does: in a democratic society, one's ability to sign a contract indicates one's equal standing as a citizen. Actually, it may capture very little of the complexity of the parties' situations that produce different de-grees of agency. For Anna Johnson, the rule of intent did not account for the possibility that upon carrying a baby for nine months, she would feel that it was biologically hers, even though she did not "intend" in a ratio-nal way to make that claim. The fact that she was a single, black mother on welfare likely did not help her case; media portrayals of her relied on the racist history of representing black women as "welfare queens." In the court's eyes, the Calverts appeared the better family to raise the baby, as their whiter, middle-class, married status indicated that they had ra-tionally planned for the child and would make good parents. Grayson comments that the rule of intent

> is often inconsistently applied because it assumes an equality between in-dividuals that does not yet exist. Gestational mothers who renege on their contracts—poor mothers, lesbian mothers, black mothers, and other mothers thought to be functioning outside middle-class, father-centered families—often find themselves without support or legal re-course in child custody disputes. Courts consistently rule against these women, favoring instead configurations of the family that fit the nuclear family model of white, middle- to upper-class heterosexual couples. (106)

As such, arguments based on intentionality "serve essentially as a means to contain the proliferation of meanings made possible by medical tech-nology and its ways of constantly altering knowledge about intimate re-lations" (107).

There is one exception to the rule of intentionality as it applies to a contract, but it also works against single mothers. Although laws vary considerably across states, it appears that courts are increasingly willing to grant men who have become fathers via sperm donation the legal status of father, even if they initially signed a contract abdicating their rights to fatherhood. This tendency derives in part from the fathers' rights movement described in the last chapter, which has influenced judges to consider fathers as equal partners to mothers, even when they have not been as fully involved in their children's lives. If the donor knows he has fathered a child (through intercourse or artificial insemination) and can prove his paternity, he can make a legal claim, no matter what agreement was initially reached with the mother. The claim for fathers' rights such as visitation is given even more credence if the donor sperm does not pass through a doctor's office—that is to say, if the insemination occurred at home, with the assistance of friends, for example.[4] The law puts women who want nothing to do with the sperm donors in a difficult position: if they want to avoid one form of patriarchal control—the infertility business, with its costs and medical procedures—they subject themselves to another form, the courts.

What should be clear by this point is that the act of dispersed conception rarely extends to the practice of shared parenting after the child is born. It is perhaps easier to point to all the possibilities that technology introduces for deessentializing the family at the moment of conception than it is to pursue these possibilities into the everyday lives of mothers and children. In this sense, assisted reproduction has not yet produced the conditions in which single mothers can thrive as domestic intellectuals. We are left with the question: How can the absence of a father become an opportunity for dispersed kinship, one that extends beyond conception?

Longing for Fathers

The choice to have a baby without any father in the picture puts these single mothers in a particular category. On the one hand, unlike single mothers by divorce, they usually don't have to worry about the father's ongoing presence in their lives. On the other hand, they still live in a society that expects there to be some kind of identifiable father, even if he's absent. In this sense, choice is still shaped by the nuclear family norm. How does one explain "sperm donor" to a three-year-old?

The freedom represented by technology is particularly reprehensible to social conservatives. Divorce is bad enough, but artificial insemination is

complete sacrilege. In *Longing for Dad: Father Loss and Its Impact,* Beth
M. Erickson is especially worried about single mothering through insemination. Urging women who are contemplating insemination through
sperm donation to consider the implications, she says that it is a "matter
of urgent importance that they grasp what their children, especially their
sons, will be up against if they never know their father. Before they make
this irreversible decision, they also need to reckon with what this could
mean for them as solo parents of children who will know the distress of
the nagging, ongoing grief of father hunger" (71).

Donor insemination has not been normalized in the media the way
other forms of single mothering have been, indicating that the "public"
still views assisted technology as not quite natural. It's too soon for
"mainstream" televisual and filmic moms to be having cyborg babies.
Televisual single mothers get that way either through divorce (like Amy
on *Judging Amy*), being widowed (Kate on *8 Simple Rules*), or during sex
with a friend in which contraception wasn't used or failed (Miranda on
Sex and the City, Rachel on *Friends*). There are humorous treatments of
assisted reproduction and science fiction representations of alien births,
perhaps because comedy and science fiction allow a displacement of societal anxieties about the fine line between technologically assisted births
and seemingly more questionable practices such as cloning.

Many accounts of women who turn to assisted reproduction suggest
that if they had the choice, they'd rather have a baby with a partner. It's
quite rare to find a "single mother by choice" who doesn't yearn for a
partner for herself and a father for her child. Is it freedom when many
women say they'd prefer to have a partner but will settle for single mothering if that's their only option? In her *Bust* piece on single mothering,
Rose Tattoo quotes a woman named Anne, who got pregnant via donor
insemination: "Sometimes you just want to roll over and say 'honey, feel
the baby.' You're alone. There's a sense of loss" (52). In the Oxygen documentary on single mothers, most of the women say they wish they had
been able to find a male partner with whom to have a child, and that they
still hope to find one to help raise their child. Janet, who is trying to conceive through insemination, relates how difficult it was when her father
died when she was twelve: "I was definitely daddy's little girl. I felt like I
had no one shepherding me into adulthood." And Janet's mother cau-
tions her: "You know what it's like to grow up without a daddy." Janet
comments, "Believe me, I'd love to have a daddy (for a baby), and I still
hope to."

The women on the documentary also worry about how to explain to their children how they were conceived. SMC founder Mattes offers contradictory advice to her readers, indicating again the impossibility of true choice in a society that still assumes a father is central to defining a family. On the one hand, she says, tell your child that there are lots of different kinds of families, and just because there's not a daddy doesn't mean you're not "normal." On the other hand, she says, you might consider relating this story to your child: "The story might tell how a woman (you, but with a different name) was yearning for a child, how she tried to find a man who also wanted a child to be her husband, that she was unable to find such a man, and so she decided to go to a doctor who helps women who do not have husbands become single mothers" (133). Mattes is clearly struggling with the issue of choice: she still wants to assert that responsible single mothers make a deliberate choice, removing them from the realm of mistakes and dependency. Yet she also reveals how many women who use donor insemination do so only because they feel they don't really have the choice to have a husband.

Beyond Biology

International adoptions are a haphazard mixture of luck and privilege that can hardly be called "choice." This is captured in John Sayles's 2003 film, *Casa de los Babys,* in which a group of North American women wait in a Mexican resort town for their adoption applications to work their way through the bureaucracy. The mothers are clearly privileged, much more so than the townspeople who depend on their tourism dollars. Babies have become one of the primary attractions, Mexico's most desirable "exportable," as one local man comments. In another manifestation of the vagaries of luck and the discrepancies in mobility, he pins his hopes for leaving Mexico on the lottery. Homeless kids roam the streets, clearly being among those who are no longer desirable candidates for adoption. One young Mexican woman, Asunción, works in the hotel where the mothers stay, and she recounts the story of her own pregnancy and decision to give up her baby for adoption. Yet within these unequal conditions, there is sympathy created for the North American mothers, most of whom are generous and caring. One is a single mother, Leslie (played by Lili Taylor), who, despite her New York cynicism, wins us over with her sensitivity to the local culture, including her ability to speak Spanish. She seems likely to be a much better mother than the married, mean-spirited and racist Nancy Hightower, played by Maggie Gyllenhaal, who says of Leslie: "I can't believe they're going to give her one when there are so many of us with husbands who want to adopt. A child needs a mother and a father." Yet she is more concerned with the stray dogs than with kids, and her only moment of caring is when she remembers her dogs back home: "They need their mama." The unfairness of the system is illustrated when Nancy bribes the Mexican officials to expedite her application; despite one official's obvious hatred of her, the film ends with her ready to receive a baby, while other prospective mothers still wait.

Like assisted reproduction, adoption is a business. Adoptable babies without any "special needs" are rare, especially in the United States, where, somewhat ironically, the very fact that more single mothers are keeping their babies rather than giving them up for adoption, along with birth control and abortion, has created a baby shortage. The number of adoptable babies dropped dramatically after *Roe v. Wade;* one agency reported that the number of children placed for adoption dropped 45 percent between 1971 and 1974 (Solinger 2001, 95). Prospective parents began looking to other countries; "one study showed a 33 percent increase in the number of foreign children admitted to the United States for adoption between 1972 and 1973" (Solinger 2001, 22). Because heterosexual married couples are the favored candidates for babies in the United States, the tendency to look abroad is even greater among single mothers. Here, women who often do not have access to birth control and adoption or the means to raise their children are more likely to have to give up their babies. Because of the complicated bureaucratic channels one must pass through, both abroad and upon returning to the United States, prospective parents sometimes spend $20,000 or more on the adoption. This expense is obviously much less affordable for single parents than for couples.

In the adoption business, no one operates as an autonomous agent, but the differences in agency and mobility are painfully clear. Still, there is no easy answer, especially when one considers the children, who are removed from their cultures for a life that will almost certainly be vastly improved in material terms. Sayles's film does an admirable job of tracing the different degrees of agency of the three main groups involved in adoption: birth mothers, adoptive mothers, and the children.

In the film, Asunción is a young woman, perhaps twenty, who works as a maid in the hotel where the North American women await their babies. She lives in a small home in a poor neighborhood far from the hotel, taking care of her younger brother and sister; they are apparently orphans and she barely makes enough money to support the family. One day, Asunción is cleaning the room of Eileen, a kind person from Boston, who is eagerly awaiting a baby girl. Eileen tells Asunción all about her hopes and dreams for the child, and even though Asunción can understand very little English, she listens to Eileen's story as she changes the sheets, pausing occasionally to register the joy on Eileen's face as she imagines making hot chocolate for her daughter on a snowy day. At the end of Eileen's story, Asunción sits on the bed and begins talking:

> I have a little girl up north. Four years old now. I was so young. I had to work, take care of my brother and sister. The nuns came to me. They said it would be best to give her up. Sometimes when a group of new mothers comes, I seek one, a good one. I try to imagine her face, her voice when I think of Esmeralda with her other mother up north. I hope she has found a good mother like you.

At the end of the film, Eileen receives her baby and names her Esmeralda. What saves this scenario from kitsch is the fact that the two women cannot communicate in the same language. Their empathy is more a product of feeling and observation. Asunción has seen that Eileen is unlike some of the prospective mothers who condescend to the local people. Eileen is aware of the huge differences in wealth and mobility and appears grateful for this opportunity. "In a moment my life is going to change forever," she says at the end, awaiting the nuns who will bring her daughter. She begins to cry, in contrast to Nancy Hightower, who sits woodenly next to her. The film represents the complexity of these women's lives without turning them into political combatants, victimizers and victimized.

Still, there are obvious good guys and bad guys. Nancy Hightower represents the ultimate consumer, able to buy a baby even though the Mexican officials recognize her racism. After she storms into his office and lectures him, adding "You don't want my husband to have to come down here," a Mexican official rejects her bribe and as she leaves his office says, "We don't accept American Express for our children. . . . You'll never get one of our precious children." At the end, however, Hightower is apparently about to receive her baby, indicating that enough money can override racism. Clearly, she could care less about the birth mother and why she had to give up her baby for adoption. In this situation, Rickie Solinger's critique applies: in the "free market," the privileged consumer insists "that child acquisition have no strings attached. This argument for ICA (inter-country adoption) wants to entirely efface the biological mother in order to make things easier for the consumer" (2001, 31).

Yet what if the biological mother is not effaced? If her situation is represented as well as the adoptive mother's, it becomes possible to see the relationship not as a binary struggle between adoptive parents and birth mothers, but as part of a larger struggle over the definitions of parenting and family that is taking place within global economic relations. The latter, however, should not preclude us from thinking about the former; that is to say, structural inequities of a global scale do not negate the national politics of family in which it is difficult for some women in the United States who do not fit hetero norms to have children. In relation to assisted reproduction, for example, adoption gives women the choice of not subjecting themselves to endless rounds of drugs. Elizabeth Bartholet, a Harvard University law professor who wrote a memoir about her adoption of two Peruvian children, tried for many years to conceive a child through assisted reproduction, encountering numerous biases against single mothers, before she decided on adoption. She argues in her memoir for the possibilities generated by adoption:

> As a society, we define personhood and parenthood in terms of procreation. We push the infertile toward ever more elaborate forms of high-tech treatment. We are also moving rapidly in the direction of a new child production market, in which sperm, eggs, embryos, and pregnancy services are for sale so that those who want to parent can produce a child to order. At the same time, we drive prospective parents away from children who already exist and who need homes. We do this by stigmatizing adoptive parenting in myriad ways and by turning the adoption process into a regulatory obstacle course. (xx)

A better construction of adoption, says Bartholet, "would help free the infertile from the obsession to restore their personhood by obtaining a medical fix" (xxii).

We can also situate adoptive single mothers and gay and lesbian couples in relation to adoptive heterosexual couples. Adoption gives the former groups a chance to form families that counter the norm. Yet as with ARTs, there is a systemic impulse to favor the heterosexual, married couple. Although only the state of Florida categorically prohibits gay/lesbian adoption, Utah prohibits adoptions by people who aren't married and Mississippi prohibits "adoption by people of the same gender" (National Center for Lesbian Rights Web site). However, many adoption agencies are private and will not accept single applicants, and others will take the application but put it on the back burner. Says the Single Parent Central Web site, "Despite the greater acceptance of single parent adoption, the traditional view of parenting, that a child needs a mother and a father for healthy growth and development, still exists. Mental health experts say that the 'ideal' is to place a child in a two-parent home with a mother and father who are compatible and loving." All adoptions must be finalized in court, and the National Center for Lesbian Rights has found that judges vary widely in their rulings on homosexual adoption: "In practice, judicial reaction to openly lesbian, gay, and bisexual adoptive parents ranges from supportive acceptance to overt hostility" (Kendell and Haaland).

Singles are also subjected to more intense home studies by the agencies and more intensive questioning about financial stability and preparation for parenting. As one adoption Web site stated, trying to put a positive spin on the process and explaining why single parents are such good parents, "The screening process for singles is so exhaustive that only the most persistent survive" (Preconception.com). Given this assumption that single parents are less qualified or able to care for children than two parents, it seems contradictory that when U.S. agencies grant them children, they are often matched with children considered more challenging—older boys, for example, or children with mental or physical disabilities. About 25 percent of adoptions of children with special needs are by single men and women; 5 percent of all other adoptions are by singles.[5] Money can offer a way around this—if one is going through private agencies or dealing directly with the birth mother—but again single parents are less likely to have the kind of money necessary to bypass the system, and, in fact, they may not want to engage in such overtly commodified and arguably unethical practices.

Many single mothers turn to international adoption, and there they are met with both old and new obstacles. While a number of countries accept applications from single parents, the adoption agencies are often homophobic. In her memoir *Meeting Sophie* about adopting a baby girl from China in the late 1990s, Nancy McCabe describes the news she got from the Center for China Adoption that her application had been put on hold.

The center was suspicious that McCabe was a lesbian. They had recently passed a rule saying all adoptive parents had to be heterosexual and requiring all single applicants to swear they did not have same-sex roommates. McCabe describes the difficulty of writing this statement, sitting at her computer and typing, deleting, then retyping: "'I am heterosexual.' Writing that sentence feels like a betrayal of everything I believe. That my sexuality is no one's business. That labels are always lies because sexuality exists on a spectrum. That, even though I am in fact heterosexual, I am selling out" (48). She polled her adoption listserv and found one other prospective single parent who "was flagged by China as 'potentially gay.' Jennifer in Salt Lake City had to write an affidavit swearing that she will marry should an appropriate man become available" (49). In Peru some ten years earlier, Elizabeth Bartholet frequently ran into a nuclear family bias as she made her way through the various interviews with government officials. When asked to draw a picture of a family, for example, she was advised by other prospective parents to draw a man, woman, and child. It's not just international officials who are homophobic. In South Carolina, McCabe was asked by a police officer taking her fingerprints, "Why don't you just get married and have babies like everyone else? . . . Or don't you like men?" (40).

The paperwork requirements in international adoptions are formidable. McCabe describes her odyssey through the United States and China: filling out forms for the adoption agency, for the U.S. immigration service and the Chinese government; securing references, copies of birth and marriage certificates, her divorce decree, pictures of her house, photocopies of years of income tax forms, verification of employment, criminal clearance from the police station, passport. She also took on extra work freelance writing and editing to make enough money to pay for the adoption. In China, there were many more bureaucratic hurdles to clear and Chinese officials who seemed disapproving of her single status. What Bartholet describes as the "obstacle course," both in the United States and internationally, works to establish the idea that adoptive parents are less worthy than parents seeking assisted reproduction. Why, asks Bartholet, should the former be subjected to more scrutiny than the latter? "Regulation sends a powerful message about the essential inferiority of adoption as a form of parenting. By subjecting adoptive but not biological parents to regulation, society suggests that it trusts what goes on when people give birth and raise a birth child but profoundly distrusts what goes on when a child is transferred from a birth to an adoptive parent" (34).

We come at last to the final group involved in adoption: the children. *Casa de los Babys* opens with a scene of the orphanage, a clean, well-lit place where dozens of babies await the transfer. An older Mexican woman cares for them, singing them to sleep. She calls them her "army of souls, ready to travel to distant lands." When they cry, she soothes them: "You're so lucky. You'll have a car and your own house. You'll go to a pretty school with all the Yankee children. You'll have perfect teeth and a huge bedroom." The woman's reference to "Yankee children" indicates she's perfectly aware of the power differences, yet she still recognizes the children's opportunities for a better life. This point is driven home by the stories of the local street children, young boys for whom adoption is no longer an option, who sniff glue and scramble for coins, barely eating, old before their teens. Can we subsume these children's experiences within a global political critique? Although adoptive parents like McCabe and Bartholet possess considerably more mobility in the global power geometry than the birth mothers, they may be able to deploy their privilege to keep the children as connected as possible to their home countries, teaching them, as these mothers have, about China and Peru as they grow up and eventually making them aware of the very reasons for their adoptions—not that their mothers didn't love them but rather that they loved them enough to want a better life for them.

Adoptive parents of U.S. children may have an even more tangible option for keeping children close to their birth mothers. This option is linked to the move in the United States for more open adoptions. Most adoptions are still secret, with records sealed at the time the adoption is formalized; in most cases, the child is issued a new birth certificate, the original one goes into a file, and both families are denied access to this information. The files can be opened only for "good cause." There is some reason for the secrecy, as adoptive parents fear that birth parents may seek to regain custody of their children or otherwise impede the children's attachment to the adoptive family. Some critics have argued, however, that the secrecy of the process is not good for parents or children, and that an open process that still guaranteed the adoptive parents' legal rights would lessen the stigma of adoption for birth parents and adopted children. Why can't the child know the birth parents, asks Bartholet? "Implicit in these arguments (for sealed records) is the sense that there is something deeply shameful in giving birth to a child that one is not prepared to raise and in the decision to surrender, and that there is something very threatening to adoptive families about the existence of blood-linked relatives" (58).[6] More open adoptions would both expand kinship possibilities and give the child more autonomy, says Bartholet, lessening the sense that the adoptive parents have become the child's "new owners."

"Sharing Katie: Open Adoption Allows Two Families to Be Active in Child's Life," read a recent headline in my local newspaper, the *Centre Daily Times*. A Knight-Ridder story that ran in the "Saturday Values" section, it indicated not only the trend toward open adoptions but also the shift in national conceptions of family. It is now acceptable for a newspaper in a fairly traditional community to run in its "values" section a story about how two sets of parents are raising a child. Three-year-old Katie was given up for adoption by her seventeen-year-old unemployed single mother, Kit Sawyer of Bedford, Texas. Kit and the baby's father, Dustin, were not ready to raise a child. Laurie and Jim Saunders of Charlotte, North Carolina, were grateful to find Katie and offered to keep Kit involved in her life after the adoption. Now, the families gather for Katie's birthday and several other times during the year. Katie says proudly that she has "two mommies and two daddies"; she calls Kit "Mama Kit" and Dustin "Dustin Daddy" (Leland C2). When Kit and Dustin decided to get married, about eighteen months after Katie was born, the Saunders flew out for the wedding, and Katie was the flower girl. These cases of shared parenting present the possibility that dispersed kinship does not have to begin and end with conception.

Conclusion
From Identity Politics to Human Rights

A cartoon reprinted in *Chicken Soup for the Single Parent's Soul* shows two women, presumably both mothers, sitting at a kitchen table, drinking coffee. Says one mother to the other: "I'd like to get married again, but I'm afraid I won't be able to get the 'Single Parent and Proud of It' bumper stickers off my car" (21).

The sentiment, expressed as it is in a wildly popular self-help manual, indicates how little stigma is currently attached to the state of single mothering—especially when it can be represented in a clearly middle-class kitchen. It also indicates how acceptance is predicated on the possibility, perhaps even the expectation, of remarriage. It is within this temporary and contingent state of acceptance that we as domestic intellectuals must work, deploying the category "single mother" to create the conditions in which women can choose to remain single mothers if they wish because they feel fully supported in their everyday lives. Ironically, what this support would eventually produce is the dissolution of the category "single mother," for so many people would be involved in the work and pleasure of caring that it would no longer be necessary to advocate a strong identity politics. Of course, mothers would still be mothers and revel in that role, but they would not have to constantly advance a politics based on that identity.

We must, however, play the game of identity politics for now, given the many different ways in which marriage or at least the heterosexual couple is still assumed to be the preferred model. The chapters in this book detail and analyze the various sites at which single mothers encounter the nuclear family norm—in divorce and adoption decisions, in limited access to child care and to assisted reproduction technologies, through welfare and immigration policies that demonize dependency, and in the general pressure to go it alone. Dominant discourses and institutions are slow to change and adapt to the demographic realities of the United States—slower than television and film representations that celebrate the single mother. How much cultural work these representations do is unclear, however, especially because of their articulation to an autonomous consumer identity.

I have also shown that single mothers are emerging in various spaces as domestic intellectuals formulating an alternative ethical politics grounded in the details of everyday life. In this conclusion, I'd like to describe one space that illustrates especially well how the domestic intellectual creates conditions for the sustenance of single mothering.

It's a warm day in the southeast corner of D.C. in March of 2004. People are hanging around outside the Anacostia Professional Building, joking, smoking cigarettes, chasing after kids. On the fourth floor, at the Center for Mental Health, people—mainly women, mainly single mothers—gather for the weekly Crossing the River workshop on the spoken and written word. There's lots of chatter as the women filter in, some with their children. Since it's a Friday, the talk turns to what they'll be doing this weekend. "If you feel like you want to use this weekend, what are you going to do?" asks Carrie. "Say a serenity prayer," she answers herself. Carrie has been clean and sober for three years and eight months. She's fifty-four, a single mother of four children ranging in age from thirteen to thirty-six. She graduated from the Crossing the River workshops in 2001 and credits it and the drug treatment program for her new lease on life.

Rosetta Kelly walks into the room a few minutes late. "My name's Rosetta and I'm an addict," she says in greeting. A chorus of "Hello, Rosetta" in response. She's an energetic presence, pacing the room, explaining today's activity. "We're going to write a poem, a 'Who am I' poem, using all the senses," she says. A woman in the room balks: "I don't think I'm ready for that," she says. "It just seems like too much for me right now." Rosetta is tenacious: "If not now, when? When will you be ready? My recovery is important to me. I keep the focus on me in recovery. If anybody feels like she doesn't want to do the poem, she can go." The woman, a bit chagrined, stays in her chair. And Rosetta asks, "What will keep you focused in recovery?"

She writes "touch, hear, see, taste, smell" on the board and draws the column markers. What's something that you touch? she asks, and participants call out their ideas: people, animals, flowers, grass, money, chairs, floors, TV, windows. Hear? Music, voices, children crying, children laughing, chaos, thunder. See? Sun, moon, my baby's smile, stars, weight gain, colors, places, God. To this last one, which Rosetta herself adds to the list, a woman disagrees: "How can you see God? Explain what you mean." And a heated exchange ensues. Rosetta says, "When I see God, he tells me what to say." But that's not sight, says the woman. If we're really talking about seeing, what I want to know is what did you *see?* And Rosetta complies: "I see bronze feet, hair that's nappy like mine, dark, compelling eyes." And her critic seems satisfied.

Taste? Food, mangos, watermelon, soda, water, smoke, strawberries, sweat, salt, ice cream, crack. Carrie offers this last one. "I'm not going to put crack up there," says Rosetta. But Imani, also facilitating, says go ahead and put it up. Other women agree—you can taste crack, they say. Smell? Fear, trouble, gasoline, farts, sea, fire, tobacco, lavender, incense, feet, roses.

Rosetta explains how to write a poem using the words they've brainstormed, combining across categories. She looks at the board: "I am windows whose music touches the sun." Women start volunteering to read; each one rises to her feet, goes to the center of the room, and says, "My name is _____, and I claim this space." Carrie wrote:

> Today I'm proud of my
> 4 children hearing their voices
> touches me. I don't go to the
> places I used to. I smelled
> crack at a friend's house did not
> go there again. I have no fear
> of the crack man. I don't use
> anymore. Today is a good day.

The Crossing the River workshops began as a way for women in drug treatment programs to express their suffering and joys through poetry, dance, and sculpture, often specifically linked to African American cultural practices. Culture becomes a way to reconnect to a body that has been lost through addiction; reclaiming the body also means reclaiming a personal space. The participants listen to one another's stories and realize their struggles are not due purely to individual weakness but rather part of a larger social struggle against poverty, racism, and other structural issues.

These women are tacticians as well as strategists, making do with what they have and also using these resources to transform strategic sites, such as Congress. After graduating from Crossing the River, many join Sacred Authority, a leadership network that advocates on Capitol Hill, talking to congressional representatives about welfare reform, drug addiction, and incarceration. Sacred Authority started in 2000 after they were invited by Catholic Charities to meet with staffers from the House Ways and Means Committee and the Senate Finance Committee to talk about their experiences with substance abuse and treatment. In 2001, they received a Ford Foundation grant and developed the policy work, putting all their endeavors under the rubric of the Rebecca Project. Here's Sacred Authority director Imani Walker's description of the intersections of everyday life and policy:

> One of the things that's powerful in terms of how we do policy work is that the mothers have the lived experience. One of our goals is to bridge the wide divide between policy makers and the lived experiences of women in recovery. We're able to reach them in a way that other advocates aren't. We may be the only ones at the table with the lived experiences. The other representatives are talking about this population of women and that population of women, something other than what they are, so for us to go and talk about our own experiences, we connect in a human way with the staffers in a way that the other folks don't.

This strategy has had some immediate successes. One of the main goals is to expand options for treatment to include children so that when a mother identifies a substance abuse problem and has to get help, she doesn't have to make a choice between taking care of her children and undergoing treatment. The Rebecca Project persuaded Pennsylvania Senator Arlen Specter to increase funding for family treatment by $10 million. As mentioned in the introduction, they also persuaded senators to propose welfare legislation that allows six months of treatment time to be considered as work under the welfare-to-work requirements. The group also has taken on the issue of incarceration of mothers. They now conduct Crossing the River workshops in the D.C. women's jail, and they're advocating on Capitol Hill for alternatives to incarceration for mothers who need addiction treatment.

This activist work informs everyday life. For example, Carolette is thirty-six, a single mother of a three-year-old disabled boy. She used drugs for twenty-three years and has been clean for two years, thanks to Crossing the River, and now participates in Sacred Authority:

Imani will give me a call saying we need you to be at such and such a place. It's so personally rewarding, and when I come home after speaking on the Hill or talking to any panel or foundation or anything, I whisper in my son's ear "Guess what your mommy did today?" and when I'm on my way, on the bus, I'm wondering while he's at school, does he know what I'm trying to do. That makes me feel warm inside, just trying to make things better. To even think that I can make a difference, is so rewarding.

The spatial practices—the movement between home, Capitol Hill, work, day care, Sacred Authority—produce a sense of possibility, of both individual and social change. Care of the self, care of one's children, and care of the community are interwoven.

The Rebecca Project organizers are domestic intellectuals in the best sense, for, like the cultural studies methodology I have tried to demonstrate in this book, they are intensely pragmatic and ethical at the same time. They have figured out what works now, at this moment in time and at this place, for improving their members' lives while simultaneously having a vision of a better world for everyone. This ethical pragmatism meshes the discourse of self-help/twelve-step programs, both of which appeal to the individual subject, with social strategies in the realms of both policy and grassroots activism. These realms of individual/social and activism/policy are not necessarily contradictory; rather, their effects are contingently determined, in particular spaces.

Ultimately, the work of the domestic intellectual does not just benefit single mothers and their children. Tellingly, the group calls itself the Rebecca Project for Human Rights. The embodied interests of single mothers and their children speak to what all citizens need to fully participate in a life of freedom, formed in the overlapping spaces of the domestic, the local, the national, and the global.

Notes

NOTES TO THE INTRODUCTION

1. Solinger says that in 1957, for the first time, the official number of illegitimate births in the United States broke 200,000, but that is considered a serious undercount.

2. In *Ordway v. Hargraves* (1971), the U.S. Supreme Court made it illegal for schools to expel unwed pregnant girls. In 1975, with the passage of Title IX, Congress denied federal funding for schools that did not comply with Ordway (Solinger 96).

3. As governor of California, Reagan proposed that "the third child and subsequent illegitimate children of an unwed mother 'should be statutorily removed for adoption'" (Solinger 132).

4. *Caught in the Crossfire* is an important analysis of economic, political, and cultural conditions that have made it seem like America's youth are to blame for a host of social problems. It does not deal much, however, with mothering and everyday domestic issues.

5. I realize that I am raising but not directly confronting the difficult question of what constitutes work in cultural studies. By focusing on these two journals, major publications, and major figures, I do not mean to preclude other work but rather to point to exemplary sites where cultural studies has developed.

6. I should acknowledge that *Cultural Studies* published my article on mothering, "Dirty Diapers and the New Organic Intellectual," 17(2) (2003), 168–192.

7. Hardt and Negri did include a short section on maternal work as a kind of "biopolitical production," but this section was cut, later appearing in a special issue of *Cultural Studies* along with other omitted sections.

NOTE TO PART I

1. Since the passage of the Personal Responsibility Act, several studies assessing its effects have shown that when single mothers move from welfare to full-time work, they continue to live below the poverty level. The *Illinois Welfare News* (June 2002), for example, summarized a study by the Chicago Jobs Coun-

cil called "Paychecks and Poverty: Real Household Budgets of Welfare-to-Work Participants," which analyzed in detail the lives of four single mothers, none of whom could make ends meet after finding full-time jobs.

Notes to Chapter 1

1. Network and advertising executives describe a growing desire for programming that families can watch together, and, reports the *New York Times,* "the networks have broadened their definition of family friendly" to "embrace nontraditional households, reflecting the changing composition of audiences" (Elliott 2002, C9).

2. Carmen Inoa Vazquez and Rosa Maria Gil, clinical psychologists, argue in their book *The Maria Paradox* that single mothering still carries a significant stigma in Latino culture.

3. I'm using pseudonyms in this section.

Notes to Part II

1. You can purchase *Chicken Soup* for the souls of the African American, bride, cat and dog lover, Christian family, college student, expectant mother, fisherman, horse lover, kid, nature lover, pet lover, preteen, sports fan, teenager, and more.

2. In referencing anthropology and ethnography, I do not mean to suggest that I am doing full-scale ethnographies in these chapters. Rather, my interviews are one component of an investigation into how space shapes and is reshaped by the practices of single mothering.

Notes to Chapter 2

1. The AAUP "Statement of Principles on Family Responsibilities," while including many important recommendations, also assumes marriage when children are involved: "Probably the most serious handicap facing married women desirous of a teaching career in higher education, especially in research-oriented universities, is that the very age range in which men are beginning to achieve a reputation through research and publication, 25 to 35, married women are likely to be bearing and rearing their children" (7).

2. The report here is drawing on a study by Finkel and Olswang.

3. Joan Williams cites a number of studies which show that retention increases with improved child-care policies. For example, Patagonia Co. estimated that it saved $160,000 in recruitment and retraining costs in 1993 alone when it began offering on-site child care (*Unbending Gender,* 90).

NOTES TO CHAPTER 3

1. The PRA barred most immigrants from food stamps and supplemental security income, cash assistance for the poor, elderly, and disabled. Food stamps for legal immigrants were restored in 2002 via an agricultural bill.

2. For example, the 1986 Immigration Reform and Control Act offered amnesty to undocumented people who had been in the country since 1982. However, it included a provision that denied amnesty to anyone "likely to become a public charge" and included a five-year ban on welfare and food stamps for anyone who did qualify for amnesty.

3. Congress passed these amendments in response to an INS claim that 30 percent of immigration visa petitions based on marriage were fraudulent. The most intrusive restriction requires an "alien" who marries during deportation or exclusion proceedings to leave the United States for two years before the INS will approve the petition.

4. Many of the single mothers I interviewed were clients of Proyecto Libertad's applying under VAWA, and I relied heavily on this group not only to examine the effects of VAWA but also because it is difficult to locate undocumented women who want to be interviewed. Thus, it may seem that my study reproduces a stereotype of the macho Latino, which is obviously not my objective. I would cite Latina critics including Anzaldúa who have argued that machismo is a social reality, but one that is the product of political and economic conditions rather than biology.

5. The numbers of women crossing the border into the United States has increased steadily over the past twenty years. Women now make up 41 percent of the estimated 9.3 million undocumented immigrants in the United States. Furthermore, there are about 1.6 million undocumented children in the country.

6. The border is plagued by many problems common to "third world" regions—substandard living conditions, environmental degradation, shortages of health-care professionals, and high rates of communicable and infectious diseases. Many of these problems have been exacerbated under the administrations of Presidents Clinton and Bush, who, with a willing Congress, have pushed through cuts in Medicaid to documented and undocumented mothers and children and to newly arrived legal immigrants. Furthermore, even when women are eligible for social services for themselves or their children, they often do not apply either due to language barriers and/or due to a fear that the process will negatively affect their immigration status.

7. The applicant must also pay $130 at the start of the process and, if she makes it through the first phase, $130 in order to receive work authorization. To renew the work permit, she must pay $120 a year. Due to a large backlog of cases, it may take years for the woman finally to win legal permanent residence

status, so each year she must pay another $120 to renew her work authorization. For adjustment to residency, she must pay a $255 application fee plus $55 for fingerprints.

NOTES TO CHAPTER 4

1. Cohabitation is common, so many women classified as single mothers may actually live with partners. Sal Oropesa and Nancy Landale, drawing on a study of Puerto Ricans in the United States, say that "boundaries across households tend to be relatively fluid in impoverished ethnic groups because a kin-based network is necessary to ensure that basic needs are met" (946).

2. In the year 2000, Flores says, there were 2.8 million Puerto Ricans on the mainland and 3.8 million on the island.

NOTES TO CHAPTER 5

1. The Clinton administration also enforced a public housing policy whose main objective was reuniting low-income fathers with their families. For more on this, see Crooms.

2. The book claims to be based on the most comprehensive examination of divorce ever conducted—"an in-depth examination of nearly 1,400 families and over 2,500 children, many followed for more than three decades" (3).

3. Many legal scholars have commented on this phenomenon. In a survey of 149 judges in Alabama, Louisiana, Mississippi, and Tennessee, for example, Leighton Stamps found that judges consistently demonstrated a preference for mothers over fathers, based on traditional gendered assumptions about caretaking and nurturing.

4. According to LaFrance, "In 1993, of the 17,872,000 children living with only one parent, 15,586,000, over eighty-seven percent, lived with their mothers." Also in 1993, "38.4 percent of children living with their divorced mothers were below the poverty line, compared to only 18.1 percent of children living with their fathers" (LaFrance 5–6).

NOTES TO CHAPTER 6

1. Ironically, feminism also gets "blamed" sometimes for the fact that women who focused on their careers and put off having kids until their late thirties or early forties have trouble getting pregnant. The choice to have a career cost them the choice to have a baby, goes the reasoning.

2. West's use of the concept of rights here differs from Solinger's use of rights above. For Solinger, the discourse of rights worked to guarantee women the right to reproductive freedom until it devolved into a discourse of choice. For

West, the discourse of rights has always been contaminated by its emphasis on individualism.

3. Cussins received permission from the clinics to observe many of the procedures; she dressed in a white coat, went by the title "Dr. Cussins," and was identified as a "visiting researcher."

4. If the sperm is routed through a sperm bank, then the donor is not presumed to be the father, and the donor cannot find out the identity of his child(ren).

5. Information from the Internet site Preconception.com.

6. There are popular texts supporting Bartholet's argument that adoption is seen as inferior to biological parenting. In *The Primal Wound: Understanding the Adopted Child,* Nancy Newton Verrier says, "It is my belief, therefore, that the severing of that connection between the adopted child and his birthmother causes a primal or narcissistic wound, which affects the adoptee's sense of self and often manifests in a sense of loss, basic mistrust, anxiety and depression, emotional and/or behavioral problems, and difficulties in relationships with significant others" (21).

Works Cited

Abramovitz, Mimi. *Regulating the Lives of Women: Social Welfare Policy from Colonial Times to the Present.* Boston: South End Press, 1988.

American Association of University Professors. "Statement of Principles on Family Responsibilities and Academic Work." May, 2001.

Amott, Teresa L. "Black Women and AFDC: Making Entitlement out of Necessity." In *Women, the State, and Welfare.* Editor Linda Gordon. Madison: University of Wisconsin Press, 1990.

Anderson, Joan. *The Single Mother's Book: A Practical Guide to Managing Your Children, Career, Home, Finances, and Everything Else.* Atlanta: Peachtree Publishers, 1990.

Anzaldúa, Gloria. *Borderlands/La Frontera: The New Mestiza.* San Francisco: Aunt Lute Books, 1987.

Bailyn, Lotte. *Breaking the Mold: Women, Men, and Time in the New Corporate World.* New York: Free Press, 1993.

Bartholet, Elizabeth. *Family Bonds: Adoption and the Politics of Parenting.* Boston and New York: Houghton Mifflin, 1993.

Bassoff, Evelyn. *Between Mothers and Sons: The Making of Vital and Loving Men.* New York: Plume, 2000.

Behar, Ruth. *Translated Woman: Crossing the Border with Esperanza's Story.* Boston: Beacon Press, 1993.

Belluck, Pam. "With Mayhem at Home, They Call a Parent Coach." *New York Times,* March 13, 2005, A1, 23.

Bennett, Tony. "Putting Policy Into Cultural Studies." In *Cultural Studies,* 23–37. Editors Lawrence Grossberg, Cary Nelson, and Paula Treichler. New York: Routledge, 1992.

———. "The Invention of the Modern Cultural Fact: Towards a Critique of the Critique of Everyday Life." In *Contemporary Culture and Everyday Life,* 21–36. Editors Elizabeth B. Silva and Tony Bennett. Durham, UK: British Sociological Association, 2004.

Bhattacharjee, Anannya. "The Public/Private Mirage: Mapping Homes and Undomesticating Violence Work in the South Asian Immigrant Community." In *Feminist Genealogies, Colonial Legacies, Democratic Futures,*

308–329. Editors Chandra Talpade Mohanty and Jacquin Alexander. New York: Routledge, 1997.

Boney, Virginia M. "Divorced Mothers' Guilt: Exploration and Intervention through a Postmodern Lens." *Journal of Divorce and Remarriage* 37(3/4) (2002): 61–84.

Bourdieu, Pierre. *The Weight of the World: Social Suffering in Contemporary Society.* Stanford, CA: Stanford University Press, 1999.

Brown, Wendy. *States of Injury: Power and Freedom in Late Modernity.* Princeton, NJ: Princeton University Press, 1995.

Butler, Judith. "Is Kinship Always Already Heterosexual?" *differences: A Journal of Feminist Cultural Studies* 13.1 (2002): 14–44.

Carbone, June. "The Missing Piece of the Custody Puzzle: Creating a New Model of Parental Partnership." *Santa Clara Law Review,* Symposium. 1999.

Carroll, Jill. Post to the *Chronicle of Higher Education* colloquy, November 6, 2001.

Carsten, Janet. *After Kinship.* Cambridge, UK: Cambridge University Press, 2004.

Chang, Grace. *Disposable Domestics: Immigrant Women Workers in the Global Economy.* Cambridge, MA: South End Press, 2000.

Chodorow, Nancy. *The Reproduction of Mothering: Psychoanalysis and the Sociology of Gender.* Berkeley: University of California Press, 1978.

Clifford, James. *Routes: Travel and Translation in the Late Twentieth Century.* Cambridge, MA: Harvard University Press, 1997.

Coetzee, J. M. *Boyhood: Scenes from Provincial Life.* New York: Viking Penguin, 1997.

Cott, Nancy F. *Public Vows: A History of Marriage and the Nation.* Cambridge, MA: Harvard University Press, 2000.

Council on Anthropology and Reproduction. "Reproduction in (and of) the Profession of Anthropology." www.geocities.com/anthrorepro/#statementon-repro.

Crittenden, Ann. *The Price of Motherhood: Why the Most Important Job in the World Is Still the Least Valued.* New York: Henry Holt and Co., 2002.

Crooms, Lisa A. "Families, Fatherlessness, and Women's Human Rights: An Analysis of the Clinton Administration's Public Housing Policy as a Violation of the Convention on the Elimination of all Forms of Discrimination Against Women." *Journal of Family Law* 36 (1997–98): 1–27.

Curphey, Shauna. "Lesbian, Single-Mother Families Still Face Hurdles." *Women's E News,* August 5, 2004. www.womensenews.org.

Cussins, Charis. "Producing Reproduction: Techniques of Normalization and Naturalization in Fertility Clinics." In *Reproducing Reproduction: Kinship, Power, and Technological Innovation,* 66–101. Editors Sarah

Franklin and Helena Ragone. Philadelphia: University of Pennsylvania Press, 1998.

Das, Veena, and Renu Addlakha. "Disability and Domestic Citizenship: Voice, Gender, and the Making of the Subject." *Public Culture* 13(3) (2001): 511–531.

DeBroff, Stacy. *The Mom Book: 4,278 of Mom Central's Tips—For Moms from Moms.* New York: Free Press, 2002.

De Certeau, Michel. *The Practice of Everyday Life.* Berkeley: University of California Press, 1984.

D'Espana, Manuel. Post to the *Chronicle of Higher Education* colloquy, November 6, 2001.

Dolgin, Janet L. "Why Has the Best-Interest Standard Survived? The Historic and Social Context." *Children's Legal Rights Journal* 16(1) (1996).

Drago, Robert. *Striking a Balance: On Work, Family, and Life.* Boston: Dollars and Sense, 2005.

Duggan, Lisa. *The Twilight of Equality? Neoliberalism, Cultural Politics, and the Attack on Democracy.* Boston: Beacon Press, 2003.

Duncan, Simon, and Rosalind Edwards. *Lone Mothers, Paid Work and Moral Gendered Rationalities.* New York: St. Martin's Press, 1999.

Edin, Kathryn, and Laura Lein. *Making Ends Meet: How Single Mothers Survive Welfare and Low-Wage Work.* New York: Russell Sage Foundation, 1997.

Elliott, Stuart. "Family Friendly TV, with Crucial Support of Advertisers, Wins More Time in Prime Time." *New York Times,* June 3, 2002, C9.

Engber, Andrea, and Leah Klungness. *The Complete Single Mother: Reassuring Answers to Your Most Challenging Concerns.* Holbrook, MA: Adams Publishing, 1995.

Erickson, Beth. *Longing for Dad: Father Loss and Its Impact.* Deerfield Beach, FL: Health Communications, 1998.

Farquhar, Dion. "Gamete Traffic/Pedestrian Crossings." In *Playing Dolly,* 17–36. Editors E. Ann Kaplan and Susan Squier. New Brunswick, NJ: Rutgers University Press, 1999.

Fathalla, Mahmoud F. "Fertility Control Technology: A Woman- Centered Approach to Research." In *Population Policies Reconsidered: Health, Empowerment, and Rights,* 223–234. Boston: Harvard School Public Health, 1994.

Feldstein, Ruth. *Motherhood in Black and White: Race and Sex in American Liberalism, 1930–1965.* Ithaca, NY: Cornell University Press, 2000.

Felski, Rita. "The Invention of Everyday Life." *New Formations* 39 (1999–2000): 13–31.

Final Report to the Alfred P. Sloan Foundation for the Faculty and Families Project/The Pennsylvania State University. Work-Family Working Paper #01-2, March 14, 2001.

Fineman, Martha Albertson. *The Neutered Mother, the Sexual Family and Other Twentieth-Century Tragedies.* New York: Routledge, 1995.

Finkel, Susan Kolker, and Steven G. Olswang. "Child Rearing as a Career Impediment to Women Assistant Professors." *Review of Higher Education* 19 (1996).

Firestone, Shulamith. *The Dialectic of Sex: The Case for Feminist Revolution.* New York: Quill William Morrow, 1970.

Flores, Juan. *From Bomba to Hip-Hop: Puerto Rican Culture and Latino Identity.* New York: Columbia University Press, 2000.

Flores-Gonzalez, Nilda. "Paseo Boricua: Claiming a Puerto Rican Space in Chicago." *Centro Journal* 13(2) (Fall 2001): 8–23.

Fogg, Peter. "Family Time: Why Some Women Quit Their Coveted Tenure-Track Jobs." *Chronicle of Higher Education,* June 13, 2003, A10–A11.

Folbre, Nancy. *The Invisible Heart: Economics and Family Values.* New York: The New Press, 2001.

Foucault, Michel. "Truth and Power." In *Power/Knowledge: Selected Interviews and Other Writings, 1972–1977,* 109–33. Editor Colin Gordon. New York: The New Press, 1980.

———. *Michel Foucault: Ethics, Subjectivity and Truth.* Editor Paul Rabinow. Translator Robert Hurley. New York: New Press, 1997.

Franklin, Sarah. "Making Miracles: Scientific Progress and the Facts of Life." In *Reproducing Reproduction,* 102–117. Editors Sarah Franklin and Helena Ragone. Philadelphia: University of Pennsylvania Press, 1998.

Fraser, Nancy, and Linda Gordon. "Contract versus Charity: Why Is There No Social Citizenship in the United States?" In *The Citizenship Debates.* Editor Will Kymlicka. Minneapolis: University of Minnesota Press, 1998.

Ginty, Molly M. "Single Mothers-to-Be Face Bias, Race Ticking Clock." *Women's E News,* August 3, 2004. www.womensenews.org.

Giroux, Henry. *Corporate Culture and the Attack on Higher Education and Public Schooling.* Fastback. Bloomington, IN: Phi Delta Kappa Educational Foundation, 1999.

———. *Public Spaces, Private Lives: Beyond the Culture of Cynicism.* Lanham, MD: Rowman and Littlefield, 2001.

Gonzalez, Juan. *Harvest of Empire: A History of Latinos in America.* New York: Penguin, 2000.

Gore, Ariel. *Breeder: Real-Life Stories from the New Generation of Mothers.* Editors Ariel Gore and Bee Lavender. Seattle: Seal Press, 2001.

Gramsci, Antonio. In *An Antonio Gramsci Reader: Selected Writings, 1916–1935.* Editor David Forgacs. New York: Schocken Books, 1988.

Grayson, Deborah. "Mediating Intimacy: Black Surrogate Mothers and the Law." In *Biotechnology and Culture: Bodies, Anxieties, Ethics,* 99–120. Editor Paul E. Brodwin. Bloomington: Indiana University Press, 2000.

Greenhouse, Steven. "Child Care, the Perk of Tomorrow?" *New York Times,* May 13, 2001, 4.14.

Grossberg, Lawrence. "Identity and Cultural Studies: Is That All There Is?" In *Questions of Cultural Identity,* 87–107. Editors Stuart Hall and Paul Du Gay. London: Sage, 1996.

———. *Caught in the Crossfire: Kids, Politics, and America's Future.* Boulder, CO: Paradigm Publishers, 2005.

Grossberg, Lawrence, Cary Nelson, and Paula Treichler. Introduction. *Cultural Studies,* 1–22. Editors Grossberg, Nelson, and Treichler. New York: Routledge, 1992.

Grossberg, Michael. *Governing the Hearth: Law and the Family in Nineteenth-Century America.* Chapel Hill: University of North Carolina Press, 1985.

Hetherington, Mavis E., and John Kelly. *For Better or for Worse: Divorce Reconsidered.* New York: W. W. Norton, 2002.

Hill Collins, Patricia. "Black Women and Motherhood." In *Rethinking the Family: Some Feminist Questions,* 215–245. Editors Barrie Thorne and Marilyn Yalom. Boston: Northeastern University Press, 1992.

Huntington, Samuel P. "The Hispanic Challenge." *Foreign Policy,* March–April 2004. http://www.foreignpolicy.com.

Jacobs, Susan Beth. "The Hidden Gender Bias behind 'The Best Interest of the Child' Standard in Custody Decisions." *Georgia State University Law Review,* June 1997.

Joseph, Miranda. *Against the Romance of Community.* Minneapolis: University of Minnesota Press, 2002.

Kaplan, E. Ann, and Susan Squier, editors and introduction. *Playing Dolly: Technocultural Formations, Fantasies and Fictions of Assisted Reproduction.* New Brunswick, NJ: Rutgers University Press, 1999.

Kendell, Kate, and Robin Haaland. "Lesbians Choosing Motherhood: Legal Implications of Donor Insemination, Second Parent Adoption, Co-Parenting, Ovum Donation, and Embryo Transfer." Third edition. National Center for Lesbian Rights, 1996. www.NCLRights.org.

Kittay, Eva Feder. *Love's Labor: Essays on Women, Equality, and Dependency.* New York: Routledge, 1999.

Kline, Marlee. "Complicating the Ideology of Motherhood: Child Welfare Law and First Nation Women." In *Mothers in Law: Feminist Theory and the Legal Regulation of Motherhood,* 118–141. Editors Martha Albertson Fineman and Isabel Karpin. New York: Columbia University Press, 1995.

LaFrance, Arthur B. "Child Custody and Relocation: A Constitutional Perspective." *University of Louisville Journal of Family Law* 34(1) (1995–96): 1–27.

Lamott, Anne. *Operating Instructions: A Journal of My Son's First Year.* New York: Ballantine Books, 1994.

Landale, Nancy, and R. S. Oropesa. "Father Involvement in the Lives of Mainland Puerto Rican Children: Contributions of Nonresident, Cohabiting and Married Fathers." *Social Forces* 79.3 (2001): 945–968.

Lazarre, Jane. *The Mother Knot.* New York: McGraw-Hill, 1976.

Leland, Elizabeth. "Sharing Kate: Open Adoption Allows Two Families to Be Active in Child's Life." *Centre Daily Times,* July 31, 2004, C1–C2.

Lewis, Oscar. *La Vida.* New York: Random House, 1966.

Martin, Randy. *Financialization of Daily Life.* Philadelphia: Temple University Press, 2002.

Massey, Doreen. *Space, Place, and Gender.* Minneapolis: University of Minnesota Press, 1994.

Masson, Mary Ann, and Marc Goulden. "Do Babies Matter? The Effect of Family Formation on the Lifelong Careers of Academic Men and Women." *Academe,* February 2003. http://www.aaup.org.publications/Academe.

Mattes, Jane. *Single Mothers by Choice: A Guidebook for Single Women Who Are Considering or Have Chosen Motherhood.* New York: Random House, 1994.

McCabe, Nancy. *Meeting Sophie: A Memoir of Adoption.* Columbia: University of Missouri Press, 2003.

Meckler, Laura. "President Proposes Welfare Overhaul." *Centre Daily Times,* February 27, 2002, A1, A3.

Mink, Gwendolyn. "From Welfare to Wedlock: Marriage Promotion and Poor Mothers' Inequality." *Good Society* 11.3 (2002): 68–73.

Moi, Toril, editor. *The Kristeva Reader.* New York: Columbia University Press, 1986.

Montejano, David. *Anglos and Mexicans in the Making of Texas, 1836–1986.* Austin: University of Texas Press, 1987.

Moore, Pamela. "Selling Reproduction." In *Playing Dolly,* 80–86. Editors E. Ann Kaplan and Susan Squier. New Brunswick, NJ: Rutgers University Press, 1999.

Morley, David. *Home Territories: Media, Mobility, and Identity.* London and New York: Routledge, 2000.

Moses, Kate. *Wintering: A Novel of Sylvia Plath.* New York: Anchor Books, 2003.

National Center for Lesbian Rights. www.NCLRights.org.

Navarro, Mireya. "Latino TV Embraces Reality Shows." *New York Times,* September 8, 2003.

Nealon, Jeffrey. "The Associate Vice Provost in the Gray Flannel Suit: Administrative Labor and the Corporate University." Talk, Modern Language Association, Philadelphia, PA, December 29, 2004.

Negri, Antonio, and Michael Hardt. "'Subterranean Passages of Thought': Empire's Inserts." Compiled by Nicholas Brown and Imre Szeman. *Cultural Studies* 16(2) (2002): 193–212.

"Paid Parental Leave in Academia Is Rare, U.Va. Study Shows." University of Virginia News, January 29, 2004. www.virginia.edu/topnews/releases2004.

Pateman, Carole. *The Sexual Contract.* Cambridge, UK: Polity Press, 1988.

Perales, Nina. "A Tangle of Pathology: Racial Myth and the New Jersey Family Development Act." In *Mothers in Law: Feminist Theory and the Legal Regulation of Motherhood.* Editors Martha Fineman and Isabel Karpin. New York: Columbia University Press, 1995.

Pérez, Gina. "An Upbeat Westside Story: Puerto Ricans and Postwar Racial Politics in Chicago." *Centro Journal* 13(2) (Fall 2001): 47–68.

Perry, Joan. *A Girl Needs Cash: How to Take Charge of Your Financial Life.* New York: Times Books, 1999.

Quayle, Dan. *The American Family: Discovering the Values That Make Us Strong.* New York: HarperCollins, 1996.

Radway, Janice. *Reading the Romance: Women, Patriarchy, and Popular Literature.* Chapel Hill: University of North Carolina Press, 1984.

Ramos-Zayas, Ana Y. *National Performances: The Politics of Class, Race, and Space in Puerto Rican Chicago.* Chicago: University of Chicago Press, 2003.

Rapp, Rayna, and Faye Ginsburg. "Enabling Disability: Rewriting Kinship, Reimagining Citizenship. *Public Culture* 13(3) (2001): 533–556.

Readings, Bill. *The University in Ruins.* Cambridge, MA: Harvard University Press, 1996.

Rich, Adrienne. *Of Woman Born: Motherhood as Experience and Institution.* New York: W. W. Norton, 1986.

Rimke, Heidi Marie. "Governing Citizens through Self-Help Literature." *Cultural Studies* 14(1) (2000): 61–78.

Robson, Ruthann. "Mother: The Legal Domestication of Lesbian Existence." In *Mothers in Law: Feminist Theory and the Legal Regulation of Motherhood,* 103–117. Editors Martha Fineman and Isabel Karpin. New York: Columbia University Press, 1995.

Rose, Nikolas. *Inventing Our Selves: Psychology, Power, and Personhood.* New York: Cambridge Studies in the History of Psychology, 1996.

———. *Powers of Freedom: Reframing Political Thought.* Cambridge, UK: Cambridge University Press, 1999.

Rosenberg, Lee Fletcher. "Child Care Benefits May Get Boost from Tax Credit." Crain Communications, July 30, 2001. web.lexis-nexis.com.

Rúa, Meredith. "Colao Subjectivities: PortoMex and MexiRican Perspectives on Language and Identity." *Centro Journal* 13(2) (Fall 2001): 117–133.

Seltzer, Judith A. "Father by Law: Effects of Joint Legal Custody on Nonresident Fathers' Involvement with Children." *Demography* 35(2) (May 1998): 135–146.

Semans, Anne, and Cathy Winks. *The Mother's Guide to Sex: Enjoying your*

Sexuality through All Stages of Motherhood. New York: Three Rivers Press, 2001.

Shapiro, Julie. "Custody and Conduct: How the Law Fails Lesbian and Gay Parents and Their Children." *Indiana Law Journal*, Summer 1996.

Silverstone, Roger. *Television and Everyday Life*. London: Routledge, 1994.

Single Mothers by Choice Web site. http://mattes.home.pipeline.com/index.html.

Solinger, Rickie. *Beggars and Choosers: How the Politics of Choice Shapes Adoption, Abortion, and Welfare in the United States*. New York: Hill and Wang, 2001.

———. "Dependency and Choice: The Two Faces of Eve." In *The Subject of Care: Feminist Perspectives on Dependency*, 61–77. Editors Ellen K. Feder and Eva Kittay. New York: Rowman and Littlefield, 2002.

Stamps, Leighton E. "Maternal Preference in Child Custody Decisions." *Journal of Divorce and Remarriage* 37(1–2) (2002): 1–11.

Stanworth, Michelle. "Birth Pangs: Conceptive Technologies and the Threat to Motherhood." In *Conflicts in Feminism*, 288–304. Editors Marianne Hirsch and Evelyn Fox Keller. New York: Routledge, 1990.

Strathern, Marilyn. *Reproducing the Future: Essays on Anthropology, Kinship, and the New Reproductive Technologies*. New York: Routledge, 1992.

———. "Displacing Knowledge: Technology and the Consequences for Kinship." In *Conceiving the New World Order: The Global Politics of Reproduction*, 346–364. Editors Faye D. Ginsburg and Rayna Rapp. Berkeley: University of California Press, 1995.

Sullivan-Boss, Carmen. "Single Mothers Unite." In *Chicken Soup for the Single Parent's Soul: Stories of Hope, Healing, and Humor*. Deerfield Beach, FL: Health Communications, Inc. (2005): 31–34.

Swank, Drew A. "The National Child Non-Support Epidemic." *Michigan State DCL Law Review* Summer 2003.

Tattoo, Rose. "Having My Baby." *Bust*. Summer 2001, 50–54.

Thomas, Cal. "Uncle Sam May Enter the Marriage Business." *Centre Daily Times*, February 22, 2002.

Thompson, Charis. "Strategic Naturalizing: Kinship in an Infertility Clinic." In *Relative Values: Reconfiguring Kinship Studies*, 175–202. Editors Sarah Franklin and Susan McKinnon. Durham: Duke University Press, 2001.

Trattner, Walter. *From Poor Law to Welfare State: A History of Social Welfare in America*. New York: Free Press, 1999.

Vazquez, Carmen Inoa, and Rosa Maria Gill. *The Maria Paradox: How Latinas Can Merge Old World Traditions with New World Self-Esteem*. New York: Putnam, 1996.

Verrier, Nancy Newton. *The Primal Wound: Understanding the Adopted Child*. Baltimore: Gateway Press, 1993.

Wajcman, Judy. "Delivered Into Men's Hands? The Social Construction of Reproductive Technology." In *Power and Decision: The Social Control of Reproduction,* 153–175. Cambridge, MA: Harvard School of Public Health, 1994.

Walden, Elizabeth. "Cultural Studies and the Ethics of Everyday Life." *Culture Machine,* Culturemachine.tees.ac.uk. Retrieved May 26, 2002.

Warner, Michael. *The Trouble with Normal: Sex, Politics, and the Ethics of Queer Life.* New York: Free Press, 1999.

Warner, Michael, and Lauren Berlant. "Sex in Public." In Michael Warner, *Publics and Counterpublics,* 187–208. Zone Books: New York, 2002.

West, Robin. "The Right to Care." In *The Subject of Care: Feminist Perspectives on Dependency,* 88–114. Editors Ellen K. Feder and Eva Kittay. New York: Rowman and Littlefield, 2002.

"Why Women Opt for Sperm Donation." *BBC News,* June 30, 2002.

Williams, Joan. *Unbending Gender: Why Family and Work Conflict and What to Do about It.* New York: Oxford University Press, 2000.

———. "How the Tenure Track Discriminates Against Women." *Chronicle of Higher Education Career Network,* October 27, 2000. http://chronicle.com/jobs.

Williams, Raymond. "Culture Is Ordinary." In *Resources of Hope: Culture, Democracy, Socialism.* Editor Robin Gable. Originally published 1958. London: Verso, 1989.

———. *Keywords: A Vocabulary of Culture and Society.* New York: Oxford University Press, 1976.

Wilson, James Q. *The Marriage Problem: How Our Culture Has Weakened Families.* New York: HarperCollins, 2002.

Wilson, Robin. "A Push to Help New Parents Prepare for Tenure Reviews." *Chronicle of Higher Education,* November 9, 2001, A10.

———. "Working Half Time on the Tenure Track." *Chronicle of Higher Education,* January 25, 2002, A10–A11.

Zaino, Jeanne S. "Expecting on the Tenure Track." *Chronicle of Higher Education Career Network,* October 10, 2002.

Index

About the Author

Jane Juffer is an associate professor of English and Women's Studies at Pennsylvania State University, where she specializes in cultural studies, Latina/o studies, and feminist theory. She is the author of *At Home with Pornography: Women, Sex, and Everyday Life* (New York University Press) and other work on pornography and domesticity. She has also published on lingerie, Sammy Sosa, Latina/o studies at the corporate university, and various aspects of the U.S.-Mexican border.